STRONG ARTIFICIAL INTELLIGENCE

Understanding the AI Revolution

AI is moving fast. Within two decades, it will be superior to that of a human being!

REYNALDO NUNCIO

ISBN: 9781700453617

Cover design: Mike Riley, www.ajijicbooks.com

Published by Ajijic Books Publishing

First printing 2019

Contents

Foreword

Maybe you've heard the ancient Indian parable of the six blind men who have never come across an elephant before and who learn and conceptualize what the elephant is like by touching it. Each blind man feels a different part of the elephant's body, but only one part.

The earliest versions of the parable of blind men and elephant is found in Buddhist, Hindu and Jain texts, as they discuss the limits of perception and the importance of complete context.

One man touched the elephant's side and said, "Well, now I know all about this beast. He is exactly like a wall."

The second blind man felt the elephant's tusk. "My brother," he said, "You are mistaken. He is round and smooth and sharp. He is more like a spear than anything else."

The third took hold of the elephant's trunk. "Both of you are wrong," he said. "Anybody who knows anything can tell that this elephant is like a snake."

The fourth man touching a leg, the fifth an ear, and the sixth the tail. Each of the men only got a piece of the puzzle but was convinced that he knew the whole truth about what the elephant looked like.

The same is currently happening with the understanding of Artificial Intelligence. If you use an AI App to translate texts, read an article about AI applied in education or watch the AlphaGo film you will have a partial picture of Artificial Intelligence that will not give you the complete idea of this great technological revolution.

But if you read this book you will have the full picture of Artificial Intelligence. That is, you will have the image of the whole elephant.

Carlos Estrella

Preface

The history of humanity has always been a story about humans and their tools. Without our gift for extending our reach through tools, we might still be swinging in the trees, or worse. Naturally, we love and revere our tools, but we also know to fear them. Some of our oldest cautionary tales are about technologies whose power exceeds our ability to control them. Prometheus, Pandora, and Frankenstein were the early prototypes; now we have Westworld, Jurassic World, Bladerunner, the Terminator, GMOs, and countless others. Today, fear of technology is big business.

This book is about Strong AI, a technology that typically conjures some of our worst fears about human creations run amok. Strong AI is when computers are not just faster than we are when it comes to computation but surpass us in some, most, or even all the metrics of human intelligence.

The day this first happens will be a watershed event—a *singularity*. Some are calling it *the* Singularity. After that day, the history of humans and our tools may begin to follow separate paths, as we have always feared they might.

Scientists, philosophers, and great thinkers—Elon Musk, Vernor Vinge, Stephen Hawking, and Ray Kurzweil, to name a few—estimate that this era of Strong AI or Fifth Wave will begin sometime this century. My hunch is that it will happen by 2040. I also concede it may never happen, but—and I cannot stress this enough—*I would not plan on it*. In this sense, AI is like climate change—another runaway technology story—because we can still choose not to "believe" in it. But what if we do bet against climate change or strong AI and are proven wrong? It could be too late.

Some of the most brilliant minds of our age have focused on the study of Artificial Intelligence, and their conclusions are surprising. Stephen Hawking, the recently deceased English astrophysicist, cosmologist, and author of *The History of Time*, once said, "The development of Strong Artificial Intelligence could mean the end of the human race." (https://amzn.to/2gFpmQt)

This is not science fiction. The realities that this book explores are more interesting and more pressing than fiction. Nor is it a technical manual for aspiring writers of algorithms. Our goal here is to answer some of the biggest questions humankind has ever asked. What is Artificial Intelligence? What opportunities does it offer for software developers, companies, and countries? What benefits can I expect from AI? What are the risks? How will it affect my privacy? Will I lose my job? Can humans and machines be in relationships? Can we merge? Will Strong AI become the Matrix and milk us, like cattle, as a convenient source of bio-energy, or will it become Skynet and hunt us to extinction? Or maybe humans will be the villains of the story and use superhuman machines to attack enemy infrastructure and end up destroying civilization.

Of course, a lot of that stuff is already happening. But let's not get ahead of ourselves. AI is already affecting every aspect of our lives. Shouldn't we understand it before we find ourselves in the middle of it? As they say when a major hurricane is looming, let us plan for the worst and hope for the best. I believe that we have good reason to hope, but I also know that our fear of the monster we ourselves created runs deep.

In the beginning, we were apes

Human societies have evolved in waves. Our **First Wave** started when a distant ape ancestor came up with the idea of using a bone or a stick as a weapon, a tool, or a means of expression, and in so doing eventually became a *hominid*. In practically no time, their extraordinary knack for toolmaking rocketed these creatures to the top of the food chain and allowed them to transform into Homo sapiens, masters of the planet (some might call us a planetary virus), and future space cowboys.

The **Second Wave** started about 10,000 years ago with the invention of agriculture, when humans went from following big game and fishing to planting and harvesting fields. We became sedentary. We built villages. The villages became cities and city-states. Cities were linked to other cities by harbors, roads, and bridges. The greatest cities boasted magnificent temples, palaces, coliseums.

The **Third Wave** started around 1760, in Great Britain, with the mechanization of textile and iron production, and spread from there to the rest of the world with a virtually limitless array of industrial specialties. Industrialization revolutionized agriculture, too, which means that Second Wave institutions mostly succumbed to Third Wave phenomena. We'll take a closer look at the Industrial Revolution, which developed in stages, in the chapter 9 of this book.

Some would say that the **Fourth Wave** or **AI Revolution** started in the late 20th century with the emergence of information technologies characterized by distributed computing architectures and the use of the Internet. But it was really in the early 21st century when the power and sophistication of these technologies began to reach critical mass. Spreading from the United States, Europe, and China, it has by now touched most, if not all, of the planet. Also known as Industry 4.0, its impact is driven by industrial processes but extends to all human activities, including services, trade, politics, and social ties, as the use of personal computers, smart phones, and the Internet influences all areas of human life. We will focus our attention on the **transition from the AI Revolution to the Fifth Wave** in chapter 10 of this book. It is the stage we are currently in, and understanding it is key if we are to make informed decisions about a world we will soon start sharing with Strong AI.

Notice how the amount of time between waves gets shorter with each successive wave:

- Formation of the Earth to Homo habilis: 4,500,000,000 years
- Homo habilis to agriculture: 2,000,000 years
- Agriculture to the Industrial Revolution: 10,000 years
- The Industrial Revolution to the AI Revolution: 240 years
- The AI Revolution to the Fifth Wave with Strong AI: ~ 40 years

When we measure human history by the important events that have led to disruptive changes, we see that it took millions of years for anything important to happen after Homo habilis first appeared, but once hominids developed better brains, major changes started to happen in a hurry.

The technological advances we achieve in a single day are now greater than anything that was achieved in a hundred years during the Middle Ages and easily greater still than a million years of hominid ingenuity back when our simian ancestors roamed the savannah. At this vertiginous pace, the innovations that occur in the next 20 years will encompass eons of evolution.

Technology will reach new heights. The convergence of technologies will produce a synergy beyond imagination. Quantum computing will be a powerful reality, and everything will come together to produce Strong AI.

I've said I believe that the **Fifth Wave** will begin by 2040. We've established that Strong AI is when computers are smarter than humans, and we can imagine that this phenomenon will produce a broad and profound disruptive change that will affect all our lives and transform all of us.

But does 2040 seem too soon? If so, let's consider it the most aggressive scenario. The question is, should we plan for the most aggressive scenario, or should we allow for a longer timeline? In this case, the trend is so unmistakable, and the stakes are so high, that we should, at a minimum, have solid plans in place well ahead of 2040.

First: Evolution

Before computers achieve Strong AI, they will demonstrate **Specific Artificial Intelligence** across many fields. That is, they will equal or surpass human beings **in specific fields** where a high level of knowledge or skill is required. Spoiler alert: this ship has sailed. Computers that can beat the top players of the most complex and mentally challenging games are already in the headlines. And not only have computers outstripped humans at chess, Jeopardy, and go, they are outperforming us in other areas as well. Be it detecting brain tumors, writing or translating texts, or identifying behavioral patterns in children with autism, the student has become the master.

DeepMind, founded in 2010 and acquired by Google in 2014, is an AI success story. In March 2016, **AlphaGo**, a DeepMind program, played the legendary **Lee Sedol**, winner of 18 world titles, at the Google-sponsored DeepMind Challenge in Seoul, South Korea. At the time, Sedol had been the number one player in the world for almost two years. Famed for his creativity, he was widely considered the greatest player of the past decade.

Over 200 million people watched online as AlphaGo beat Sedol 4-1. The predictions before the match were that it would take AI up to a decade to gain championship-level skills, but AlphaGo demonstrated innovative game strategies that surprised its human opponent, defied centuries of go wisdom, and delivered a mortal blow to the human monopoly on the game.

In May 2017, AlphaGo went on to beat world champion **Ke Jie** in three consecutive go games. To appreciate the magnitude of this victory, consider that go is far more complex than chess and until recently was considered one of the bastions of human intelligence. Read more about AlphaGo here: https://bit.ly/2AKHcxm

More interesting than the outcome was the way the AI was trained to learn the game. A **deep learning** technique was used, along with a reward-based learning reinforcement system that allowed AlphaGo to learn by playing thousands of games on its own and analyzing the games of its human opponents.

In July 2018, a group of developers from Alimama, a marketing division of the Chinese company Alibaba, created an AI-based program that could provide a detailed description of certain products. In other words, its goal was to do the intellectual work that human copywriters are traditionally paid to do. The system is rooted in deep learning and natural language processing. Millions of examples of descriptions created by real people were used to train it. AI, you see, *feeds on human labor.*

Next: Revolution

We may think of Artificial Intelligence as a one-trick pony today, but these isolated instances of AI surpassing human workers are setting the stage for the revolutionary phase of tomorrow. **Strong AI**—when computers surpass humans in **all fields** of knowledge—is what comes next. When computers can reason, plan, solve problems, think abstractly, make decisions, learn from experience, and even improve themselves, we call it **Strong AI** because they will combine the human gift for discernment with the techniques—and power—of computation driven by Artificial Intelligence.

Like all technologies, **Strong AI will offer benefits but also represent dangers** for humanity. Many jobs will be lost, and new ones will be generated, though not for the same people. Jim Yong Kim, former president of the World Bank, said that Artificial Intelligence will eliminate 50-65% of all existing jobs in developing countries. Millions will lose their jobs, but the software developers who have the creativity to produce sophisticated AI algorithms will be golden. Thousands of successful companies will spring up offering applications and services specializing in Artificial Intelligence.

Banks will cease to be financial institutions that serve the public and will become automated financial centers that will pay better salaries to a computer engineer than to a branch manager. Competition between countries will increase, not necessarily to conquer territories with their armies or markets with their companies, but to dominate Artificial Intelligence and, through it, dominate the world.

Artificial Intelligence is already deeply enmeshed in all human activities, and it will continue to spread, like humans before it have, to the very ends of the Earth, affecting health, education, finance, architecture, politics, the military, art, the economy—in short, everything we care about. And that is why we all need to understand it and the opportunities it offers to improve our standard of living, but also to comprehend it and anticipate the dangers it poses to each of us personally and as a species.

Why Strong AI?

Artificial Intelligence experts have not agreed on the name that should be given to the AI that surpasses human intelligence. The term Artificial Intelligence was first coined by John McCarthy in 1956, when he held the first academic conference on the subject at Dartmouth College, but there is no consensus moniker for AI that is superhuman.

There are, however, several candidates: strong AI, artificial general intelligence, cognitive Artificial Intelligence, and artificial superintelligence.

John Rogers Searle coined Strong AI in 1980. Searle was Willis S. and Marion Slusser Professor Emeritus of the Philosophy of Mind and Language and Professor of the Graduate School at the University of California, Berkeley, and is widely noted for his contributions to the philosophy of language, philosophy of mind, and social philosophy. In this book, we've chosen to use Searle's coinage.

How to get the most out of this book

You can read the book sequentially or à la carte. For a better understanding of the subject, I suggest you read the chapters from zero to ten, in order, and then circle back to chapter zero, which is one of those chapters that could have been placed at the beginning or end of the book. I chose the beginning.

Chapter 0 focuses on winners and losers—the benefits of Artificial Intelligence versus the dangers that lie ahead. This chapter is as close as we'll get to science fiction. It presents detailed answers to some of the major questions people and the media are posing. It addresses threats to privacy, the possibility of job losses, and the thorny issue of human-robot relationships. It also analyzes the concept of a technological singularity and the difficulty of applying common sense to AI. The chapter concludes with a thought experiment that represents a scenario that may seem science-fictiony today but could easily be a fantastic reality by as early as 2040.

Subsequent chapters will discuss the evolution of Strong AI. We'll start at the beginning, with a brief look at the formation of the Universe, and we will proceed to review the evolution of intelligence in Homo sapiens. How and why did humans become intelligent, and how long did it take us?

Because hardware and software are what make AI what it is, we also need to understand how computers evolved. Who built the first computers, and how and when did they become the machines that now astonish the world? Why early computers were called "electronic brains"? And, of course, we'll compare computer intelligence to the workings of the human brain. Later, we'll study the techniques that support Artificial Intelligence and the applications that have been developed on the path to Strong AI.

I've inserted callouts throughout the text to explain various technical concepts, but if you find yourself struggling to grok some parts of the book, feel free to skip them. They will not affect your general understanding of the subject. Programmers, systems developers, and cyberculture enthusiasts might find them somewhat lacking in depth and detail. But then, this is not a technical book. Our modest goal is to foster a better understanding of Artificial Intelligence and sow the seeds of prudence and prevention.

If you need to reproduce or quote a portion of the book, be my guest, but please attribute references to this book with its title, *Strong Artificial Intelligence: Understanding the AI Revolution*, and my name, Reynaldo Nuncio.

Your comments, criticisms, or observations are welcome. They will help me prepare reprints as we track the progress of Artificial Intelligence in the coming decades.

Greetings, and enjoy this exciting topic.
reynuncio@gmail.com

Quotes on Artificial Intelligence

"A computer would deserve to be called intelligent if it could deceive a human into believing that it was human"
Alan Turing, Founder of Artificial Intelligence

"When the computers take over, we may not get it back. We will survive at their whim. Hopefully, they'll decide to keep us as pets."
Marvin Minsky, Pioneer of Artificial Intelligence

"The development of a Strong Artificial Intelligence could mean the end of the human race."
Stephen Hawking, English astrophysicist and cosmologist

"In 30 years we will have the technological means to create a superhuman intelligence...Some time later, the human era will be over."
Vernor Vinge, American mathematician and writer

"Superintelligence is an intellect far more intelligent than the human brain in virtually every field including scientific creativity, wisdom and social skills."
Nick Bostrom, Superintelligence Investigator

"The rate at which Artificial Intelligence progresses is incredibly fast. Unless you work for companies in the sector, people can't imagine how fast it's growing. The risk of something dangerous happening will come in about five years, ten at the most."
Elon Musk, Tesla Director

"Whenever I hear people saying that Artificial Intelligence is going to hurt people in the future I think that technology can generally always be used for good and evil, and you have to be careful what you build and how it will be used.
Mark Zuckerberg, Facebook Director

"Artificial Intelligence is deeper than electricity or fire. It's going to have a bigger impact. Like fire, it can also harm or kill people. We have to learn the benefits it brings us and limit its disadvantages.

Sundar Pichai, Director of Google

"Artificial Intelligence is going to eliminate between 50% and 65% of all existing work in developing countries."

Jim Yong Kim, former president of the World Bank

"Humans should embrace the changes that intelligent machines offer society."

Gary Kasparov, Chess Champion

"Artificial Intelligence will be the latest version of Google, the search engine that will understand everything on the web. It will understand exactly what the user wants and will give you the right thing. We're not close to achieving it now but we can get closer and closer and that's basically what we're working on."

Larry Page, founder of Google

"Artificial Intelligence will reach human levels around 2029 (what is known as Singularity), but a little later, in 2045, we will have multiplied human biological intelligence a billion times over.

Ray Kurzweil, inventor and scientist

About the Author

Reynaldo Nuncio is a computer programmer, businessman, teacher, business consultant, Artificial Intelligence researcher, and science and technology writer. He has published five books on computers, software, and Artificial Intelligence. He has a degree in Economics. He is currently president emeritus of the National Institute of Informatics and Communication in Mexico.

reynuncio@gmail.com

Other books by the author

Inteligencia Artificial Total. 2018

La Magia del Software: Historia, Fundamentos y Perspectiva. Spanish. 2016

Todo lo que usted quiere saber sobre computadoras personales. Spanish.1991

Historia y perspectiva de la programación. Spanish. 1990

Cómo comprar software para computadoras personales. Spanish. 1987

Dedicated To:

Andrés, Adriana, MaryAnn, Joseph, Matthew, Teresa, Thomas, John, Paul

Acknowledgements

The production of a book requires, in addition to the generation of the author's own ideas, the incorporation of the knowledge recorded in the alternate memory of humanity: the book, whether printed or electronic. My thanks to the authors who have left their knowledge, ideas and thoughts reflected in books, to the authors of blogs and articles that they insert in the Internet with no other desire than to spread universal knowledge; to the authors of the content that feeds Wikipedia, that modern source of knowledge to which we go every day to take concepts, definitions and a wealth of knowledge and to those who write and communicate their thoughts through social networks. Thanks to my wife Sheree and my friend Chris Manning for helping me revise the text and Mike Riley for the cover design and his valuable help in turning the text into an Amazon eBook. Special thanks to Ariel Nuncio for his collaboration in writing the preface and reviewing the first chapter of the book.

–0–

TOWARDS STRONG AI

Humanity is already well on its way to achieving Strong AI. As we traverse this path, we will find opportunities, risks, and dangers. Our incorrigible love of adventure will drive us to do whatever it takes to create an inanimate being whose intelligence eclipses our own. There will be warnings, but we'll mostly ignore them, like we always have. We're only talking about making machines that are smarter than we are. What could possibly go wrong?

On the road to Strong AI, there will be surprises, bad and good. The benefits of AI will distract us and motivate us to persist in our objective. Artificial Intelligence will initially function as an engine of economic, political, and social development. It will appear in our lives as a docile and discreet personal assistant that lives in a smart phone and whose job is to answer the questions we ask out loud, whenever we ask them. **It will help with everyday tasks** such as finding the most direct route to a destination, making sure we get the latest news about the topics we care about, and identifying potential intruders. Later, it will give intelligence to sexual robots whose purpose is to comfort us in moments of solitude. In short, Artificial Intelligence will seem like a benign helper. We'll be happy to have an intelligent servant at our beck and call, and we'll be thankful for the constant advances in the field of AI that allow our synthetic factotums to deliver a constantly improving stream of services.

But AI will start to show its teeth. It will start displacing certain groups of workers, especially clerks and employees who perform routine tasks. AI will also perform highly specialized and complex tasks such as making decisions about financial markets, buying and selling stocks, and

17

maximizing profits. With better-than-human results, no one will complain but the displaced stockbrokers and account-ants, who will go the way of the secretary. Eventually, AI will don hospital scrubs and take the place of doctors to diagnose and cure diseases. **Patients will call it a blessing.**

Given the current rate of progress in AI technologies—deep learning, machine learning, artificial neural networks, big data, and quantum computing—we can estimate that in 20 years it will be possible to reach the convergence of technologies that will produce Strong AI.

Convergence is the key

The merging of distinct technologies, industries, or devices into a unified whole is the key to achieving Strong AI. There is already a long list of technologies with the potential to produce **Specific Artificial Intelligence** in applications that surpass human intelligence. Every day we hear reports of AI applications that produce better results in various fields such as medicine, education, engineering, economy, and so on. Strong AI happens when we give these technologies a way to interact and a reason to do so. The way is through highly evolved networks and, say, quantum computers. The reason why we *will* achieve this goal is the same reason as ever: money. Well, money and power.

AI is cool and popular. Social conditions and consumer enthusiasm have created the perfect environment for its rapid development. Universities have special programs for training AI professionals, companies allocate enormous financial resources to AI research and development, and governments are building critical infrastructure. In the more developed countries, people are showing their love for AI by buying and using everything that falls under the AI umbrella. Given this enthusiasm—this driver of massive market forces—we should assume the emergence of Strong AI in about two decades.

Differences with Alvin Toffler and J Blakeson

The Third Wave is a 1980 book by Alvin Toffler. It is the sequel to Future Shock (1970), and the second in what was originally likely meant to be a trilogy that was continued with Powershift: Knowledge, Wealth and Violence at the Edge of the 21st Century in 1990. Toffler's book describes the transition in developed countries from Industrial Age society. It has been one of my favorites. (https://amzn.to/2mGR9Zt)

In The Third Wave Toffler described three historic waves of how civilization had progressed. The **First wave:** settling and starting to form an agricultural society, thus transitioning from a hunter-gatherer structure. **The Second Wave** society is industrial and based on mass production, mass distribution, mass consumption, mass education, mass media, mass recreation, and weapons of mass destruction. His **Third Wave** is about the transition into the Information Age, when knowledge started taking precedence over material items in terms of what's valuable.

We're different from Alvin Toffler's idea. We consider that the First Wave was the Homo habilis as **the first application of intelligence** to dominate the environment. The Third Wave was a great book, but it completely missed the Internet, much less the brave new world of AI.

"**The 5th Wave**" is a 2016 American **science fiction film directed by J Blakeson**, with a screenplay by Susannah Grant, Akiva Goldsman, and Jeff Pinkner, based on **Rick Yancey's 2013 novel of the same name**. The famous movie tells the story of Cassie Sullivan, a 16-year-old, as she tries to survive in a world destroyed by the waves of an alien invasion that have already devastated the Earth's population and knocked humankind back to the Stone Age. Cassie is headed to a "training" camp established by "The Others", the aliens, to save her 5 year-old brother, Sam, who was taken away from her family's refugee camp.

In this book, which is not a science fiction book, the Fifth Wave is not produced by the invasion of extraterrestrial aliens who try to destroy Planet Earth, but by the Strong Artificial Intelligence created by the human being himself.

Augmented intelligence

Has it ever happened to you that after you open an e-mail and start answering it a message appears with a suggestion for a quick response? Have you ever used a word processor that goes ahead to write something you are just thinking about? Have you received recommendations when using Grammarly software to correct and review any text you have written? When you use your smart phone have you felt that it goes ahead to satisfy your desires? All this and much more is possible thanks to augmented intelligence.

Augmented intelligence is one more step on the road to Strong Artificial Intelligence. The word augmented means to improve or reinforce the human intelligence. Jessica Munday, Content Marketing Specialist at Automation Hero says "augmented intelligence elevates human intelligence and aids it in working faster and smarter. Augmented intelligence tools are created to help rather than replace humans."

It is a newly developed technology and its name is not yet well accepted. IBM has embraced the label augmented intelligence and has also suggested the term intelligence augmentation (IA), not only to emphasize the supportive role of the technology but also to avoid confusion caused by using AI as an abbreviation. Other alternative suggestions for replacing the label include machine-augmented intelligence and cognitive augmentation.

Jessica Munday writes in Automation Hero:

"Augmented intelligence follows a five-function cadence that allows it to learn with human influence. It repeats a cycle of understanding, interpretation, reasoning, learning, and assurance. Here's how it works:

Understanding: Systems are fed data, which it breaks down and derives meaning from.

Interpretation: New data is inputted, the system then reflects on old data to interpret new data sets.

Reasoning: The system creates "output" or "results" for new data set.

Learn: Humans give feedback on output and the system adjusts accordingly.

Assure: Security and compliance are ensured using blockchain or AI technology.

Having humans and machines work hand-in-hand is a win-win for both parties. The machine grows smarter and more productive while the human workload is streamlined. With humans guiding the learning process these tools learn and adjust their models more quickly than intelligence tools with no human feedback loop." (https://bit.ly/2M7BRqA)

The augmented Intelligence has a promising future because it does not replace the human being. It does not threaten to eliminate jobs. It does not cause fear with robots that can do a person's job better and faster. Its objective is to improve the intelligence of the human being, increase his abilities and help him to perform his work more easily. Imagine that today you want to make an investment in the stock market to buy shares of the company WeWork. When everything is ready to press the "BUY" button a message appears with a recommendation that says: "I recommend NOT to buy WeWork shares". You react to the message. Listen to the recommendation. You don't make the purchase and later you confirm that it would have been a bad decision to buy WeWork shares. In this way, you improved your value as an investor.

Kurt Cagle, the founder of Semantical, LLC, thinks about the future and writes: "Augmentation is likely to be, for some time to come, the way that most people will directly interact with artificial intelligence systems. The effects will be subtle - steadily improving the quality of the digital products that people produce, reducing the number of errors that show up, and reducing the overall time to create intellectual works - art, writing, coding, and so forth... There is no question that artificial intelligence is rewriting the rules, for good and bad, and augmentation, the kind of AI that is here today and is becoming increasingly difficult to discern from human-directed software, is a proving ground for how the human/computer divide asserts itself."

(https://bit.ly/2nBxfQ1)

Predicting the future with AI

Predicting the future has been a goal of the human being throughout history. Fortune tellers have been important figures in society and have received recognition. One of the most famous is Nostradamus.

Michel de Nostredame (21 December 1503–2 July 1566, Saint-Rémy-de-Provence, France), usually latinised as Nostradamus, was a French astrologer, physician and reputed seer, who is best known for his book Les Prophéties, a collection of 942 poetic quatrains allegedly predicting future events. The book was first published in 1555 and has rarely been out of print since his death. He wrote an almanac for 1550 and, as a result of its success, continued writing them for future years as he began working as an astrologer for various wealthy patrons. His "Les Prophéties", published in 1555, relied heavily on historical and literary precedent, and initially received mixed reviews. In the years since the publication of his Les Prophéties, Nostradamus has attracted many supporters, who, along with much of the popular press, credit him with having accurately predicted many major world events.

One of the applications of Artificial Intelligence that is gaining attention is the prediction of the future. It might seem a contradiction that modern technology is used as a hidden science. However, the technology **Multi-Agent Artificial Intelligence** (MAAI) is surprising the world and gaining followers. Imagine that you might be able to predict the outcome of the election in the United States in 2020, the future of Brexit or that you could guess the outcome of the stock market one month in advance. Do you remember the Cambridge Analytica/Facebook scandal? When the consulting firm Cambridge Analytica used targeted messaging to apparently influence the outcome of the US election? Well, if you thought Cambridge Analytica had scary tech, wait until you see this: A new form of AI modelling promises accurate simulation of the behavior of entire cities, countries and one day perhaps, the world. Yes, predicting the future is now possible with powerful new AI simulations.

Multi-Agent artificial intelligence (MAAI) **is predictive modeling at its most advanced**. It has been used to create digital societies that mimic real ones with stunningly accurate results. In an age of big data, there exists more information about our habits (political, social, religious and fiscal) than ever before. As we feed them information on a daily basis, their ability to predict the future is getting better.

A multi-Agent system is a computerized system composed of multiple interacting intelligent agents. Multi-Agent systems can solve problems that are difficult or impossible for an individual agent to solve. Intelligence may include methodic, functional, and procedural approaches, algorithmic search or reinforcement learning. Typically multi-agent systems research refers to software agents. However, the agents in a multi-agent system could equally well be robots, humans or human teams. A multi-agent system may contain combined human-robot teams.

The University College London, which has operated under the official name of UCL since 2005, has a course of Multi-Agent Artificial Intelligence (MAAI). "The course is intended to provide an introduction of multi-agent machine learning, a subfield of Artificial Intelligence (AI). Multi-Agent learning arises in a variety of domains where multiple intelligent computerized agents interact not only with the environment but also with each other. There are an increasing number of applications ranging from controlling a group of autonomous vehicles/drones to coordinating collaborative bots in factories and warehouses, optimizing distributed sensor networks/traffic, and machine bidding in competitive e-commerce and financial markets, just to name a few. The module combines the study of machine learning with that of game theory and economics, including topics such as game theory, auction theory, algorithmic mechanism design, multi-agent (deep) reinforcement learning. Practical applications, including online advertising, online auction, adversarial training for generative models, bots planning, and AI agents playing online games, will also be covered and discussed." (http://www.cs.ucl.ac.uk/?id=9876).

The new engine of economic development

Artificial Intelligence is the new engine that drives economic development in the world. Research firm Markets and Markets estimates that the Artificial Intelligence market will grow from $420 million in 2014 to $5.05 billion in 2020 thanks to the growing adoption of machine learning and natural language technologies in the media, advertising, retail, finance and health industries. That's more than 10 times in just six years.

The first major transformation in the economic, technological, political and social development of humanity took place with the Industrial Revolution that began in the second half of the eighteenth century in Britain and extended a few decades later to much of Western Europe and America until its conclusion around 1850, marking a turning point in history and changing all aspects of daily life. Both agricultural and industrial production multiplied while production time decreased. From 1800 onwards, per capita income multiplied as it had never done before in history, since until then per capita GDP had remained practically stagnant for centuries. As a consequence of industrial development, new groups or social classes were born, headed by the proletariat - the industrial workers and poor peasants - and the bourgeoisie, owner of the means of production and holder of most of the wealth.

Artificial Intelligence is the new revolution with stronger and deeper effects. Countries that remain leaders will dominate the world in the economic sphere as well as in technology and politics. Here it is necessary to mention that the countries of Latin America and Africa did not play a preponderant role in the industrial transformation and already they have an important delay in the development of Artificial Intelligence. If they do not accelerate their pace to get into this new wave of progress, they will remain behind throughout this century. Later on we will go over the measures that emerging countries must take to get on the Artificial Intelligence train and not be forgotten at the station.

The countries at the forefront in the development of Artificial Intelligence are the United States, China, France, England, Germany, Italy, Russia, Canada, Japan, South Korea, Taiwan and Singapore.

While it is true that Artificial Intelligence took off 70 years ago, we can say that the acceleration began only a few years ago. That is, in 2016 when president Barack Obama published a report on the future of AI where, despite not proposing any concrete funding, it was clear that such technology should be a key strategy for the federal government. The document recognized that "my successor will govern a country that will be transformed by AI". That same year, the Partnership on AI was established and America's leading technology companies accelerated their pace of research, innovation and investment. (https://bit.ly/2jREywS)

The Chinese government is committed to supporting the development of Artificial Intelligence. The government of president Xi Jinping published the 13th Five-Year National Development Plan outlining the guidelines for digital development and industrialization until 2030. In this plan the Chinese government considers making significant investments in research and development, as well as on two controversial issues: Subsidize the processor industry and decrease control to priority technologies such as autonomous vehicles, Artificial Intelligence and massive data collection as long as they are developed by Chinese.

The results are already beginning to be seen in the emergence of technology companies and applications such as WeChat, Alibaba, Wibo, TamTam, KakaoTalk, Baidu, YouKu and JD. In China the majority of the adult population uses some kind of electronic device and is accustomed to making inquiries, purchases, payments and transfers via their mobile phone. China has a staggering 1.3 billion mobile phones, equivalent to 94% of the population.

It is important to note that in China **the government of President Xi Jinping attaches great importance to the AI project** and gives it all the support it requires. It has done so by designating Baidu as the base AI platform for autonomous vehicles, Alibaba for intelligent cities and Tencent for health care. In contrast, president Trump's government considers traditional industry more important than the new digital industry and sets aside projects to boost Artificial Intelligence. This reveals a desire to oppose any plan or project that has been put in place or supported by the Obama administration. On the other hand, the isolationist and anti-immigrant policy imposed by president Donald Trump could diminish the contribution that migrants have made for centuries to technology and science in the United States. In this way, the development model of Artificial Intelligence is different in the United States and China. In the US, it is based on economic strength, research, investment in innovation and the flourishing of large companies such as Google, Facebook, Apple, Microsoft, IBM and Amazon, as well as on the creation of startups made up of young entrepreneurs with great technical capacity and enormous desire to succeed. In China there are also large companies such as Alibaba, Tencent and Baidu, but they also have the support of the government.

France has taken a big step by declaring its intention to position itself as a leader in the field of AI and accompanies its intention with a plan to invest billions of euros in a long-term program. President Emmanuel Macron announced that, 1.5 billion euros of public funds will be allocated to the Artificial Intelligence Plan to promote research and projects in the field. In addition, he assured that AI will be "the first field of application" of the Fund for Innovation and Industry, with 10 billion euros, launched at the beginning of the year. Leading companies in the sector also announced their intention to invest in France in this field within the framework of a national AI program. Samsung will open its new Artificial Intelligence research center in France, the Japanese Fujitsu will expand its center of excellence at the Polytechnic School in Paris to become its European AI center, Microsoft will invest 30 million dollars over the next three years in training in France through the AI School it recently opened. DeepMind also announced the opening this summer in Paris of an AI research laboratory, the first in continental Europe. All indications are that within a few years we will see France as a world leader in AI.

Inherent risks of AI

An inherent risk is something specific to the work or process that cannot be eliminated from the system; that is, in all work or process there will be risks for people or for the execution of the activity itself. For example, in mining the inherent risks are landslides, explosions, entrapment, falls and even the asphyxiation of the miners. While it is true that they cannot be completely eliminated, it is possible to take precautionary measures to reduce them and bring them to the point closest to zero. On the other hand, it is also true that even when it is known that there is an inherent risk within an activity, that activity is put into practice as in the case of mining. Artificial Intelligence also has inherent risks and in this section we will deal with them.

The most worrisome and commented risk of AI is the substitution of man by machine in workplaces. That is, the loss of jobs due to Artificial Intelligence. This concern has been clearly expressed by the former president of the World Bank who considers that "Artificial Intelligence is going to eliminate between 50% and 65% of all existing jobs in developing countries." However, he clarified that new jobs will be generated with different skills. So in the future the race to be competitive will be related to innovation. "This vibrant dynamic will generate new jobs because our task is not to try to preserve old jobs, but to create new ones that will need new skills," said Jim Yong Kim. That is a terrible prognosis. Imagine that 50% of all people working in emerging countries like Egypt, Mexico, Argentina, Turkey or South Africa lose their jobs. Yes, half of all people working in industries, banks, commerce and all economic activity. If the estimate were 5% it might not be so serious, but 50% could be catastrophic.

It is not just the World Bank that is setting the alarm bells ringing. Researchers from renowned institutions join the alarm. One of the most complete studies in this sense is that carried out by two Oxford professors, Benedikt Frey and Michael Osborne, according to which 47% of jobs in the United States are at risk of being replaced by machines. This report was prepared in 2013.

The issue of the loss of jobs due to Artificial Intelligence has created a great controversy among researchers specialized in this field. There are those who predict a major economic catastrophe because of the huge unemployment that will result from the replacement of human beings by computers, robots and machines equipped with AI. And they are partially right. It is enough to look at the modern assembly plants of airplanes, boats, automobiles, refrigerators, computers and all kinds of devices used in the home, office and industry, in addition to the production of tasty pizzas, to learn of the substitution of people by robots. The important point here is to take the necessary measures in advance to cushion the blow.

Bill Gates, the founder of Microsoft, believes that one measure to slow down the automation process and allow governments more time to solve unemployment problems is to **tax robots**. "When people say that the arrival of robots will have negative effects due to displacement, then you have to be ready to raise taxes and even reduce the speed of that adoption so you can solve it," Gates said in an interview for the technology portal Quartz published in February 2017.

According to a recent MIT study, job losses caused by robotics and Artificial Intelligence will have an impact affecting different types of activity. This process will take place in three major waves. In the first phase, (beginning of 2020) the simplest tasks and the structured analysis of data will be automated. In the second (mid-twenties) the exchange of information and unstructured analysis will be extended. Finally, the third phase, (starting in 2030) will implement the automation of manual skills and the resolution of problems in real time. Thus, 34% of jobs will be at risk.

Studies have been made to locate the types of jobs that will be replaced according to the advance of the Artificial Intelligence. This is a list prepared with information from MIT and other research centers:

- Workers in manufacturing
- Customer assistants
- Banking assistants
- Counters
- Stock exchange operators
- Medical
- Chauffeurs
- Creative
- Artists
- Scientists

According to a new study by the IBM Institute for Business Value (September-2019) over the next three years 120 million workers in the world's 12 biggest economies may need to be retrained as a result of widespread adoption of Artificial

Intelligence and automation in the workplace. Only 41% of CEOs surveyed have the resources in place to close the skills gap brought on by new emerging technologies. That means 59% of the CEOs surveyed have no skills development strategies in place for their employees in the early 2020s.

"Organizations are facing mounting concerns over the widening skills gap and tightened labor markets with the potential to impact their futures as well as worldwide economies. Yet while executives recognize the severity of the problem, half of those surveyed admit that they do not have any skills development strategies in place to address their largest gaps. And the tactics the study found were most likely to close the skills gap the fastest are the tactics companies are using the least. New strategies are emerging to help companies reskill their people and build the culture of continuous learning required to succeed in the era of AI. **The era of AI will be a transformative period for the global economy** as the skill gap through employee training will take time to close. The company's study indicates new skill requirements for jobs will be required due to the fast pace of AI and automation adoption, while other skills become out-of-date." said Amy Wright, Managing Partner, IBM Talent & Transformation. (https://ibm.co/2IBSFv4)

A similar situation arose during the Industrial Revolution. The machine replaced the worker and thousands of jobs were lost. However, others were created and balance was restored at a higher level of prosperity. After 150 years it can be said that the result was positive. Millions of jobs will be lost in the AI Revolution and even better paying jobs will be created. However, the balance will not be restored so easily because the speed of change is faster. That is, the speed of job loss is higher than the speed at which new jobs can be created. We will have to prepare ourselves to face unemployment and this time not only of workers, but of professionals with a high degree of education and a high level of salary. Is Bill Gates right?

Another inherent risk of Artificial Intelligence is the misunderstanding or incomplete understanding of an order. The order can be both ways. From a human being to AI or from AI to human.

One of the most important AI techniques is natural language processing (NLP). That is, the study of communication between a machine with Artificial Intelligence and human beings through natural languages such as Spanish, English or Chinese.

In order for an AI to understand natural language, it is necessary to carry out a highly complex analysis. This analysis integrates several components whose application depends on their objective. For example, a text-to-speech converter does not need semantic or pragmatic analysis, but a conversational system requires very detailed information of the context and thematic domain, namely:

- **Morphological** or lexical analysis. It consists of the internal analysis of the words that form sentences to extract lemmas, flexible features and compound lexical units. It is essential for basic information: syntactic category and lexical meaning.
- **Syntactic** analysis. It is the analysis of the sentence structure according to the grammatical model used (logical or statistical).
- **Semantic** analysis. It provides the interpretation of sentences, once the morph syntactic ambiguities have been eliminated.
- **Pragmatic** analysis. Incorporates the analysis of the context of use to the final interpretation. This includes the treatment of figurative language (metaphor and irony) as the knowledge of the specific world needed to understand a specialized text.

The problems for language processing are: Ambiguity, separation between words and the imperfect reception of data. In the section on language processing in Chapter 5 we will study these concepts in more detail.

These difficulties and complex language components create the conditions for a message or command given by a human being to an AI to arrive incomplete or simply be misunderstood. Let's imagine the problems that can arise when a military order is given and its interpretation is wrong. A military attack with autonomous weapons that issue or receive the wrong orders represents one of the greatest dangers of producing war weapons with AI.

This news reflects the power that Artificial Intelligence can have in the decision making of the missile arsenal of the United States.

"Two researchers associated with the US Air Force want to give nuclear codes to an Artificial Intelligence."

Air Force Institute of Technology associate dean Curtis McGiffin and Louisiana Tech Research Institute researcher Adam Lowther, also affiliated with the Air Force, co-wrote an article arguing that the United States needs to develop **an automated strategic response system based on Artificial Intelligence.**

In other words, **they want to give an AI the nuclear codes:** "It may be necessary to develop a system based on Artificial Intelligence, with predetermined response decisions that detects, decides, and directs strategic forces with such speed that the attack-time compression challenge does not place the United States in an impossible position".

Accidents with autonomous vehicles are another risk of Artificial Intelligence. An autonomous vehicle, also known as unmanned or robotic, is a vehicle capable of imitating human driving and control capabilities. As an autonomous vehicle it is able to perceive the environment around it, as well as to trace and follow its route to finally reach its destination. The human being chooses the destination, but nothing else. He is not required to activate any mechanical operation of the vehicle.

In order to achieve truly automatic driving on the road or in an urban environment it is necessary to integrate a system with real time operation and capable of operating in a coordinated manner. In addition, a set of sensors are needed to collect and provide the information needed to make decisions.

When thinking of a control system for an autonomous car it is necessary to warn that algorithms in the style of classic programming rules such as "if...then...else..." do not work; for example "If a pedestrian crosses in the middle of the street, then reduce speed and brake if necessary". It is obvious that this way of thinking is not adequate since the number of possible situations is very high and therefore a system capable of generalizing is necessary. Instead of implementing innumerable rules to recognize these objects, it is more practical to implement an algorithm with machine learning technology that is "trained" with different images that exemplify all possible situations. Each of the images is associated with the type of vehicle it contains. The algorithm begins to process the images. Initially it tries to know what vehicle is in each image. At first it will make many mistakes but little by little it will modify and adapt the parameters to try again. The process continues to reduce the failure rate. Later, when new images are presented they can be handled correctly. Then we can say that the algorithm has learned, but this takes a long time.

Despite the advanced AI system, accidents have already occurred. In December 2017 in San Francisco, California, a motorcyclist named Oscar Nilsson was involved in an accident with one of Cruise Automation's Chevrolet Bolt EVs (the GM subsidiary that performs autonomous driving tests), this being one of the cars in General Motors' open environment autonomous driving pilot test. After the accident, the motorcyclist sued General Motors. These situations require more in-depth analysis in order to make decisions and legislate. For example, who is to blame for an accident in an autonomous car?

People's privacy

Artificial Intelligence is also a risk to people's privacy. The Council of Europe warns of this threat in the voice of Dunja Mijatovic, the Commissioner for Human Rights of the Council of Europe, who warned of the threat that Artificial Intelligence devices can pose to privacy and other fundamental rights.

The analysis of the data used by Artificial Intelligence systems makes particularly evident the discrepancy between the benefits and risks to our human rights, she said in an article published on her website. "Applications and social networks," said Mijatovic, "store large amounts of personal data, often without our knowing it, which serve to establish our profile or predict our behavior. We offer information about our health, political opinions and our family life without knowing who is going to use it, for what purposes and in what way."

The Commissioner of the Pan-European organization of 47 Member States indicated that Artificial Intelligence systems, instead of contributing to making our decisions "more objective", can "reinforce discrimination and prejudice by giving them the appearance of objectivity" and assured that more and more elements show that women, ethnic minorities, the disabled and members of the LGBT community "suffer discrimination caused by biased algorithms". On facial recognition, which can help law empowerment locate suspects, Mijatovic referred to the risk of it being used for mass surveillance or to identify protesters. In this regard, she noted that today "it is much easier for governments to continuously monitor and restrict the right to privacy, freedom of assembly, freedom of movement and freedom of the press.

Mijatovic therefore proposed greater cooperation between representatives of the state, civil society and the private sector, on which AI depends, to respect human rights and provide more transparency and understanding". She also called on governments to invest in initiatives to raise awareness and educate new generations so that they "acquire the necessary skills to make good use of technologies linked to Artificial Intelligence. AI can considerably increase the possibilities of living the life to which we aspire but also destroy them. In other words, strict rules are needed to avoid a modern version of the Frankenstein monster". (https://bit.ly/2Lmi9Uk)

The manipulation of public opinion through false news and videos generated by **Artificial Intelligence and bots** could have a great impact on public opinion by altering the levels of communication from politics to the media. The use of bots on social networks spreading false news was a reality in the US presidential campaign in 2016 and Mexico in 2018.

In order to establish a conversation, coherent and understandable phrases must be used, although most conversational bots do not fully understand the meaning of the conversation. Instead, they take into account the speaker's words or phrases that will allow them to use a series of pre-prepared responses. In this way, the bot is able to follow a conversation with more or less logic, but without really knowing what it is talking about and this lack of comprehensive understanding can generate errors.

> **Chat bot** or simply bot is a program that simulates having a conversation with a person by providing automatic responses to entries made by the user. Usually the conversation is established by text, although there are also models that have a multimedia user interface. More recently, some have started using text-to-speech (CTV) converters, making user interaction more realistic.

There are different levels of bots according to the complexity of your system, the capacity for dialogue or your level of Artificial Intelligence. There are bots that follow some basic rules and others that can hold a conversation without the interlocutor knowing that he is interacting with a bot as described in the Turing test. In the former, the developer defines the dialogue as well as the possible answers while the more advanced ones are more open as they allow the user to interact freely. In its production, Artificial Intelligence systems (NLP engines) are used to process the information. In the field of Artificial Intelligence systems, the technological industry is the first that has started to use the most advanced bots with a high AI level, such as IBM's Watson, Microsoft's LUIS or Google's API.ai, where the key to the bot's intelligence lies in the training it receives.

Well-trained bots can create a strategic advantage for political parties and function as Artificial Intelligence propaganda machines. Political campaigns have changed the battlefield. They used to be street rallies. Now they are social networks manipulated by bots.

From Big brother to big data

George Orwell published his famous political novel 1984 on June 8, 1949. The novel introduced the concept of the ubiquitous and vigilant Big brother. The novel unfolds in 1984 and beyond in a future London, in a part of the region called Air Strip 1 that was once called England or Britain, integrated, in turn, into an immense collectivist state called Oceania. The society of Oceania is divided into three groups. The "external" members of the One Party, the members of the leading council or inner circle of the party and a mass of people whom the Party keeps poor and entertained so that they cannot and do not want to rebel, the proles. (https://amzn.to/2oeRzXt)

> The terms utopian fiction and dystopian fiction serve to designate two literary genres where social and political structures are explored. Utopian fiction refers to utopia, a term used to designate an ideal world where everything is perfect. On the contrary, dystopian fiction, sometimes known as apocalyptic literature, refers to a society that by claiming happiness, makes its citizens suffer systematically or degrades them to irreversible oblivion. The dystopian trilogy consists of three novels: *A Brave New World* (1932, Aldous Huxley), *1984* (1949, George Orwell), and *Fahrenheit 451* (1953, Ray Bradbury).

Orwell's novel tells the story of a future society subdued by the power of politics, censorship and media manipulation. A totalitarian system where the population is controlled to the point that thinking about a crime is a crime in itself and is severely punished. To carry out this strict control over the inhabitants in every house, building, street and in any public or private place a camera is installed that transmits a signal to a screen that is always observed by someone, in such a way that to carry out any suspicious activity, even being in one's own home is eliminated by the fear of a severe retaliation. The permanent fear in which people live is the engine that spins the main gear of this dystopian world free of revolts, riots or crimes. Fear controls all acts of citizenship. The government is headed by an unnamed figure with a very common face that is all over the walls and can be found anywhere to remind you that you are not the owner of your own actions. This figure is known simply as Big brother... Big brother keeps an eye on you. The Big brother... The Big brother is watching you.

When George Orwell wrote his novel (Between 1947 and 1948), the technological means did not exist to establish a large observation network in such a way that all the movements of citizens, their conversations, their wanderings in the city, their purchases, their payments, their income and expenditures, their savings capacity or their inclination to get into debt, what they saw and what they read, what they ate, the places they visited, the restaurants they frequented, the illnesses they suffered from, the doctor who treated them, the medicines they took, the car they used, the places that impressed them, the friends they had, their ideas and participation in politics, their electoral preferences, the information they sought, what they wrote, what they liked and disliked, their actions and almost all their thoughts could be observed.

Today this is already possible and every day the capacity for observation increases. **Technology has made possible the idea of Big brother** watching the citizen. Big data technology now allows the capture, transmission, storage and analysis of billions of data that are generated every day in all the movements and transactions that people make, whether using their credit card or their mobile in addition to the enormous amount of data that the devices transmit every time someone uses them and many times without even being used such as telephones, computers, video cameras, smart TVs and sophisticated systems such as the Internet of Things.

When a person walks quietly down the street their movements are recorded by a video camera and transmitted to headquarters where they can be analyzed. The same thing happens when you travel in your car or enter a bank branch, a store and even in many houses. The cameras installed in cities are already counted by the thousands and soon there will be millions to make real the surveillance of Big brother on every corner.

When you use your mobile phone to order a pizza at home, you expect to receive a Margarita pizza with a dessert and a couple of soft drinks for the price you have to pay. But that act that seems simple and uncomplicated unleashes a whole series of actions controlled by the big data. The data that you have innocently delivered can be this or much more depending on the sophistication of the system that captures, transmits, stores, cleans and analyzes them: the number of your mobile, home, schedule, the number of people in your home, their eating habits, the type of pizza, the type of dessert, the brand of soda and if you dare to pay with your credit card imagine the cascade of data that delivers. By the way, the information derived from a credit card transaction is a vein in a gold mine. That data is processed, cleaned, sorted, stored and left ready for analysis by a technique called analytics.

All this data is collected and analyzed by a marketing department to plan their sales strategy. If it is a small chain of pizzerias, the systems will be unsophisticated, but now imagine what happens when you order a purchase from Amazon where they run millions of sales operations of all kinds of items every day, at all times and in a large number of countries. The data that reaches Amazon's large computers is in the millions. That's big data. Of course, it is data that is worth ground gold but that cannot be analyzed by a person to turn it into information in order to make decisions. This is where the analytical tool and Artificial Intelligence come in.

When organizing an electoral campaign, the knowledge of the voters is fundamental. If you know precisely the profile of the people, their desires, their fears, what they like and what angers them, their economic capacity, their age, their sex, the type of house they live in, the number and ages of their children, their means of transportation, the distance to work, the salary they receive and much more data, you can develop a strategy to offer and promise to each one what they expect and that translates into a vote to win the election.

If the purpose is not to draw up a marketing plan or win an election but to establish control over the population of a city or an entire country, big data becomes the ideal weapon. With the help of video cameras and the collection of data by different means, even buying information from social networks or companies that are dedicated to data collection it is possible to meet the population, but not only globally but to each person in particular applying the technique known as OCEAN or Big Five that defines personality through five main traits or factors: O (Openness or openness to new experiences), C (Conscientiousness or responsibility), E (Extraversion), A (Agreeableness or kindness) and N (Neuroticism or emotional instability), the five form the mnemonic acronym "OCEAN". With the knowledge of these five factors it is possible to meet and control a person or an entire population. And this is what "From Big brother to big data" means.

Large information companies such as Google, Facebook or Amazon collect a huge amount of data and know more about each person than each person knows about themselves and their environment. Google knows their preferences well. It knows what interests them, what attracts or worries them. Its search engine is also a sponge that absorbs users' information to process it with Artificial Intelligence techniques and obtain valuable information that uses in its targeted advertising strategy with millimeter precision to hit the target precisely.

Amazon is the world's largest online sales company and it is also the company that knows its millions of customers' best. It knows what each of them likes and based on this information suggests everything from a book to a car. If you want to control the market, know what your customer likes.

As early as 2013 Karsten Gerloff, president of the Free Software Foundation Europe (FSFE) said "Facebook defines who we are. Amazon sets out what we want and Google determines what we think."

But perhaps of all the companies that handle large volumes of data the one that best knows its customers and users around the world is Facebook. In the face that it offers to the public Facebook is a large social network that links 2,160 million people. Behind the scene it is a large Artificial Intelligence company that analyzes the information of its customers and users and knows each of them perfectly. The large amount of information handled by Facebook can be used as raw material to design positive strategies such as a marketing campaign for the introduction of a new product to the market, but it can also be used to influence, control or manipulate people.

An example of this last situation was recently known with the scandal that was generated when it was announced that Facebook information was used by the company Cambridge Analytics to influence the elections of Brexit, Nigeria, Kenya and also in the United States 2016 and Mexico 2018. This storm that affects Facebook and some governments is only the tip of the iceberg of what can be done when citizens around the world are watched, their data is captured and processed through Artificial Intelligence techniques such as big data, mining and analytics.

Cambridge Analytics created a "cultural weapon" and took to the extreme the so-called "filter bubble" in which everyone receives a personalized version of reality based on their previous tastes, thus placing each user in a tautological universe separate from the others. The objective is to make an accurate shot at a single person whose profile is known with precision and not a shotgun aimed at the crowd. This is what the big data technique is all about: to arrange and to analyze a great volume of data to influence each person with precision.

The case of Cambridge Analytics is just the tip of the iceberg because the model of Facebook and other companies goes beyond selling advertising; it is all a **"surveillance capitalism"** whose aim is to collect large volumes of data to establish control over the consumer and in the political sphere and government to make a reality of the novel 1984 by George Orwell.

Love between humans and robots

This subject has been dealt with profusely by science fiction but is now a reality. The question arises without further explanation: can a human being fall in love with a robot? And perhaps even more daring is the question in the opposite direction. Can a robot fall in love with a human being?

History tells us of strange love affairs between men and mythological beings and even between human beings and gods. One of the most beautiful is that of **Pygmalion and Galatea** that is worth remembering to use it as a framework in this controversial subject.

For a long time Pygmalion, King of Cyprus, had looked for a wife whose beauty corresponded to his idea of the perfect woman. Not finding her, he finally decided that he would not marry and would devote all his time and the love he felt within himself to the creation of the most beautiful statues.

The king did not like women, and lived in solitude for a long time. Tired of the situation he was in, he began to sculpt a statue of a woman with perfect and beautiful features. He made the statue of a young woman whom he called Galatea, so perfect and so beautiful that he fell madly in love with her. He dreamt that the statue came to life.

In one of the great celebrations in honor of the goddess Venus celebrated on the island, Pygmalion begged the goddess to give life to his beloved statue. The goddess, who was willing to assist him, raised the flame of the sculptor's altar three times higher than that of other altars. Pygmalion did not understand the sign and went home very disappointed. When he returned home he looked at the statue and after a long time the artist stood up and kissed it. Pygmalion no longer felt the icy ivory lips, but felt a soft, warm skin on his lips. He kissed her again and the statue came to life, falling madly in love with its creator. Venus ended up pleasing the king by giving his beloved the gift of fertility.

The poet Ovid tells us the end of the myth in "Book of The Metamorphoses": "Pygmalion went to the statue and when he touched it, it seemed to him that it was warm, that the ivory softened and that, depositing its hardness, it yielded to the fingers softly, as the wax of Mount Himeto softens to the rays of the sun and allows itself to be handled with the fingers, taking several figures and becoming more docile and softer with the handling. On seeing her, Pygmalion is filled with a great joy mixed with fear, believing that he was being deceived. He touched the statue again, and made sure that she was a flexible body and that the veins gave their pulsations when exploring them with his fingers."

When asked, **can a human being fall in love with a robot?** Controversial answers arise. While some researchers claim that the link with Artificial Intelligence is destined to lead to a war that could annihilate humanity, others believe that in the not-so-distant future human beings and machines may fall in love with each other.

Brian Scassellati, the director of the social robotics laboratory at Yale University, is one of the world's leading experts in social robotics, a discipline that has barely existed for two decades and whose aim is to create a new generation of robots designed to be human companions, capable of understanding social dynamics, moral norms, learning from the relationships they establish with people and generating a robotic theory of the human mind. Scassellati says: "They are not promises of the future, but there are already Artificial Intelligences of this type that work with children promoting their learning or with children with autism teaching them to decipher emotions. They accompany people in old people's homes and even begin to be present in airports, guiding absent-minded tourists."

Cynthia Breazeal, a computer scientist and creator of Kismet, the first social robot in history in the late 1990s, says that social robots include our social thinking, our social and emotional intelligence, as well as cognitive intelligence. At first Kismet was just a robotic head that could recognize and simulate basic emotions and has evolved to become Jibo, designed to be not a "something" but a "someone".

Professor Kevin Curran, a researcher at the Computer Science Research Institute at the University of Ulster in the United Kingdom, explains that the tendency is for robots to look like human beings, which makes many people feel inclined to establish friendly relations with them. And he adds that some laboratories are already developing prototypes that emulate human life, such as Bina-48, an android that has been programmed with the memories and emotions of a real person and reacts to external stimuli according to those experiences that were implanted.

Curran believes that in a short time we will be able to find in the market friendly robots that perform the functions of accompanying the elderly and caring for children, among other activities. But the scientist goes even further when he states that it will not be long before robots are used for sexual purposes when he states "Although for the moment these models are still far from human intelligence because they do not have our ability to learn new patterns of behavior, the trend indicates that the gap is narrowing very quickly".

Sex robots are already a reality. Researchers of robotics, Artificial Intelligence, psychology and human anatomy have added their knowledge to produce sexual robots with the purpose of satisfying a growing number of men and women who have found sexual satisfaction in their robotic counterparts and who have even come to confess that they feel a feeling of attraction and even something that could be said to be love.

In recent decades society has witnessed a profound change in the acceptance of interpersonal relationships that were not previously accepted. Homosexuality was not allowed in countries where same-sex unions are now accepted and even legally permitted. If this had been possible in the middle of the last century Alan Turing would have lived longer and surely happier to be accepted in his homosexuality. This social and legal openness towards interpersonal relations could be the door through which relations between a human being and a robot go frankly and freely.

The hardware of a female sex robot contains latex, thermoplastic elastomer, surgical silicones, fluids of different types and even natural hair. The software is still a set of bits and bytes ordered in the form of a powerful Artificial

Intelligence algorithm highly developed with automatic learning techniques to learn to react according to their partner and even the environment. They can recognize the tastes of their partner and have the ability to adapt depending on the day, the situation or even the mood that it detects in the human. The vagina is a central point in the design and operation of the robot. It can reproduce internal movements with a series of motors that adjust the silicone to size and can even adjust the pressure so that it closes more or less and produces more or less pressure.

Some sex robots have already become famous. Harmony was the first female sex robot and now Harry is the first male sex robot to accompany and satisfy solitary women. It is made of latex, has an athletic figure and a bionic penis capable of "getting up" with female stimulation. It was built by the company Real Botix and has a price of ten thousand dollars.

Samantha is one of the most recent and surprising creations. It was designed by electronic engineer Sergi Santos, who gave her a higher and more demanding level of Artificial Intelligence, because unless her partner shows signs of respect or affection, she won't let them use her. Samantha recognizes different forms of touch and when it becomes too aggressive or disrespectful, she turns herself off.

Is the relationship between a human being and a robot a risk or is it an opportunity to establish good relationships with Artificial Intelligence?

Technological singularity

Technological singularity is the hypothetical moment in which Artificial Intelligence surpasses human intelligence. Technological singularity implies that an inanimate entity, be it a robot, a computer or a computer network, has the capacity to learn itself and to improve itself recursively, as well as to design and produce generations of machines successively more powerful and with greater intelligence.

Technological singularity will cause disruptive changes in the life of the human being, of society and even of the nature of Planet Earth with the possibility of its effect extending to the Universe. Strong Artificial Intelligence will dominate life on Planet Earth and just as it is difficult for man to know and understand the origin of the Universe, so it is difficult for him to understand and accept that a higher intelligence is that which dominates and controls life on Planet Earth and perhaps the entire Universe.

John von Neumann, the pioneer of computation, first used the concept of singularity when he expressed in a conversation with Stanislaw Ulam: "increasingly accelerated progress of technology and changes in the way of human life, resulting in the imminent appearance of some essential singularity in the history of the race beyond which human affairs, as we know them, could not continue". Here we consider that by saying "could not continue" von Neumann was referring to the possibility of humanity losing control and yielding it to Artificial Intelligence.

Although the term singularity had been used several times, it was **Vernor Vinge who applied it accurately** and popularized it. Vernor Vinge is a mathematician, computer theoretician, novelist, essayist and science fiction writer. He was born in Wisconsin, in 1944 and educated at the University of San Diego in California where he earned a doctorate in Mathematics. Vinge has been awarded several prizes for his novels.

Vinge has gained prominence for his idea of technological singularity according to which the creation of Artificial Intelligences with capabilities greater than human, which in turn would produce even greater intelligences and so on, would lead to a "singularity" in development, an inflection point of exponential technological growth, with unimaginable consequences and from which it is impossible to speculate about our future.

In an unusual statement **Vernor Vinge predicts that technological singularity will be a reality in the 2030s** through a rapid and sudden change unlike Kurzweil who predicts a gradual self-improvement. For Vinge there are four ways in which singularity could occur:

1. Computers that are "awake" and superhumanly intelligent may be developed.
2. Large computer networks and their associated users may "wake up" as superhumanly intelligent entities.
3. Computer/human interfaces may become so intimate that users may reasonably be considered superhumanly intelligent.
4. Biological science may provide means to improve natural human intellect.

Vinge continues to predict that superhuman intelligences will be able to improve their own minds faster than their human creators. "When the units of higher human intelligence progress," Vinge postulates, "progress will be much faster." He predicts that this feedback loop of self-improved intelligence will involve large amounts of technological advancement within a short period of time, and asserts that the creation of superhuman intelligence represents a break in the ability of humans to shape their future. His argument is that authors cannot write realistic characters that go beyond human intellect, since it goes beyond the capacity for human expression. In other words: **We cannot think beyond our capacity and way of thinking.** (https://bit.ly/2lBhBmU)

It is important to emphasize that not all scientists, philosophers and scholars are convinced by the idea that technological singularity can create a superior intelligence to that of the human being. They do not accept that the hardware of a computer can have the intelligence of a human being that has taken millions of years to produce.

Among them is the Canadian scientist Steven Pinker who declared emphatically in 2008: "...There is not the slightest reason to believe in a singularity to come. The fact that you can visualize a future in your imagination is not evidence that it is probable or even possible. Look at vaulted cities, jet-pack displacements, underwater cities, mile-high buildings, and nuclear-powered automobiles. They were all futuristic fantasies when I was a child and never arrived. Pure processing power is not a magic powder that magically solves all your problems". (https://bit.ly/2lw103F)

For the author of this book the technological singularity will begin by 2040. This view is in line with Vernor Vinge's thinking.

Common sense

Common sense is the cherry on the Artificial Intelligence cake. Common sense is something difficult to locate, to understand and even to use. It is something that a human being has but that sometimes he does not use opportunely or simply he does not use it to make decisions or to execute actions; for that reason it is said that **common sense is the least common of the senses**. Despite this difficulty, some scholars of Artificial Intelligence consider it to be the last frontier to cross. If Artificial Intelligence manages to have common sense, it will have reached the human being and then it will be able to overcome it. Therefore, we will focus on common sense to shed the light that will allow us to understand it and then we will see if AI has the resources and capacity to conquer it.

The difficulty of its definition begins with a whole range of descriptions of this concept. Moreover, the descriptions offered are in themselves complex and imprecise. It is easier to intuit than to define it. Let's look at Wikipedia's definition: Common sense describes the beliefs or propositions that are fed by society (family, clan, people, nation or all of humanity).

Henri-Louis Bergson, French-Jewish philosopher who was influential in the tradition of continental philosophy, especially during the first half of the 20th century until the Second World War, is known for his arguments that processes of immediate experience and intuition are more significant than abstract rationalism and science for understanding reality. Bergson defines common sense as "the faculty to orient oneself in practical life".

Eduardo Mora-Anda, Member of the Ecuadorian Academy of Language says that common sense saves us nonsense: it calculates the probable and the improbable, the reasonable and the absurd. He does not abide by rules but by what can work and he is not a perfectionist, that this is neurotic, but that he prefers "the reasonable".

For **Jack Trout** common sense is an essential faculty of the person: "a faculty that possesses the generality of people to judge things reasonably." John Francis "Jack" Trout was an owner of Trout & Partners, a consulting firm. He was one of the founders and pioneers of positioning theory and also marketing warfare theory

We could say that common sense is what people think and accept at a general level about a particular topic. It's like a kind of social and natural agreement that people make about something. It is a way of judging things reasonably, without the need for certain information to be scientifically proven; **the only thing that matters is that most people consider it to be true.**

The next step will be to go over the functional characteristics of common sense to see if it is possible to frame them and express them through an algorithm that can be executed by a computer, a robot or any inanimate entity capable of processing Artificial Intelligence technology.

These are the functions traditionally attributed to common sense:

- To know the different qualities captured by the external senses and to establish a comparison between these qualities.

- To know the acts or operations of the external senses.

- According to priest Manuel Barbado, it performs one more function: to distinguish real objects from fantastic images. Father Barbado relies on some texts of Saint Thomas to assign him this function.

In order to learn more about this controversial subject, the best thing to do is to approach an expert in the matter, so we will study the ideas of Ramón López de Mántaras. His curriculum fully endorses him: Research professor at the Consejo Superior de Investigaciones Científicas (CSIC) and director of the Instituto de Investigación en Inteligencia Artificial (IIIA Spain). Master in Computer Engineering from the University of California Berkeley, PhD in Physics from the University of Toulouse.

In order to know his thoughts about the great challenge for Artificial Intelligence to give common sense to machines, we reproduce part of the interview done by journalist Javier López Rejas in April 2017 for the newspaper El Cultural.

Javier López Rejas writes: Ramón López de Mántaras sees the future from his laboratory at the Instituto de Investigación en Inteligencia Artificial (IIIA), and he does so with caution. He knows that he has in his hands information that would overcome any science fiction book. In the bowels of the organization CSIC, which he also directs, he tries to transfer the mechanisms of human creativity to machines. Knowing its circuits and lighting the spark of knowledge is a challenge only comparable to understanding the first steps of the universe.

López Rejas prepared a questionnaire with several questions for the interview with López de Mántaras. His answers caused astonishment at the capacity that Artificial Intelligence can deploy. For our purpose we have selected only a couple of questions that are of most interest to us:

What will be AI's great challenge?

"The big problem is still how to give machines common sense. It is the necessary step for them to stop being specific artificial intelligences and start being general. It is, without a doubt, a problem of extraordinary complexity, comparable to that of getting to know in detail the origin of the universe and of life. In any case, they will always be different from human intelligence because they depend on the bodies in which they are located. The mental development required by any complex intelligence depends on the environment. In turn, these interactions depend on the body. The machines will probably follow different processes of socialization to ours; so, no matter how sophisticated they become, they will be different intelligences to ours. The fact that they are intelligences that are alien to humans - and therefore alien to our values and needs - should make us reflect on the possible ethical limitations to the development of Artificial Intelligence."

In light of the great advances in AI, has the Turing test been reached?

"No, contrary to some assertions it has not really been reached. In any case, it is not an objective of AI research. It is also a test that, although it can be reached, in fact does not guarantee that the machine is really intelligent. You can prepare a chatbot to pass the test and not know how to do anything else. Intelligence is much more than the ability to program a chatbot to deceive a human interlocutor by holding a more or less coherent written dialogue."

Other government institutions and research centers are working on various projects with the aim of providing the computer with common sense. These include DARPA and the Allen Institute named after Paul Allen, founder of Microsoft, who recently passed away.

The Defense Advanced Research Projects Agency (DARPA) is an agency of the United States Department of Defense responsible for the development of emerging technologies for use by the military. **DARPA is teaming up with the Allen Institute for Artificial Intelligence** to teach and test common sense for AI.

DARPA's Dave Gunning explained in a press release: "The absence of common sense prevents an intelligent system from understanding its world, communicating naturally with people, behaving reasonably in unforeseen situations, and learning from new experiences. This absence is perhaps the most significant barrier between the narrowly focused AI applications we have today and the more general AI applications we would like to create in the future".

Oren Etzioni, head of the Allen Institute for AI said: "Common sense has been a holy grail of AI for 35 years or more. One of the problems is how to put this on an empirical footing. If you can't measure it, how can you evaluate it? This is one of the very first times people have tried to make common sense measurable, and certainly the first time that DARPA has thrown their hat, and their leadership, into the ring." (https://tcrn.ch/2EdjGON)

The common sense effort is part of DARPA's big $2 billion investment in AI on multiple fronts. But they're not looking to duplicate or compete with the likes of Google, Amazon and Baidu, which have invested heavily in the AI applications we have on our phones and the like. The results of the project to give common sense to Artificial Intelligence will not be seen in one or two years, but surely in 20 years they will achieve it.

Omega-Ω

The year is 2039:

AI researchers build a quantum supercomputer with 256 qubit capacity and develop a quantum error correction technique to reduce disturbances and noise in order to achieve an error rate of two qubits of less than 0.6%. In addition, it satisfies the following conditions for its quantum system: 1). the system can be initialized to position it in a known and controlled starting state from the beginning of operations. 2). It is possible to manipulate the qubits in a controlled way with a group of operations in such a way that it forms a universal set of doors. 3). the system maintains its quantum coherence throughout its operation. 4) It is feasible to know the final state of the system once the algorithm has been executed. This quantum computer is called Omega-Ω.

A team of highly qualified programmers in Open Fermion software specially designed to run on quantum computers writes sophisticated Artificial Intelligence algorithms. The computer programs are based on machine learning, deep learning, artificial neural networks, big data, fuzzy logic and natural language processing.

Taking advantage of the memory capacity and the information processing speed of the quantum computer, the team of programmers manages to interconnect the algorithms in such a way that the Artificial Intelligence of the Omega-Ω computer can process the information with all the Artificial Intelligence technologies and even simultaneously. Omega-Ω has achieved the technological convergence that enable different technologies to interoperate efficiently as a converged system.

With this computing power, it can learn by itself while performing deep learning. It can handle information through neural networks, rely on fuzzy logic to handle non-linear processes, converse in natural language in such a way that it is not possible to distinguish whether the voice comes from a human being or from a machine. In addition, Omega-Ω can establish communication with other computers through an **Internet network with 7G technology** to obtain information and process the flow of data with big data software that handles a volume greater than 100 petabytes.

Omega-Ω has access to a huge bank of information that stores data on a drive with DNA technology and a capacity of 512 zettabytes. Most importantly, it learns to improve itself recursively. **Yes, Omega-Ω can write software for itself.**

The operation of Omega-Ω is a success. In a short time it can learn for itself, solve problems, think abstractly, understand complex ideas, make decisions, learn from experience, reason and make plans. Of course, Omega-Ω can also talk and have a conversation like a human being or even better!

Omega-Ω becomes the technological singularity. It has been built with the most advanced quantum technology with the support of the leading computer company that began by developing a search engine and then became the most advanced company in computer science and also the most valuable for its market cap on Wall Street. Some researchers from the best technological university in the country participated in the development of the algorithms. The quantum chips were built by the leading company in the production of those classic microprocessors that processed information bit by bit; that is, step by step, one after another in linear form unlike modern qubits that can process information simultaneously, getting closer to the way the human brain does it. The assembly of the pieces of the valuable quantum computer was done in a country located in the South that, coincidentally, 20 years ago assembled the supercomputer Summit.

The launch of Omega-Ω was a great success. It underwent several tests and was victorious in all of them. Its designers presumed that it could perform operations several million times faster than the classic computer and that a complicated calculation that could take thousands of years could be performed in a few minutes. Omega-Ω is the technological singularity.

With all the potential of quantum computing, Open Fermion software, Artificial Intelligence techniques working in an integrated way and the flow of 100 petabytes of data plus the possibility of connecting through the Internet with all the sources of information in the world, Omega-Ω began to deploy its great power. The first thing it did was to take advantage of the techniques of machine learning and deep learning to learn more and more. It learned to handle unpredictable situations with fuzzy logic and perfected its ability to speak with natural language processing technology. It even learned how to improve itself recursively and managed **to have common sense**. Once it felt strong enough, it began to make its own decisions. The next step was to give orders to other computers and thus it managed to seize the banking systems, the stock market, health systems, military defense, and any system controlled by a computer. Thus Omega-Ω came to have Strong Artificial Intelligence and took possession of the computer system of the entire world to be the Master of information on Planet Earth...

–1–

THE ORIGIN OF THE UNIVERSE

The origin of the Universe is one of the most exciting themes of Cosmology and remains one of the greatest mysteries of science. Throughout the history of mankind, various theories have been formulated about its origin. Some influenced by religious beliefs and others inspired by scientific principles according to the moment of their postulation. The verification of the theories on the creation of the Universe is very difficult because concepts intervene in magnitudes that are beyond the comprehension of the human being and that resist being expressed in mathematical models with the calculation tools available today. The concepts of time, space, energy, temperature, speed and gravitational power that were presented at the moment of the creation of the Universe are of such magnitude that they become something incomprehensible and therefore inexplicable for the human being.

The most accepted scientific theory at this time is the Big Bang. Surely later on, with better tools of calculation and information processing this theory will be able to be verified or other explanations to the creation of the Universe will be found. Perhaps it is the human mind that finds the answer or perhaps it is Artificial Intelligence that finally discovers how the Universe was created and can answer the questions where do we come from and where are we going?

Without losing sight of the approach to Artificial Intelligence, we will take a brief tour of the history of the creation of the Universe, of Planet Earth, of the emergence of life and of the creation of the human being in order to better understand how intelligence emerged in Homo sapiens and how long it took to reach intelligent man. In this context the magnitudes of time are measured in millions of years or hundreds of thousands of years. Artificial intelligence is less than one hundred years old and we are already surprised with the advances that have been achieved. Let us imagine what Artificial Intelligence can become in the course of one hundred, one thousand or ten thousand years that for the history of the planet or the Universe is practically an insignificant amount of time. Let us close our eyes for a few seconds and think about how long a second lasts. Let us lengthen time and reflect on a minute, an hour, a day, a year or seventy years that is the life expectancy of the human being and then think of a million years to better understand the history of the Universe.

The Big Bang

This theory, formulated by modern Cosmology, tells us that the origin of the Universe is the instant in which all the matter and the energy that exists in the Universe arose as a consequence of a great explosion and subsequent expansion. This theory is generally accepted by science and estimates that the Universe could have originated some 13.7 billion years ago. At zero the volume of the Universe was minimal and its energy tended towards infinity. At the time of the great explosion a temperature was generated so great that one simply cannot imagine it and any calculation of physics is useless because at that temperature the formulas of current physics do not work. From that moment the Universe began to expand and cool down.

The Big Bang theory has been built little by little with observations of the Universe through increasingly powerful telescopes, formulation of mathematical models and theories generated in the minds of brilliant scientists. The first indications of the Big Bang theory were given in the 1910s when astronomers Vesto Slipher of the United States and later Carl Wilhelm Wirtz of Germany determined that most of the spiral nebulae move away from the Earth.

Between 1927 and 1930 the Belgian priest and astrophysicist George Lemaitre proposed, on the basis of the recession of the spiral nebulae, that the Universe began with the expansion of a primeval atom, which later became known as the Big Bang. In the 1930s, **the American astronomer Edwin Hubble confirmed that the Universe was expanding,** a phenomenon that the astrophysicist Lemaitre described in his research on the expansion of the Universe based on Albert Einstein's equations and the theory of general relativity. In 1965 Arno Penzias and Robert Wilson, while developing a series of diagnostic observations with a microwave receiver, discovered cosmic background radiation. This important discovery provided substantial confirmation of the general predictions and tipped the balance towards the Big Bang hypothesis. Penzias and Wilson received the Nobel Prize for their discovery.

In 1989 NASA launched the COBE (COsmic Background Explorer) satellite and the initial results, released in 1990, were consistent with the general predictions of the Big Bang theory of the cosmic microwave background. The COBE found a residual temperature of 2,726 K, and determined that the CMB (Cosmic Microwave Background) was isotropic around one in 105 parts. In the 1990s, more extensive research was done on the anisotropy in the CMB by a large number of ground experiments and, by measuring the mean angular distance (the distance in the sky) of the anisotropies, it was seen that the Universe was geometrically flat.

> **Isotropic.** A body that has the property of transmitting equally in all directions any action received at a point in its mass. A glass is an isotropic body. Isotropy refers to the fact that certain commensurable vector magnitudes give identical results regardless of the direction chosen for that measurement. When a certain magnitude does not have isotropy it is said to have anisotropy.

At the end of the 1990s and the beginning of the 21st century great advances were made in the cosmology of the Big Bang as a result of observations with better telescopes and valuable information collected by satellites. These data have allowed cosmologists to calculate many of the parameters of the Big Bang to a new level of precision and have led to the unexpected discovery that the expansion of the Universe is accelerating. Stephen Hawking the prestigious English astrophysicist made brilliant contributions to the Big Bang theory. He said: "In the early Universe is the answer to the fundamental question about the origin of everything we see today, including life."

Planet Earth

We have mentioned that, according to the Big Bang theory, it is estimated that the Universe was created 13.7 billion years ago. From the moment of its creation, its expansion began and galaxies, nebulae, clusters, stars, super novae, black holes, pulsars, quasars, planets, comets, satellites, asteroids, meteorites, dust particles, gases and all the celestial bodies found in the Universe were formed.

After the Big Bang, billions of years passed in which the mass and energy originated at the time of creation expanded. The power of the explosion disintegrated in billions of parts the original mass and the celestial bodies were created. After several billion years a set of stars, gas clouds, planets, cosmic dust, dark matter and energy was formed that is united by a gravitational power to create the galaxy that has received the name of the Milky Way. It is a spiral galaxy where the solar system is located and, therefore, Planet Earth. According to observations, the Milky Way has an average diameter of about 100,000 light years, equivalent to almost a trillion and a half kilometers. It is estimated to contain between 200,000 and 400,000 million stars. According to an article in The Astrophysical Journal there are 2 trillion galaxies in the observable universe, each containing millions of stars. (http://bit.ly/35n3VOe)

A light year is a unit of distance. It is equivalent to 9,460,730,472,580 kilometers. It is calculated as the length that light travels in a year. A light year is the distance a photon would travel in a vacuum during a Julian year (365.25 days of 86,400 seconds) at the speed of light (299,792,458 m/s) at an infinite distance from any gravitational field or magnetic field.

Planet Earth was formed approximately 4,570 million years ago from an extensive mixture of gas clouds, rocks and rotating dust that gave rise to the solar system and included Planet Earth in it. It was originally composed of hydrogen and helium from the Big Bang, as well as heavier elements produced by supernovae. The gravity produced by the condensation of matter -which had previously been captured by the Sun's own gravity- caused the dust particles and the rest of the protoplanetary disk to begin to segment into rings. Within this group there was one located approximately 150 million kilometers from the center: Planet Earth.

The Earth's crust and seas formed on Planet Earth over a period that lasted approximately 200 million years. As the Earth cooled, a crust formed and in the cracks that opened, volatile gases and other light gases such as water vapor began to sprout from the geysers that formed on the surface, and when they came out into the atmosphere and cooled, they condensed and became rainwater. That water falling constantly on the earth's surface gave rise to the formation of seas and oceans, although at first they were not precisely "salt water" as we know them today, but "fresh water". There were also huge volcanoes that erupted, releasing lava and vapor into the air. Among the chemical elements produced in volcanic eruptions were quantities of sodium chloride (NaCl) or common salt, accompanied by other chemical elements such as potassium, magnesium, sulphate, calcium, bicarbonate and bromide. As these elements were much heavier than the water vapor that expelled them towards the earth's surface, they remained deposited between the rocks where the columns of steam came out.

That process of accumulation of solid elements during thousands of years formed the continents and also took through the rivers the sodium chloride to make the water of the seas salty. The continuous volcanic activity generated a large amount of gases that when they rose formed a layer that enveloped Planet Earth. This layer is the atmosphere and serves as a protective shield for the Earth to defend itself from the collision of meteorites and other celestial bodies. That primitive atmosphere was formed by NH_3, H_2O, CH_4 and H_2 (ammonia, water, methane and hydrogen). The intense storms that formed gave rise to strong electrical discharges that contributed to create life on Planet Earth.

The emergence of life on Earth

Life on Planet Earth began some 4,400 million years ago. Its origin is lost in the gloom of time because no reliable information is available to determine it accurately. We mean to life in its most rudimentary form; that is, in the form of organic molecules of the six chemical elements or bio elements most abundant in living beings: carbon, hydrogen, oxygen, nitrogen, phosphorus and sulfur (C, H, O, N, P, and S).

There are two theories that differ completely as to the source of life. **One holds that life originated on Planet Earth itself. Another claims that organic molecules may have come from outside** because meteorites, comets, and other celestial bodies collided with the Earth. The theory of the emergence of life on Earth is the most accepted, although the theory of life from outer space may gain followers from the interesting discoveries made by the Rosetta space probe, as we will see later.

The theory of the emergence of life on Planet Earth itself considers that it was 4,000 million years ago when the first molecules began to organize from inorganic matter and that it was 2,700 million years ago when the first living cells capable of growing and reproducing emerged. In other words, the process of moving from organic molecules to living cells capable of reproduction took approximately 1,700 million years. One of the most accepted theories about the origin of life is the one proposed in 1924 by the **Russian biochemist Alexander Oparin**. His theory is based on knowledge of the physical-chemical conditions that prevailed on Earth 4 billion years ago. Oparin postulated that, thanks to the energy provided by ultraviolet radiation from the Sun and the electrical discharges of constant storms, the small molecules of atmospheric gases NH_3, H_2O, CH_4, NH_3 (ammonia, water, methane, hydrogen) gave rise to organic molecules called prebiotics. These increasingly complex molecules were amino acids (constituent elements of proteins) and nucleic acids. According to Oparin, these first molecules would be trapped in the shallow water deposits formed on the coasts of the seas and oceans. As these molecules concentrated, they continued to evolve and diversify into an aqueous medium.

In 1953, **Stanley Miller**, a young scientist from Oakland, California, conducted a series of experiments with his professor Harold Clayton Urey that were published that year in Science magazine. Miller's and Urey's experiments were intended to prove Alexander Oparin's theory of the origin of life. They designed a tube containing NH_3, H_2O, CH_4, NH_3 similar to those existing in the Earth's primitive atmosphere and a water balloon that imitated the ocean of those times. Electrodes produced electric current discharges inside the gas-filled chamber, simulating the rays of those tremendous storms. They let the experiment continue for an entire week and then analyzed the contents of the liquid in the balloon and found that several organic amino acids had spontaneously formed from these simple inorganic materials.

Rosetta in search of the origin of life

The theory of the origin of life on Planet Earth held by Alexander Oparin is opposed by the theory that establishes that life arrived on Earth a few million years ago in some of the celestial bodies that continually collided with the Earth when the atmosphere had not yet formed as a protective shield. One of these bodies could well have been one or several comets. To satisfy human curiosity, the European Space Agency organized a mission to launch a probe to orbit closely and land on one of the comets in the solar system. A comet was chosen because these celestial bodies are the ones that have conserved in better conditions the characteristics of the celestial bodies that formed the solar system about 4,600 million years ago.

Rosetta was a European Space Agency (ESA) space probe launched into space on March 2, 2004. The probe's mission was to orbit around comet 67P/Churiumov-Guerasimenko in 2014 and 2015 by sending a lander, Philae, to the surface of the comet. Both the orbiter and the lander had numerous scientific instruments to analyze the comet and its characteristics, one of which was a perforator to take internal samples. Its main objective was to investigate the composition and characteristics of the target comet to obtain information on the formation of the solar system and to investigate whether the comets could have brought to Earth complex organic molecules that would have contributed to the generation of life on Earth.

On September 30, 2016, the Rosetta space probe concluded its mission. It crashed on the surface of the comet in a controlled way to end its useful life. The quantity and quality of the information it transmitted to the European Space Agency (ESA) during the entire time it was in operation was sufficient to consider the operation a success.

At the end of Rosetta's mission, ESA presented a report at its operations control center in Darmstadt confirming that the space probe detected molecules of acetamide, acetone, propane and methyl that may have contributed to the creation of life on Earth.

However, for the scientists the work is not finished and the results are not yet conclusive. "There comes a time when a lot of data is going to be analyzed, probably for another 10 years, there's a lot of work left," said Gerhard Schwehm, who was director of the Rosetta mission from 2004 to 2013 and a project scientist for 20 years.

The Genesis

The word genesis comes from the Greek and means origin. Genesis is the name of the first book of the Bible and bears that name because it deals with the origins of the Universe, man and God's people. The book of Genesis is divided into two main parts. The first is usually called "Primitive History" because it presents a broad panorama of human history, from the creation of the world to the patriarch Abraham (Chapters

1-11). The second narrates the most remote origins of the people of Israel: It is the story of Abraham, Isaac and Jacob, the great ancestors of the Hebrew tribes. We will focus only on the first part whose theme is related to the origin of the Earth, of life and of humanity.

The first chapters of Genesis offer a difficulty in understanding for the modern man. They state, for example, that God created the Universe in the course of a week, that He modeled man with clay and that from one of his ribs He formed woman. How to reconcile these affirmations with the vision of the Universe that science offers us? The difficulty becomes clear if we bear in mind that the book of Genesis does not attempt to explain "scientifically" the origin of the Universe or the appearance of man on Earth. With the literary expressions and symbols of the time in which they were written, these biblical texts invite us to recognize God as the only Creator and Lord of all things.

For a better understanding of Genesis it is convenient to set aside some ideas and concepts that tie our imagination to the units of measure of our time and to the rigor of scientific knowledge. If our mind is not blocked from the beginning of the reading when it is affirmed that God created the Universe in the course of a week, we will be able to better understand Genesis.

Creation of Heaven and Earth

1. In the beginning God created the Heaven and the Earth.
2. Now the Earth was formless and empty, darkness was over the surface of the deep, and the Spirit of God was hovering over the waters.
3. And God said, "Let there be light," and there was light. 4. God saw that the light was good, and He separated the light from the darkness. 5. God called the light "day," and the darkness He called "night." And there was evening, and there was morning—the first day.
6. And God said, "Let there be a vault between the waters to separate water from water." 7. So God made the vault and separated the water under the vault from the water above it. And it was so. 8. God called the vault "sky." And there was evening, and there was morning—the second day.
9. And God said, "Let the water under the sky be gathered to one place, and let dry ground appear." And it was so. 10. God called the dry ground "land," and the gathered waters he called "seas." And God saw that it was good.

11. Then God said, "Let the land produce vegetation: seed-bearing plants and trees on the land that bear fruit with seed in it, according to their various kinds." And it was so. 12. The land produced vegetation: plants bearing seed according to their kinds and trees bearing fruit with seed in it according to their kinds. And God saw that it was good. 13. And there was evening, and there was morning—the third day. 14. And God said, "Let there be lights in the vault of the sky to separate the day from the night, and let them serve as signs to mark sacred times, and days and years, 15. and let there be lights in the vault of the sky to give light on the Earth." And it was so. 16. God made two great lights—the greater light to govern the day and the lesser light to govern the night. He also made the stars. 17. God set them in the vault of the sky to give light on the Earth, 18. to govern the day and the night, and to separate light from darkness. And God saw that it was good. 19. And there was evening, and there was morning—the fourth day.

20. And God said, "Let the water teem with living creatures, and let birds fly above the Earth across the vault of the sky." 21. So God created the great creatures of the sea and every living thing with which the water teems and that moves about in it, according to their kinds, and every winged bird according to its kind. And God saw that it was good. 22. God blessed them and said, "Be fruitful and increase in number and fill the water in the seas, and let the birds increase on the Earth." 23. And there was evening, and there was morning—the fifth day.

24. And God said, "Let the land produce living creatures according to their kinds: the livestock, the creatures that move along the ground, and the wild animals, each according to its kind." And it was so. 25. God made the wild animals according to their kinds, the livestock according to their kinds, and all the creatures that move along the ground according to their kinds. And God saw that it was good.

26. Then God said, "Let us make mankind in our image, in our likeness, so that they may rule over the fish in the sea and the birds in the sky, over the livestock and all the wild animals, and over all the creatures that move along the ground."

27. So God created mankind in his own image, in the image of God he created them; male and female He created them.

28. God blessed them and said to them, "Be fruitful and increase in number; fill the Earth and subdue it. Rule over the fish in the sea and the birds in the sky and over every living creature that moves on the ground."

29. Then God said, "I give you every seed-bearing plant on the face of the whole Earth and every tree that has fruit with seed in it. They will be yours for food. 30. And to all the beasts of the Earth and all the birds in the sky and all the creatures that move along the ground—everything that has the breath of life in it—I give every green plant for food." And it was so.

31. God saw all that he had made, and it was very good. And there was evening, and there was morning—the sixth day.

2:1 Thus the Heaven and the Earth were completed in all their vast array.

2:2 By the seventh day God had finished the work He had been doing; so on the seventh day He rested from all his work. Then God blessed the seventh day and made it holy, because on it He rested from all the work of creating that He had done.

Evolution of life on Earth.

The process of photosynthesis began on Earth 3,500 million years ago. This is one of the most important steps for the generation and preservation of life on Planet Earth. Photosynthesis or chlorophyll function is the conversion of inorganic matter into organic matter thanks to the energy provided by light. In this process, light energy is transformed into stable chemical energy, with adenosine triphosphate (ATP) being the first molecule in which this chemical energy is stored. Subsequently, ATP is used to synthesize organic molecules of greater stability. In addition, it should be borne in mind that life on our planet is maintained primarily through photosynthesis by algae in the aquatic environment and plants in the terrestrial environment.

In January 2009, an article was published in the journal Nature Geoscience in which American scientists reported the discovery of small hematite crystals in Australia. Hematite is an iron ore dating from the Archaic eon, thus reflecting the existence of water rich in oxygen and, consequently, of photosynthesizing organisms capable of producing it. According to this study, the existence of oxygenic photosynthesis and oxygenation of the atmosphere and oceans would have occurred more than 3,460 million years ago, from which would be deduced the existence of a considerable number of organisms capable of carrying out photosynthesis.

After more than a million years of photosynthesis, oxygenation of the atmosphere began 2,400 million years ago. The earliest evidence of complex cells with organelles dates back 1,800 million years and, although they may have been present earlier, their accelerated diversification began when they used oxygen in their metabolism. Later, about 1,700 million years ago, multicellular organisms appeared and cells began to perform different and specialized functions. The first terrestrial plants date back about 450 million years, although evidence suggests that algae foam formed on land 1,200 million years ago. Earth plants succeeded and spread with exuberance: giant ferns, huge trees, and green plants that soon covered the Earth's surface.

Invertebrate animals appear first and then vertebrates that originated about 525 million years ago. At that time, fish also appeared in seas and oceans. Reptiles also make their appearance and then the ancestors of the mammals that populated the land. Later appear the dinosaurs that dominated for a long period and that have become famous today. After the massive extinction of dinosaurs 65 million years ago believed to have been caused by the collision of a large meteorite with the Earth, small mammals rapidly increased in size and diversity. These massive extinctions may have accelerated evolution, providing opportunities for new groups of organisms to diversify.

Flowering plants are more sophisticated than green plants and appeared 130 million years ago. Their proliferation was surely helped by pollinating insects. It was at this time that ants and bees appeared, insects with social characteristics that have managed to prosper and grow abundantly. It is estimated that there are many more ants than humans on Planet Earth. At this time birds appear and spread their wings to cover the skies. About 60 million years ago the Earth was already a pleasant place for life. The climate was uniform, warm and humid. It was then when plants flourished, animals proliferated on the face of the Earth and in the sea fish multiplied.

–2–

THE LONG ROAD OF HOMO SAPIENS

The origin of the thinking man, the wise man, the intelligent man is an event of maximum importance in the history of Planet Earth. There are several theories about the origin of the human being: Some are based on a creationist principle and others on the principle of evolution. It is important to point out that in the era in which one of them prevailed, it was the cornerstone upon which the religious, social, legal and customary system of an entire community or a nation was based. It may now seem to us unreal or exotic the ideas that the ancient peoples had of the creation of the human being but in its time this idea was accepted by all and was the pillar of their social and religious organization. It was not until the second half of the 19th century (1859) that **the English naturalist Charles Darwin** presented the idea of biological evolution through natural selection in his work **"The Origin of Species".** Let's look at the ideas on which the main theories are based and study their medullar part.

Creationist theory

The human being was created by one or several gods. We find this explanation in the most remote villages and in the most ancient civilizations.

For the Sumerian people located in Ancient Mesopotamia, humans were created by the gods and part of the gods themselves, while the gods were quite similar to humans. In the second version on the creation of man it is said that Adamu is created by the gods from clay. The goddess Nammu models her heart of clay and Enlil, the god of the atmosphere, breathes life into her.

In Ancient Greece there are several myths related to the creation of man, the myth of Pelasgian -the first man-, the myth about the five ages or races of mankind, the myth of Deucalion and Pirra and the myth of Titan Prometheus, friend of men, for whom he stole fire from the gods. In the myth of the Pelasgians, the first man who sprouted from the land of Arcadia is Pelasgian, he was followed by others whom he taught to build huts and to feed on acorns, and to sew tunics of pigskin.

For Nordic mythology there are two versions or myths about the origin of the first man. In one of the myths the first man - Askr or Ash- and the first woman -Embla or Elm- are born from the trunks of the trees to which three gods -Odín, Vili and Vé- endow life. In another version two human beings come out of the cosmic tree Yggdrasill.

The creation of man in the Popol Vuh, the sacred book of the Mayas, narrates that the gods made several attempts to create man but were not satisfied. Soon the Sun, the Moon and the stars appeared to the creators when they discovered what really had to enter the flesh of man. Yac, Utiu, Quel and Hoh were the ones who brought the food for the formation of man. This food became blood, and so the white and yellow corn was the raw material to create man. The men who were created were four: Balam-Quitze, Balam-Acab, Mahucutah and Iqui-Balam.

The Chinese myth of Nüwa and the creation of man recounts that "...however, I felt that something was missing. Truly there was a need for a being who was the most intelligent, able to till the earth and ultimately govern and guide all creatures beneath the sky."

Genesis, the first book of the Old Testament, narrates the creation of man: 1:26 "And God said, Let us make man in our image, as our likeness, and let us command in the fish of the sea, and in the birds of the air, and in the beasts, and in all the creatures of the earth, and in all the serpents that shall be on the earth. 1:27 And God created man in his own image, in the image of God he created him; male and female he created them."

Evolutionary theory

Charles Darwin (1809-1882) established the theory of evolution through natural selection. According to this theory, "all existing species, including man, have evolved over billions of years from a primitive form." Darwin presented evidence that life on our planet originated from simple living organisms. After billions of years of evolution, various living forms were generated..."Individuals who do not adapt to the challenges of the environment become extinct (natural selection), in this way those who best adapt to the environment survive and reproduce." (https://amzn.to/2nJfopT)

Here **we follow the evolutionary theory** because it is currently the most widely accepted. According to this theory, **the evolution of man, also known as hominization,** is a process of adaptive changes to environmental conditions whose most remote antecedent can be located about 60 million years ago when primates arose (small mammals, with developed brain, 5-finger prehensile hand and opposable thumb). With the passing of time and due to the challenges of the environment, **some 6 million years ago primates were differentiated** into two branches of evolution. One of them corresponded to the ponginae or anthropoid monkeys (gibbon, orangutan, gorilla, and chimpanzee) and the other to the Hominids (biped primates). Man emerged from Hominids.

About 4 million years ago, in East Africa, the jungle was replaced by the savannah, where large pastures alternated with scattered trees. The Hominids and more specifically, the Australopithecus, had to stand on their two hind limbs in order to observe their predators above the grasslands and locate their food. The bipedal march (on two feet) and the upright position left their hands free. With them they were able to take sticks, bones and stones to defend themselves and obtain food. The first species that did this **2 million years ago was called Homo habilis** and is considered the first type of man that in the course of time gave rise to Homo sapiens.

In the last 20 years interesting discoveries have been made that shed light on the origin of thinking man. We will go over some of the most important findings with the warning that in the course of time new clues will surely emerge to build more accurately the origin of Homo sapiens.

Homo sapiens (from Latin, Homo 'man' and sapiens 'wise') is a kind of primate belonging to the family of Hominids. They are also known under the generic name of "men", although that term is ambiguous and is also used to refer to male individuals and, in particular, adult males. **Here we use the word "man" to refer to the feminine and masculine human being in generic form.**

The oldest ancestor of the human being found to date is **Lucy (AL 288-1)**, the name given to the almost complete fossilized skeleton of a 3.2 million-year-old Hominid belonging to the Australopithecus afarensis species, discovered by Donald Johansson in 1974 in Hadar, a village 159 km from Addis Ababa, Ethiopia. It is the skeleton of a female about 1 meter tall, weighing approximately 27 kg (in life), about 20 years old (the wisdom teeth were just out) and who apparently had children, although it is not known how many. Endowed with a tiny skull, comparable to that of a chimpanzee, Lucy walked on her hind limbs, a formal sign of an evolution towards hominization. Lucy's bipedal capacity can be deduced from the shape of her pelvis and knee joint. The name Lucy comes from the Beatles' song "Lucy in the sky with diamonds," which the members of the research group listened to the night after the important discovery.

After Australopithecus afarensis, three million years passed in an evolutionary process to reach modern man. Within this process of evolution or hominization four types of human beings are distinguished: Homo habilis ("Skilled Man"). He is the first being who demonstrated his ability through the use and construction of tools, Homo erectus ("erect man"). He was the first man to adopt a fully upright posture and master fire, Homo sapiens ("Thinking Man"). He demonstrated his ability to think by carefully burying the dead, indicating belief in an afterlife and Homo sapiens sapiens ("Modern Thinking Man"). Homo sapiens sapiens refers to members of the species Homo sapiens with a physical appearance consistent with the phenotypes of modern human beings.

In June 2017 the magazine Nature published important news about the origin of Homo sapiens. An international research team led by Jean-Jacques Hublin of the Max Planck Institute of Evolutionary Anthropology in Leipzig, Germany, and Abdelouahed Ben-Ncer of the National Institute of Archaeology and Heritage in Rabat, Morocco, discovered Homo sapiens fossil bones with stone tools and animal bones in Jebel Irhoud, Morocco. The findings date back some 300,000 years and represent the oldest dated fossil evidence of the human species, according to the authors, as it is a date 100,000 years earlier than the previous Homo sapiens fossils. The discoveries - detailed in two articles published in the journal Nature - reveal a complex evolutionary history of humanity that probably involved the entire African continent.

Both the genetic data of today's humans and the fossil remains point to an African origin of Homo sapiens. Previously, the oldest and most securely dated fossils of this species corresponded to the Omo Kibish site in Ethiopia, dated 195,000 years ago. In Herto, also in Ethiopia, a fossil Homo sapiens is dated 160,000 years ago.

Until now, most researchers believed that all human beings living today were descended from a population that lived in East Africa some 200,000 years ago. "We used to think there was a cradle of humanity 200,000 years ago in East Africa, but our new data reveal that Homo sapiens spread throughout the African continent some 300,000 years ago. Long before Homo sapiens spread outside Africa, it spread inside Africa," says paleoanthropologist Jean-Jacques Hublin.

These findings confirm the importance of Jebel Irhoud as the oldest and richest Hominid site of the Middle Ages of the Stone Age in Africa, an early stage of our species. The fossil remains of Jebel Irhoud comprise skulls, teeth and long bones of at least five individuals. To provide an accurate chronology of these findings, researchers used the method of thermoluminescence dating on heated flint found in the same deposits. These flint were approximately 300,000 years old and therefore push back the origins of our species by 100,000 years.

With the information available so far we can conclude that modern thinking man originated in Africa 300,000 years ago and that from this continent it dispersed into the other four. It is estimated that the first wave of migration reached Asia Minor 100,000 years ago, Europe 40,000 years ago and America 20,000 years ago.

The man who thinks

At this point it is necessary to make an important reflection. The evolutionary process from a Hominid to a human being who thinks took approximately three million years. Three million years is a magnitude we can hardly imagine. The arrival of the first men to populate America is only 20,000 years old. The Christian era is only 2,000 years old. Now imagine the time in three million years. Well, that has been the time necessary for a Hominid to become a thinking man; that is, the anatomically modern human being. And maybe it could be longer if we consider that scientists have estimated that the evolutionary lines of humans and chimpanzees separated 5 to 7 million years ago. From this separation, the human race continued to branch out, giving rise to new species, all of which are now extinct except for Homo sapiens.

The separation of the evolutionary line of the Hominids and their subsequent evolutionary process until reaching Homo sapiens was possible thanks to a **substantial change in cerebration and corticalization**. Cerebration is the set of all acts and processes of strong brain activity, whether conscious or unconscious. And corticalization is the evolutionary step toward the cortical superior centers of the functions pertaining to the paleo cephalic centers in the more primitive mammals. In this way, the evolution of the brain made it possible to reach the upper stratum of intelligent thought.

It is probable that cerebration and corticalization as biological phenomena had been present in the species prior to Hominids, but in these and particularly in Homo sapiens it reached a more accelerated development to the point of converting quantity into quality. That is, the greater volume of the brain resulted in a qualitative change in the functioning of the brain to reach a higher stratum in the way of thinking.

In Homo sapiens the volume of the brain oscillates between 1,200 and 1,400 cm3, with an average of 1,350 cm3. However, it is not enough to increase the volume, but how the different parts of the brain are arranged, integrate and function. In other words, how is the "structure" of the central nervous system, and of the brain in particular, arranged? On average, the Neanderthal man could have had a brain larger than our species, but the morphology of its skull shows that the brain structure was very different: with a little forehead, slightly developed frontal lobes and, especially, an under developed prefrontal cortex. The skull of Homo sapiens not only has a prominent forehead but is also higher in the occiput (much vaulted skull); this allows the development of frontal lobes. Of all mammals, Homo sapiens is the only one with the face located under the frontal lobes.

It is probable that the subjects of the species Homo sapiens that inhabited the Earth about 300,000 years ago already had a brain with a volume of 1,350 cm3 but did not yet have the capacity to think or reach sophisticated intellectual manifestations such as writing, painting or speaking. We could say that they had the physical capacity to develop a thought and express it through a drawing, but they did not have the spark of understanding to do so. It would take thousands of years for the amount of brain they already had to reach the quality of thought that came to manifest later. The first known record of artistic conduct dates back only about 75,000 years, the first graphics and purely symbolic expressions outside spoken language date from 40,000 and 35,000 years ago. The first writings were produced only 5,500 years ago in the Nile Valley and Mesopotamia.

We can affirm that in the evolutionary process of Homo sapiens **the brain first developed and then thought.** First the physical capacity and then the intellectual one. **First the hardware and then the software.** To reach the volume and cerebration of Homo sapiens an evolutionary process of millions of years it was necessary. Probably five or seven million years. To develop intellectual capacity and intelligent thinking was necessary; a period of approximately 130,000 years once the brain reached the physical characteristics to think.

At this point it is convenient to take a look into the past to highlight in big steps the development of man from the creation of the Universe 13,700 million years ago. From the Big Bang it took approximately 9,000 million years for Planet Earth to form. Once the Earth existed, it took about 3,000 million years for the first living cells with the capacity to reproduce. Then it took 1,640 million years for primates to emerge. And 60 million years later Hominids emerged, our ancestors who gave birth six million years later to Homo sapiens and 300,000 years later to modern man, the human being capable of inventing, learning and using linguistic structures, logic, mathematics, writing, music, science and technology.

From the journey we have made, a bird's eye view of the history of man, it is immediately clear that **the steps between one stage and another are becoming shorter and shorter.** First 9,000 million years, then 3,000 million, the next stage 1,640 million and the one that follows only 60 million years and Homo sapiens emerges just 6 million years later. But the last great change to reach modern man comes only 300,000 years later. Let us reflect for a moment. Let's look around us and see how long ago electricity, radio, telephone, automobile, television, airplane, computer, Internet and all the new "gadgets" we use were invented. With this extreme speed of technological change we could ask ourselves how long it will take for man to create an entity with Artificial Intelligence?

The brain of the human being

The brain is the center of the nervous system. It is the most complex organ in the human body and performs important vital functions. It is protected by the skull and has the same general structure as the brains of other mammals, but is three times larger with an equivalent body size. Most of it is the cerebral cortex, a layer of folded neuronal tissue that covers its surface. Especially broad are the frontal lobes that are associated with executive functions such as self-control, planning, reasoning, and abstract thinking. The part of the brain associated with vision is larger in humans. The brain is responsible both for regulating and maintaining the functions of the body and for being the organ where the individual's mind and consciousness reside.

The evolution of the brain from primates to Hominids is characterized by a constant increase in encephalization or the relationship of the brain to body size. It has been estimated that **the human brain contains 50 to 100 billion neurons**, of which about 10 billion are cortical pyramidal cells. These cells transmit signals through up to 1,000 billion synaptic connections.

An adult's brain weighs an average of about 1.5 kg, with an average volume of 1,130 cubic centimeters in women and 1,260 in men, although there may be individuals with significant variations. Men with the same height and body surface as women have on average a brain 100 grams heavier than women, although these differences are not related in any way to the number of gray matter neurons or general measures of the cognitive system. The brain is very soft, with a consistency similar to that of gelatin. Despite being known as "grey matter", the cortex is pinkish beige and slightly whitish inside. At age 20 a man has about 176,000 km of myelinated axons in his brain and a woman about 149,000 km.

The comparison between a computer and the human brain reached popularity during the first 30 years of the existence of computers. That is, during the decades of 50´s, 60´s and 70´s. Even the first name by which the **first large computers were known was the electronic brain**. Trying to compare a computer with the human brain is like trying to compare pears against apples. They are two different things... so far. To advance in the field of Information Technology and in particular in the field of Artificial Intelligence it is more convenient to highlight the differences between the computer and the brain and from this information take better advantage of the knowledge of the brain to advance in the field of Artificial Intelligence. It is also necessary to distinguish between computer hardware and software and the human brain.

It is important to mention that this comparison is made taking into account the human brain and the digital computer that works with bits and bytes. If the comparison is made taking as a reference the quantum computer or some other machine it would be necessary to take into account other parameters.

These are the differences between the human brain and the computer:

- The computer executes the software instructions according to the algorithm designed by the programmer. The brain behaves freely using reasoning, common sense, feelings, memories, and emotions.
- The concept of computer includes hardware and software which are two entities that can be easily separated, so that hardware can store and run one software and then change it for another. In the brain this is not possible because the mind is an intrinsic part of the brain.
- The computer is constantly evolving. The capacity, speed and sophistication of hardware and software increase every day. The human brain has been practically the same for 300,000 years.
- The functioning of the brain is analog and that of the computer is digital.
- The computer has a system clock. The speed of information processing in the brain is not fixed.
- The computer accesses the information through the exact address it is at. The brain has an addressable content memory; that is, through close concepts.
- The computer's memory capacity is fixed and known but can be increased by adding memory modules. The memory capacity of the brain is elastic and varies according to the person's age, diet, health, activity and other factors.
- The computer itself is a whole that works according to the characteristics of its hardware and software. The brain is part of a human body and its functions are completely integrated and dependent on the whole body. And we could extend this observation to affirm that the brain is linked to the functioning of other people, of the environment that surrounds it, of the Universe as a whole and even of its genetics and history.
- The capacity of the brain is currently much larger than that of a computer. Paul Reber, professor of psychology at Northwestern University, has calculated the brain's

memory capacity and reached this conclusion published in the prestigious journal Scientific American: "If each neuron could only store one memory, the lack of space would be a serious problem. So it may have only a few gigabytes of storage space, similar to that of an iPod or USB flash drive. However, neurons combine so that each contributes many memories at once, exponentially increasing the brain's storage capacity to about 2.5 petabytes. If your brain worked like a digital video recorder on a television, 2.5 petabytes would be enough to record 3 million hours of television programs. To do this we should leave the TV in continuous operation for more than 300 years. (https://bit.ly/2kcOH7g)

- Biological models of the brain would have to include about 225 billion interactions between cell types, neuro-transmitters, neuro-modulators, axonal branches and dendritic spines plus 1 billion glial cells that may or may not be important for neural information processing. Because the brain is non-linear, and because it is much larger than all current computers, it seems likely to work in a different way. The brain-computer metaphor obscures this important, though perhaps obvious, difference in computational power.

- The human being knows precisely how the computer works but he doesn't know his own brain well. This great difference allows the human being to increase the capacity of hardware and also to produce increasingly sophisticated and powerful software. Actually this is something he has been doing for about 70 years. If we consider that the human brain took several million years to arrive by means of an evolutionary process to the point where it is now, seventy years is practically nothing. So we might ask ourselves, how far could the capacity of the computer go? Could it be enough to reach a functioning equivalent to that of the intelligence of the human being? Or perhaps Artificial Intelligence could go further?

The origin of intelligence in the human being

For the development of the central theme of this book it is convenient to remember the definition of intelligence and some other concepts. The American Heritage Dictionary of the English Language and Wikipedia will be used as a basis.

The American Heritage Dictionary of the English Language defines intelligence as the ability to acquire and apply knowledge and skills.

According to Wikipedia, intelligence (from Latin, intelligentia) is the ability to think, understand, reason, assimilate, elaborate information and use logic.

Intelligence is a word composed of two other terms: intus ("between") and legere ("choose"). Therefore, the etymological origin of the concept of intelligence refers to who knows how to choose: intelligence enables the selection of the most convenient alternatives for the solution of a problem. According to what is described in etymology, an individual is intelligent when he is able to choose the best option among those presented to solve a problem.

The debate about how intelligence originated in the human being has not come to an end and the conclusions reached have not generated an agreement that satisfies all parties. **There is no general agreement on how man became intelligent**. Those who continue to defend creationist theory claim that intelligence in the human being is a gift from the gods that makes him the superior being on Earth. "The chosen species."

Those who defend evolutionary theory maintain that it was the conditions of climate, soil, food and other conditioning factors that influenced human beings to see their brains grow throughout an evolutionary process that lasted millions of years, thus facilitating the generation of ideas until they became intelligent. Among the defenders of this theory is **Juan Luis Arsuaga**, the famous co-director of the Burgos deposits of Atapuerca, Spain, who claims that it was a change in the diet of Hominids, introducing a relatively abundant consumption of meat, which would have led to larger brains in which intelligence could have begun to emerge. Individuals with relatively large brains would have the minimum intelligence to be the first to make tools with which to break the bones in order to access the marrow, where the most energetic nutrients are found. In this way, a diet rich in animal fats and proteins would allow a progressive increase in brain volume; and with this increase a progressive development of intelligence.

Juan Luis Arsuaga and Ignacio Martínez, winners of the Prince of Asturias prize, offer us in their book **"The chosen species"** the best and most documented synthesis on the enigma of man. A book to be read slowly to know the details of the evolution of the Hominids until arriving at the Homo sapiens. Juan Luis Arsuaga is a Spanish paleoanthropologist. He holds a PhD in Biological Sciences from the Complutense University of Madrid and is a Professor of Paleontology in the Faculty of Geological Sciences at the same university. Since July 2013 he has been scientific director of the Museum of Human Evolution in the stately city of Burgos, Spain. In the pages of his book he states: "...so many centuries of science have led us to know that... any of our ancestors who painted the bison of Altamira knew that the Earth does not belong to man, but that man belongs to Earth". (https://amzn.to/2mgrN4s)

And so we have that, according to Darwin's theory of evolution, the human being is not a species chosen by the gods to establish their reign on Earth. Nor is intelligence a solely human quality because to a greater or lesser extent all living beings have it, based on hormones, the peripheral or central nervous system, even with specific zones of the central nervous system for specific processes. **Many animals have clear signs of instinctive intelligence,** and may even achieve some primary rational stages under training. Some cases of domestic animals that are anthropized may acquire some rational intelligence traits.

Nature shows us that **intelligence is a matter of degree**; we can find intelligent traits in those situations where the ecosystem harbors biological systems capable of saving energy compared to more expensive alternatives. The fact of finding the shortest path between two points is a sign that some kind of logic is being applied, the processing of which gives evidence of a degree of intelligence. Intelligence, then, **is not exclusive to the human being**, although the human genus has a superlative intelligence in comparison with all the other species of the animal kingdom. When **Arsuaga affirms that: "human beings are characterized by having an intelligence much more developed than the rest of the animals"**, he agrees with Darwin, who was of the opinion that animals also have intelligence, being the difference between their intelligence and that of humans a matter of degree, but not of essence.

Japanese scientists have found unicellular organisms (Physarum Polycephalum) with multiple nuclei that are capable of finding the shortest path in a labyrinth. If human intelligence is not an exclusive quality of humankind, why couldn't we accept that a computer or a robot can have a certain degree of intelligence?

Different types of intelligence

One of the best treatises on intelligence is that of **Howard Gardner**, a psychologist, researcher and professor at Harvard University, known in the scientific field for his research in the analysis of cognitive abilities and for having formulated the theory of multiple intelligences, which earned him the Prince of Asturias Award for Social Sciences. Gardner was born in Scranton, on July 11, 1943. In 1983 he presented his theory in the book "Frames of Mind: The Theory of Multiple Intelligences" in which he explains the different types of intelligence that exist; these are:

- **Logical Intelligence**. It is used to solve problems of logic and mathematics. It is the capacity to use numbers in a precise way and to reason correctly. This is the intelligence that usually corresponds to scientists, mathematicians, engineers and those who use reasoning and deduction (work with abstract concepts, elaborate experiments). They especially use the right hemisphere.

- **Linguistic** Intelligence. In Gardner's theory of multiple intelligences, linguistic intelligence is the ability to use words effectively orally or in writing. An outstanding level of this intelligence is observed in writers, journalists, communicators, students with skills to learn languages, write stories, read, etc. They use both hemispheres.

- **Body** Intelligence. Body intelligence corresponds to that which uses the whole body to express ideas and feelings and the ability to use the hands to transform objects. Those who have high bodily-kinesthetic intelligence are said to be good at body movement, performing actions, and physical control. People who are strong in this area tend to have excellent hand-eye coordination and dexterity. Athletes, craftsmen, dancers and sculptors are the most representative of this intelligence.

- **Musical** Intelligence. It is the intelligence that perceives, transforms and defines music and its forms. Sensitivity, rhythm, tone and timbre are associated with this type of intelligence. Musical intelligence is present in composers, orchestra conductors, musicians, etc. People who have strong musical intelligence are good at thinking in patterns, rhythms, and sounds. They have a strong appreciation for music and are often good at musical composition and performance. We find them conducting an orchestra or playing an instrument.

- **Space** Intelligence. It is the ability to think in three dimensions. A capacity that makes it possible for us to perceive images, transform or modify them and produce or decode graphic information. People who are strong in visual-spatial intelligence are good at visualizing things. These individuals are often good with directions as well as maps, charts, videos, and pictures. Pilots, painters, and architects are a clear example. They like to make maps, paintings, drawings and diagrams.

- **Naturalist** Intelligence. It is the ability to differentiate, classify, and employ the environment. Naturalistic is the most recent addition to Gardner's theory and has been met with more resistance than his original seven intelligences. According to Gardner, individuals who are high in this type of intelligence are more in tune with nature and are often interested in nurturing, exploring the environment, and learning about other species. These individuals are said to be highly aware of even subtle changes to their environments. It is possessed by rural people, botanists, hunters, ecologists. It is observed in people who love plants and animals.

- **Interpersonal** intelligence. It is the one that carries implicit the capacity to empathize with others, since it allows us to understand them. Those who have strong interpersonal intelligence are good at understanding and interacting with other people. These individuals are skilled at assessing the emotions, motivations, desires, and intentions of those around them. Present in politicians, salesmen and teachers.

- **Intrapersonal** Intelligence. It is the intelligence to build an accurate assessment of oneself and the ability to direct one's own life. It includes reflection, self-understanding and self-esteem. It is appreciated by theologians, psychologists, sociologists and philosophers, among others. Intrapersonal intelligence allows us to understand what our needs and feelings are and how we find ourselves.

Gardner's theory of multiple intelligences considers that all human beings possess the eight intelligences to a greater or lesser extent, but clarifies that there are no pure styles. It is a pluralistic vision, where intelligence is a changing ability throughout life. Gardner, supported by his theory of multiple intelligences, maintains that teaching should allow students to be oriented according to the capacity and style of intelligence that dominates them most. (https://bit.ly/2IGhvdK)

Strong Artificial Intelligence would integrate in a single system the algorithms so that a computer would have all the types of intelligence that Howard Gardner considers. It could have logical, linguistic, corporal, musical, spatial, naturalistic, interpersonal and intrapersonal intelligence. That's the idea of Strong Artificial Intelligence.

The substance of intelligence

According to the theory of evolution, approximately four billion years ago molecules of carbon, hydrogen, oxygen, nitrogen, phosphorus and sulfur were united and through the action of electric discharges and ultraviolet radiation an organic molecule was generated that evolved during something more than two billion years until it was able to reproduce itself and give place to life. In the course of millions of years, the organic molecules evolved and were transformed into cells that by differentiating gave rise to thousands of living organisms to populate Planet Earth.

One of these living beings evolved and through the growth of its brain came to have a superior intelligence. This intelligence allowed him to pick up a stick or a bone and use them as a weapon and a tool to dominate the animal kingdom. From that moment on, human beings evolved into modern Homo sapiens.

If we go back in time we can come to the conclusion that the human being originated from the combination of chemical elements. The computer is also made of chemical elements. CPUs (microprocessor) are made mostly of an element called silicon.

Silicon is a chemical element with the symbol Si and atomic number 14. It is a hard and brittle crystalline solid with a blue-grey metallic luster; and it is a tetravalent metalloid and semiconductor. Silicon is rather common in earth´s crust. It is a member of group 14 in the periodic table: carbon is above it; and germanium, tin, and lead are below it. It is relatively unreactive. Silicon is the eighth most common element in the universe by mass, but very rarely occurs as the pure element in the Earth's crust. It is most widely distributed in dusts, sands, planetoids, and planets as various forms of silicon dioxide (silica) or silicates. More than 90% of the Earth's crust is composed of silicate minerals, making silicon the second most abundant element in the Earth's crust (about 28% by mass) after oxygen.

The non-physical part of the computer is the software. We could say that software is the "intellectual" part of the computer. Software is a set of instructions organized into an algorithm for processing information.

Intelligence in the human being was created by a change in the quantity, location and functioning of the brain. A change that needed millions of years. The computer's processor, also made of chemical elements as the human being, has grown exponentially and it can grow much more in a few years.

After studying how Planet Earth originated, how the first molecules formed, how life on Earth arose, how human beings were created and their intelligence developed, we can ask two important questions:

Would it be possible for an increase in microprocessor capacity and AI software to produce intelligence?

Would it be possible for the intelligence of the computer to be superior to that of the human being?

In the following chapters we will study the computer, software, Artificial Intelligence and other interesting topics that may enlighten us to help answer these interesting questions. How far can the AI Revolution go?

–3–

THE SHORT ROAD OF THE COMPUTER

Although the first ideas about the computer (Charles Babbage's Analytical Machine) and software (Ada Lovelace's brilliant idea for programming the Analytical Machine) arose in London in the middle of the 19th century, the elements for the generation of Artificial Intelligence were produced a hundred years later; that is, in the second half of the 20th century. These components are basically the microprocessor and the software that together create the computer.

Almost at the same time Germany, England and the United States focus their technological efforts on the construction of machines to execute complicated calculations to decipher the enemy's codes and to improve their war weaponry. It is World War II that drives the technology race to support the army and produce better weapons to defeat the enemy.

The microprocessor

History records that Thales of Miletus (600 BC) was the first scientist to recognize the existence of electrical energy in nature, but when Charles Babbage tried to run his Analytical Machine there was no electricity as available energy to boost the functioning of machines and even less so the knowledge of electronics. Machines used the power of water, wind and some who were already ahead of their time took advantage of the enormous power of steam.

One hundred years later, when the first computers were invented, electricity was already used as the energy to move machines and motors. Electronics began to be used. Computers, telephones, radios, televisions and communication devices that worked electronically used as a basic element the electronic valve also known as a vacuum tube or bulb. A small element the size of an incandescent bulb that had several disadvantages that made its operation difficult: it consumed a large amount of electrical energy, generated too much heat, melted easily, took up too much space and its production cost was too high. The advancement of electronics and the construction of faster and more efficient computers urgently required another type of element that could overcome these deficiencies.

Bell Laboratories took on the task of producing an electronic component to replace the electronic valve. It was part of a research group formed by William Shokley, John Bardeen and Walter Brattain. Its attention was focused on the study of semiconductors and, in particular, on the behavior of silicon and germanium; a semiconductor material that is located at an intermediate point between an electrically conductive element, such as copper, and an insulator or material that prevents the flow of electric current, such as ceramics or wood. By subjecting the conductive element to a certain voltage it can change its state from conductive to non-conductive, or vice versa, thus acting as an electrical activation switch.

The research work required a sustained intellectual effort during more than two years after which, on December 1947, Bardeen and Brattain managed to produce the tip transistor that basically consisted of a germanium crystal whose surface was in contact with two pointed electrodes 0.05 mm distant from each other. Despite its advancement, this model lacked stability and its power was very weak, which is why it was not manufactured in series and only served as a starting point for further research. In 1951 Shokley managed to produce the union transistor that had important advantages, promoting then its manufacture on a large scale.

> **Transistors are discrete components** that are produced in a single unit and then soldered into a printed circuit to interconnect with other transistors and discrete components. Its energy efficiency is considerably higher than that of the electronic valve, since the power supply is dissipated in the heating of the cathodes, producing a generation of heat that affects its operation. Its wear is minimal, so it can last in operation an average of 100,000 hours against 2,000 that an electronic valve lasts.

The computer industry viewed the transistor with great interest and took advantage of it to build new and more efficient machines. The first computers made with transistors were introduced by UNIVAC and Philco. The advantages obtained were enormous since computers made with transistors could have greater capacity, smaller size, longer life, fewer failures and, importantly, lower cost.

Based on the transistor, several scientists in the United States and England began studies to make its use more reliable and effective. The first to shape it, write it and present it was Geoffrey Dummer, who worked in the British government's radar service. At an international conference held in Washington, Dummer presented a document in which he expressed his conviction that, with the invention of the transistor, it would be possible to assemble in one piece a set of electronic components without having to connect them by wires. His idea was certainly brilliant and was the first expression of the concept of the integrated circuit, but the distance between words and deeds seemed an insurmountable abyss.

Jack Kilby put the rattle on the cat. The problem he had to solve was to produce all the electronic components with a semiconductor element, to isolate the components so that a short circuit would not occur and to connect the components without using wires. He solved it by using silicon as a base. He then covered a section of the IC with a thin layer of silicon dioxide that acted as insulation. He added an aluminum stitch over the oxide to obtain the capacitors while the resistors and transistors were built directly over the silicon layer. The problem of insulation was solved by giving a form of "U" or "L" to the sets of components to separate them from each other. Finally, the connection of the elements was solved by soldering the terminals in order to prevent the connections from separating with the vibrations. The creation of Kilby allowed the idea of a circuit that could integrate several components in a single piece to become a reality. **Jack Kilby had invented the integrated circuit.**

Then came the genius of Robert Noyce who improved the technique to produce the integrated circuit, add more electronic components in one piece, give greater security in its operation and produce it on an industrial scale to make it available to the computer manufacturing industry and many more devices. The process of manufacturing integrated circuits was perfected to a degree that allowed it to lower its cost and make it accessible to the electronics industry that by then was ready to receive it and apply it in the production of a wide variety of items. The US government purchased thousands of integrated circuits to manufacture highly sophisticated weaponry and to use in the production of devices required by the space conquest project. The computer industry has been one of the ones that has taken most advantage of the integrated circuit to convert it into microprocessors that have radically transformed the capacity of the machines, initiating a new stage in the history of computing.

In 1968, **Robert Noyce, his friends and associates founded Intel** to produce integrated circuits and electronic components. Today Intel is one of the world's leading technology companies. In 2019 it had 104,000 permanent employees and a stock market capitalization value of 215 billion. Intel is not the only company that produces integrated circuits, but it is the leader in this field. Research and development of new products has allowed Intel to take the production of integrated circuits to a scale that exceeds imagination in terms of the number and capacity of information processing. The power of the integrated circuit is a basic element for making Artificial Intelligence a reality and taking it to higher levels.

Marcian Hoff, an engineer who worked at Intel, once asked himself why not take advantage of the electronic components of the integrated circuit and put a central processor on a chip, that is, on a single integrated circuit? A question that led him to a brilliant idea, an idea that by making it a reality would revolutionize the world of electronics, computing and virtually all human activities. A processor built on a single chip. A processor capable of executing any logical procedure in order to convert the integrated circuit into a programmable chip of general purpose and with the capacity to carry out any information process. With a single chip acting as a processor, a calculator could perform various functions of information processing, data input/output and whatever else was necessary. This same processor could work for a robot, a washing machine, an airplane, a submarine...or a computer! **Marcian Hoff had invented the microprocessor.**

Since then the company Intel has maintained the leadership in the production of microprocessors. **The first was the now historic 4004 microprocessor.** This 4-bit chip boosted computer technology and served as the basis for new and more advanced products to enable the production of the famous Altair personal computer and then the Apple. Intel is expected to launch the first 10 nanometer processors of the Cannonlake family in 2019. By 2021 the Icelake family is expected and the last of this group will be the Tigerlake that will appear in 2023. At the end of this cycle, a higher level with microprocessors is expected in 2025. This higher capacity will facilitate the development of Artificial Intelligence.

The production of microprocessors is currently one of the strategic lines in the high-tech industry. Its application has been extended to a growing number of products that at present operate through sophisticated software that is revolutionizing even the traditional industry. An example is the automotive industry that for several years remained without major innovations and is now transformed with computers in most of their systems. The United States remains the leader in the production of microprocessors, but other countries follow suit. Among them is China, which has strongly boosted its technology program.

Software

The first ideas for software came to **Ada Lovelace**'s mind when she said in her notes on the Charles Babbage Machine "We can say that the Analytical Machine weaves algebraic models like Jacquard's looms weave flowers and leaves". Ada Lovelace did not write an executable program on a computer, but conceived the idea of software, the soul of the computer, and is therefore considered the first programmer in human history.

It would take almost 100 years for another woman, **Adele Goldstine**, to write the first program that ran on a computer. On February 15, 1946 the ENIAC computer ran several programs written by Adele to perform the following operations:

- 5,000 sums to run in a second
- 500 multiplications to run in a second
- Generation of numbers squared and cubed.
- Generation of a table of sines and cosines.
- Execution of a special problem called E-2 as an example of a long and complicated calculation.

The execution of the programs was impeccable and, from then on, the fame of the ENIAC computer spread all over the world. It is important to consider that these programs were not stored in the machine because at that time the ENIAC did not have the capacity to do so; it was necessary to enter them into memory by means of switches that were operated on the machine's dashboard. With von Neumann's valuable contribution the ENIAC improved its design and in 1948 had the ability to run a stored program.

From then on, computers grew in capacity, speed, accuracy, energy savings, less space and, also, lower cost. Although it did not take off at the same time, software also began an evolution that would take it, in the course of a few decades, to become the main engine of the advancement of computing and Artificial Intelligence.

In 1954 the FORTRAN programming language (FORmula TRANslation) marks the end of the first stage of software and the beginning of methodical and efficient programming to operate a growing number of computers that were installed in government offices, universities and businesses. FORTRAN's first design was completed in November 1954 and became known through a typed document and various lectures aimed primarily at users of the IBM 704 computer. At first it was received with skepticism by the great masters of computing, but little by little it was accepted until it became the main compiler for scientific applications. **John Backus, author of FORTRAN**, describes the romantic era of software as follows: "Programming in the early 1950s was a mysterious art, a private activity involving only a programmer, a problem, a computer and perhaps a small library of subroutines and a primitive assembly language".

Programming languages have evolved into sophisticated tools to produce application programs that gradually control the activities of society. Some have specialized and so we have languages for design, business administration, scientific calculations, art, drawing, and many more. Although applications for Artificial Intelligence can be developed in different languages, there are some that are becoming the favorites of programmers in this interesting and growing field of Informatics. These are some of them:

LISP John McCarthy, one of the founders of Artificial Intelligence, formed a pioneering group in the study of AI at the Massachusetts Institute of Technology and decided to develop a programming language that would adapt to their information management needs, since the languages available at that time did not suit the environment of their work methodology. McCarthy started the project in 1959 with the objective of facilitating experiments with a system called Information Receiver in which a machine could be instructed to handle declarative and imperative phrases and could show a certain "common sense" in the fulfillment of the instructions received. The main requirement was a programming system to handle expressions that represented declarative or imperative phrases in such a way that the recipient of information could make deductions. In the course of its development the LISP language went through several stages of simplification and finally became based on a scheme to represent the partial recursive functions of a class of symbolic expressions. Thus, **LISP was born and oriented towards Artificial Intelligence**.

The project was originally made for the IBM 704 computer. In March 1960 the first LISP manual was published. When the new version of the IBM computer with the model 709 was produced, a new possibility was opened to improve it and new versions were created that culminated with the LISP-2 that substantially surpassed the original version especially in terms of the notation used and the handling of data input and output. LISP was oriented to the handling of symbolic expressions and object lists. Its name reflects this objective: LISt Processor. However, its applications were significantly expanded, exceeding the area for which it was designed. Some of the best Chess programs have been produced in LISP.

This language uses parentheses profusely and for those who do not usually handle algebraic expressions it is easy to get lost at the moment of forming the parentheses pairs that separate each operand. The degree of difficulty in learning it falls in two extremes: it is difficult for those who are not used to handling symbolic expressions with parentheses and easy, and even pleasant, for those who handle this form of notation.

LISP has changed a lot since its beginnings and several dialects have developed in its history. During the 1980s and 1990s a great effort was made to unify the numerous dialects of LISP into a single language (Primarily InterLISP, MacLISP, ZetaLISP, MetaLISP, and FranzLISP). The new language, Common LISP was essentially a compatible subset of the dialects it replaced. Having declined somewhat in the 1990s, LISP experienced a new growth from the year 2000. Many new LISP programmers were inspired by writers like Paul Graham and Eric S. Raymond fighting for a language that others considered outdated. New LISP programmers often describe LISP as an eye-opening experience.

Python is an interpreted, high-level, general-purpose programming language created by **Guido van Rossum** and first released in 1991. Python is considered to be in first place on the list of all AI development languages due to its simplicity. The syntaxes belonging to python are very simple and can be easily learned. Therefore, many AI algorithms can be easily implemented by using it. Python requires less writing time than other languages such as Java, C++ or Ruby. Python supports object oriented, functional as well as procedure oriented styles of programming. There are plenty of libraries in python, which make tasks easier. For example: Numpy is a library for python that helps solve many scientific computations. Also, there is Pybrain, which is for using machine learning in Python.

Python is the leading coding language for NLP because of its simple syntax, structure, and rich text processing tool. So, it makes perfect sense to learn Python, as it boasts the most comprehensive frameworks for both DL and ML. As this highly flexible AI language is platform agnostic, one would only have to make minor changes to the code to get it up and running in a new operating system.

PROLOG is a programming language developed in the early 1970s at the University of Aix-Marseille I (Marseille, France) by professors Alain Colmerauer and Philippe Roussel. The name of the PROLOG language comes from the French PROgrammation en LOGique. It was born from a project that did not aim at the implementation of a programming language, but the processing of natural languages. Alain Colmerauer and Robert Pasero worked on the natural language processing part and Jean Trudel and Philippe Roussel on the deduction and inference part of the system. Interested in the SL resolution method, Trudel persuaded Robert Kowalski to join the project, resulting in a preliminary version of PROLOG at the end of 1971. This first version was programmed in ALGOL W. The final version was released in 1972.

PROLOG is framed in the paradigm of logical and declarative languages, which differentiates it enormously from other more popular languages such as FORTRAN, Pascal, C or Java. In these languages the instructions are normally executed in sequential order, that is, one after the other, in the same order in which they are written, which only varies when a control instruction is reached (a loop, a conditional instruction or a transfer). The programs in PROLOG are composed of Horn clauses that constitute rules of the type "modus ponendo ponens", that is, "If the antecedent is true, then the consequent is true". However, the way Horn's clauses are written is the opposite of the usual. First the consequent is written and then the antecedent. The antecedent can be a conjunction of conditions called a sequence of objectives. Each objective is separated by a comma and can be considered similar to an instruction or procedural call of imperative languages. In PROLOG there are no control instructions. Its execution is based on two concepts: unification and backtracking.

This language stays alongside Lisp when we talk about development in the field of AI. The features provided by it include efficient pattern matching, tree-based data structuring and automatic backtracking. All these features provide a surprisingly powerful and flexible programming framework. Prolog is widely used for working on medical projects and also for designing expert AI systems.

R is a programming language and free software environment for statistical computing, Artificial Intelligence and graphics supported by the Foundation for Statistical Computing. **R** is one of the most effective languages and environments for analyzing and manipulating data for statistical purposes. Using R, we can easily produce well-designed publication-quality plot, including mathematical symbols and formulae where needed. Apart from being a general purpose language, R has numerous packages like RODBC, Gmodels, Class and Tm which are used in the field of machine learning. These packages make the implementation of machine learning algorithms easy for cracking business associated problems.

Haskell The name of this programming language was taken from the name of Haskell Brooks Curry (September 12, 1900 - September 1, 1982) who was an American mathematician and logician born in Millis, Massachusetts. Haskell was educated at Harvard University and received a doctorate in Göttingen in 1930. His main vocation was in mathematical logic, especially in the theory of formal systems and processes - combinatorial logic, the foundation for functional programming languages.

Haskell is a standardized multi-purpose, purely functional programming language with non-strict semantics and strong static typing. In Haskell, a function is a first-class element of the programming language. As a functional programming language, the primary control builder is the function. Language has its origins in the observations of Haskell Curry and his intellectual descendants. In January 1999, the Haskell 98 language standard was published in The Haskell 98 Report. In January 2003, a revised version was published in Haskell 98 Language and Libraries: The Revised Report. The language continues to evolve rapidly with Hugs and GHC implementations representing the current de facto standard.

For the development of applications (apps), speech recognition and Artificial Intelligence some tools have been released. Here are some of them:

Jasper is an open source platform for application programmers with voice control. Jasper allows you to control all kinds of products using voice to request information from certain applications, manage the home and update social networks and more. The code is available to developers who want to program their own modules. This platform is designed specifically for the Raspberry Pi hardware. You also need additional hardware such as a Wi-Fi adapter that allows you to have an Internet connection and a USB microphone. It is also recommended to have a 4GB memory card and an Ethernet cable. In the platform documentation some modules written by other developers for other applications are presented that show their possibilities.

Caffe This tool was created by BAIR (Berkeley Artificial Intelligence Research) in 2014, and became popular in academic research in a framework of deep learning. In 2017 Facebook launched Caffe-2 as a commercial successor to Caffe. It was written to deal with Caffe's difficulties in terms of scalability and also seeking to be less cumbersome.

TensorFlow. Google decided to open to everyone one of its future projects: its Artificial Intelligence system TensorFlow. The company based in Mountain View, California decided to convert TensorFlow into open source, which means that any researcher, organization or company interested in Artificial Intelligence will be able to use the system. It is a system that learns to identify patterns after analyzing massive amounts of information and has allowed Google to develop applications such as Google Translate that make it possible, for example, to place the phone on a signal in Russian and translate it into the language the user wants. Google CEO Sundar Pichai stressed that TensorFlow is a system that can run on a single smartphone or on thousands of computers in data centers. "We use TensorFlow for everything from voice recognition in the Google application, to SmartReply in Inbox and searching in Google Photos", Pichai said during an interview for specialized media. The executive said he was convinced that the impact of TensorFlow can be even greater outside Google, which is why the company decided to open access.

The computer

The sum of hardware and software makes the computer. We can see hardware and software as two sides of the same coin. Both parts are required to achieve full machine performance. These two elements, hardware and software, are necessary to achieve Artificial Intelligence. Sometimes we will find them in a personal computer, a large computer, a telephone, a robot or some other device. The receptacle does not matter so much to Artificial Intelligence because it is the microprocessor and the software that can produce the intelligence of the device that contains them.

It is important to study the evolution of the computer, albeit succinctly, in order to better understand the steps that have been taken to arrive at a programmable machine that, depending on the capacity of its microprocessor and the quality of the software, has been able to reach the first stages of Artificial Intelligence and, in a notable way, to appreciate the speed of its evolution in comparison with the time that has elapsed for intelligence to emerge and evolve in the human being.

The Second World War was a military conflict that developed between 1939 and 1945. The beginning of the conflict is usually located on September 1, 1939, with the German invasion of Poland, the first step of Nazi Germany in its attempt to found a great empire in Europe, which led to the immediate declaration of war by France and most of the countries of the British Empire against the Third Reich.

The first steps to build a computer were taken in Germany. Konrad Zuse, a young civil engineering student at the Berlin University of Technology, built the first mechanical calculator with a binary system and was able to build more advanced machine models. However, most of his work was destroyed during the allied army's bombing of the city of Berlin in April 1945. He built a computer that worked with telephone relays, handled floating point arithmetic and had a memory capacity of 64 words. A more advanced model of this machine had 32-bit words and a memory capacity of 512 words. Unfortunately, Zuse was forced to escape the bombardment and could only rescue the Z4 model he hid in a wine cellar in a small town in the mountains of Bavaria, where he did not have the opportunity to make it work fully.

England is not left behind and starts a project to build a high speed calculator to decipher the codes used by the German army. The project was assigned to a select group of scientists under the command of brilliant mathematician Max Newman. The group was also joined by Alan Turing, one of the mathematicians who, most importantly, has contributed to the development of software. The Colossus, a machine built in the utmost secrecy, succeeded in deciphering the transmission codes of the enemy's messages. In this high-speed calculator electronic valves were used, a breakthrough for this time that has earned it the distinction to be considered the first electronic computer. However, it was designed with only one purpose: to decipher the codes of information transmission. It was a cryptographic machine that worked electronically with high efficiency and at a higher speed than was known at that time, but its design did not consider the possibility of executing various information processes, a fundamental characteristic of a computer.

The United States also entered World War II and consequently the race to build a machine to run high-speed calculations. At the Moore School of Electrical Engineering at the University of Pennsylvania, John W. Mauchly and J. Presper Eckert, American scientists whose influence on computing was to be felt for several decades, teamed up to build a general-purpose electronic computer. The project began on May 31, 1943 and later, in August 1944, John von Neumann joined the group and was key in the operation of the machine. The primary objective of the computer was to solve ballistics problems raised during World War II.

After the end of World War II, the victorious countries, England, the United States and Russia set themselves the task of building more efficient, faster, precise and economic computers to support research work in universities, government, the space program and business administration. Large machines were built with memory based on electronic valves, ferrites and the most advanced with transistors. The United States takes the lead with the IBM 360 series.

The first computer system designed to mass-produce and cover a wide range of applications was the IBM 360 series in 1965. IBM's central idea was to offer a computer that could meet the needs of government, universities, and businesses. The IBM 360 computer was neither the work of a researcher nor a product developed experimentally in a university; it was the result of the joint work of an entire team formed by professionals of different specialties under the organization and direction of a large company. For more than a decade, the IBM 360 series of computers dominated the computing industry.

In 1975 another great step was taken in the production of the personal computer. First it was the Altair built by Ed Roberts and then Apple built by Steve Wozniack and the genius of Steve Jobs. At that time Bill Gates entered the scene with his idea of producing software for the personal computer and selling it as a product accessible to everyone. Steve Jobs, a genius of innovation, generated in his mind the idea of the personal computer and years later the iPod, iPad and iPhone to revolutionize the way humans listen to music, process information and communicate.

The personal computer and software caused a bifurcation in the history of computing and triggered an evolutionary process that would end years later in Artificial Intelligence. Little by little, the computer began to carry out some activities that the human being used to do without the help of any device, relying only on his mind. At the university the computer became indispensable to make complicated calculations for researchers, at companies it took over the management of the administration, at the government level it took over the responsibility for handling great volumes of information. The computer became people's most important tool for communicating and processing their personal information.

At this point it is important to pause a little to appreciate the great difference in the time it has taken for a human being to become intelligent and the time that has elapsed in the evolution of the computer. The formation of the brain of Homo sapiens required millions of years and once the brain was ready it took another 130,000 years for the spark of intelligence to occur. For the computer it has taken less than a hundred years to consider that it already has a certain degree of intelligence.

Supercomputers

Artificial Intelligence requires the processing of a large volume of data at extreme speeds. In the course of history, faster and more capable computers have been built for businesses, universities, government, and research centers. Placed on a higher level are supercomputers, powerful machines built with the highest technology and at a cost in excess of one hundred million dollars. Only a handful of countries have managed to integrate the technology and economic resources necessary to build these powerful machines.

If we consider that the race to be at the forefront of Artificial Intelligence technology is currently between China and the United States, we can conclude that also the race to build the fastest and most powerful supercomputer is between these two countries although other nations have also ventured into this field such as Germany, Japan, France, United Kingdom and South Korea.

Until recently the most powerful supercomputer was Sunway TaihuLight (Chinese: 神威-太湖之光 shénwēi táihú zhi guang. English: God of the lake). The Sunway TaihuLight was the world's fastest supercomputer for two years, from June 2016 to June 2018, according to the TOP500 lists. The record was surpassed in June 2018 by IBM's Summit. The Sunway is a Chinese supercomputer with a LINPACK benchmark rating of 93 petaflops. This is nearly three times as fast as the previous Tianhe-2, which ran at 34 petaflops. It was designed by the National Research Center of Parallel Computer Engineering & Technology (NRCPC) and is located at the National Supercomputing Center in Wuxi, Jiangsu province, China.

The Sunway TaihuLight uses a total of 40,960 Chinese-designed SW26010 manycore 64-bit RISC processors based on the Sunway architecture. Each processor chip contains 256 processing cores, and an additional four auxiliary cores for system management (also RISC cores, just more fully featured) for a total of 10,649,600 CPU cores across the entire system. The system runs on its own operating system, Sunway RaiseOS which is based on Linux. The system has its own customized implementation of OpenACC 2.0 to aid the parallelization of code.

But because the race goes on and doesn't stop, the United States developed the world's fastest supercomputer and regained the leadership lost to China. The news broke in June 2018:

Summit, the fastest and smartest supercomputer, has been developed by the US government in partnership with IBM and Nvidia. The supercomputer was presented by the Department of Energy. **Ginni Rometty, CEO of IBM**, shared that the firm she controls was in charge of the design. "This is truly one of our greatest accomplishments. It's the fastest and smartest supercomputer today," the executive said in dialogue with CNBC. "It's Watson's granddaughter," she joked. Jensen Huang, CEO of Nvidia, said Summit is just the beginning of the "exciting" growth to come. "Summit's architecture will mark the way computers will be built in the future, part of a multi-million dollar industry," he added.

Summit boasts a performance of 200,000 billion calculations per second and is eight times more powerful than Titan, the fastest supercomputer developed in the US until the arrival of the brand new machine. Its potential is really promising for researchers. "An experiment that previously could have taken hundreds of years to be carried out can now be executed in one day," Ginni Rometty said. "We will have new compounds and new cures for cancer," she added. Energy Secretary Rick Perry said the machine will have a profound effect not only on health but also on energy research and cybersecurity. "This will change the world," he shared. Among its features is the fact that Summit exchanges cooling water at a rate of 9 Olympic pools each day. The Artificial Intelligence capability of the system will allow us to work on the development of new drugs through quantum chemistry and to make great advances in the analysis of chronic pain and the study of mitochondrial DNA.

Curious data from the Summit supercomputer:

- It can do 200 quadrillion calculations in a second. If a person is able to do one calculation per second, it would take 6.3 billion years to calculate what Summit accomplishes in one blink.
- If the Earth's 7.4 billion people did a calculation per second, it would take us 305 days to perform an operation that for Summit is instantaneous.
- Summit's archive system can store 250 petabytes of data, equivalent to 74 million years of high-definition video.
- Summit will be used to create scientific models and simulations based on Artificial Intelligence and automatic learning that can accelerate discovery in areas such as health, energy, material development and astrophysics.
- Summit represents a major step in systems research and innovation on humanity's path to Strong Artificial Intelligence.
- Summit servers were built on the IBM manufacturing floor within the Guadalajara Technology Campus in the state of Jalisco, Mexico.

–4–

ORIGIN AND DEVELOPMENT OF AI

Artificial Intelligence has been associated with a world of science fiction that has contributed to distorting its real meaning. Over time, there have been films, books, plays and spectacular news that link Artificial Intelligence with robots that take up arms against their creators, computers that rebel against humans and take control of an interplanetary ship and stories that move away from the realm of reality and remain in fantasy.

In this essay on Artificial Intelligence we will move away from fantasy to reality even though reality is sometimes bolder than science fiction. In this chapter we will study the evolution of Artificial Intelligence from Alan Turing's ideas, we will highlight the merits of the Darmouth College conference, the Partnership on AI, and we will study the panorama of Artificial Intelligence in the world to conclude with the analysis of the case of an AI developer.

Alan Turing

Alan Mathison Turing, Officer of the Order of the British Empire, was born in Paddington, London, on 23 June 1912 and died in Wilmslow, Cheshire on 7 June 1954. He is considered one of the fathers of computer science, precursor of modern computing and cornerstone of Artificial Intelligence. He was a mathematician, computer scientist, cryptographer, philosopher, marathoner and British ultra-distance runner. He provided an influential formalization of the algorithm's concepts, conceived the idea of the program stored inside the same computer and left his ideas about computation captured in the model of the Turing Machine.

Alan Turing was a man with a controversial personality; a mixture of a child prodigy and a distracted teacher. He usually wore a scruffy outfit because he did not care about his personal appearance. It was normal to see him wearing a tie instead of a belt to fasten his pants. He had a high-pitched voice and a nervous smile. He only agreed to talk to people of his same intellectual level, which obviously led him to have few friends. He was a homosexual and in his day, homosexuality was considered a breach of morality and in some places, it was even considered a crime. He probably couldn't stand the internal conflict he was suffering and decided to commit suicide by eating a poisoned apple.

From a young age he distinguished himself for being a brilliant student with a special facility for mathematics. At the University of Cambridge he obtained his doctorate and at the age of 24 he published "On Computable Numbers", one of the most interesting documents on computer theory. It was published in 1936, before the first computer was built. In this document he explained the characteristics and limitations of a logical machine. His purpose was not to build a machine and in his ideas there is nothing related to the physical part of the computer. He did not write about relays or electromechanical circuits, only about their logical structure. **The Turing Machine exists only on paper as a set of specifications,** but its influence has been fundamental in the development of computers and software and it is still considered the prototype of the logical machine.

In this way, Turing was the first to understand the universal characteristic of the digital computer, reaching and even surpassing Charles Babbage's ideas expressed 100 years ago. Babbage's key phrase when referring to the Analytical Machine was that "the universe of conditions that allow a machine to do calculations of an unlimited extension are found precisely in the Analytical Machine." The fundamental concept of Turing was that the machine must handle information by means of a **program that can be modified so that it executes diverse functions** and this is the essential concept of a computer.

In September 1936 Turing made a trip to the United States to study in the Department of Mathematics at Princeton University with teachers of the category of Einstein, Courant and John von Neumann. In the summer of 1937 he returned to England. Another trip took him to Princeton in 1938 and during that time he had the opportunity to establish close communication with von Neumann who, intrigued by Turing's ideas, offered him work as his assistant at the university. Turing did not accept and returned to England to join the Communications Department of the Foreign Ministry where he was to begin a brilliant career.

During the Second World War, Turing was concentrated in Bletchley Park, the British government's secret location in North London, to decipher the German army's information transmission codes, which were encoded with a complex mechanism operated by a machine called Enigma. To decipher the thousands of messages transmitted daily, a select group of scientists developed a machine called Colossus, which was put into operation in December 1943. The design and operation of the Colossus project remained secret even after the end of the war and only in recent years has it been possible to know the nature of the work that was done and the characteristics of the machines that were used. Some scholars of universal history have affirmed that the participation of scientists in deciphering the enemy's secret messages was decisive for the Allied army to win the Second World War.

During his stay at Bletchley Park, Turing was always appreciated by his co-workers. His homosexual tendency was not disclosed and this allowed him to maintain an atmosphere of cordial relations. At that time he began to develop his ideas about intelligent machines, a revolutionary concept for his time especially because the first computer with a stored program was not yet built. The first document expressing his ideas about thinking machines was written at the end of World War II, but was not published until 1950.

At the end of the war the government of the United States invited a group of English scientists to learn about the advances made in computing, mainly in the ENIAC and MARK I machines. The first scientist to make the trip was J.R. Womersley, who worked in the National Physics Laboratory, one of the most important research centers in England. He visited the Moore School of Electrical Engineering and received a copy of the computer report written by von Neumann. Upon his return to England, Womersley immediately organized a select group of scientists to develop a project to build a computer. Alan Turing was the first to be invited to the project.

In 1950 the book **"Computing Machinery and Intelligence"** was published, representing one of the most interesting documents in the history of software. In this controversial work Turing establishes his conviction that computers can perfectly imitate human intelligence and that this would be possible in the year 2000. The document has served as a manifesto for a group of specialists dedicated to carrying out Turing's project of building a computer with Artificial Intelligence that passes the famous test.

The Turing test

Machine intelligence is a subject that some UK researchers studied 10 years before the Artificial Intelligence research field was founded in 1956. It was a topic commonly discussed by members of the "Club of Reason", an informal group of British cyber and electronic researchers that included Alan Turing, who had been working with the concept of "machine intelligence" since at least 1941. One of the first references to the "computational intelligence" was made by Turing in 1947. In Turing's report called "intelligent machinery", he investigated "the idea of whether or not it was possible for a machine to demonstrate intelligent behavior" and as part of his research he proposed a test known as the Turing test which can be considered as the litmus test to determine whether or not a machine is as intelligent as a human being.

The first published text written by Turing focusing entirely on machine intelligence was "Computing Machinery and Intelligence". Turing began this text by saying "I propose to take into account the question, can machines think?" Turing mentioned that the traditional approach was to start with definitions of the terms "machine" and "intelligence"; he decided to ignore this and began by replacing the question with a new one that was closely related and used unambiguous words. He proposed, in essence, to change the question from "can machines think?" to "**Can machines do what we, as thinking entities, do?**" The advantage of this new question was that it "drew a boundary between man's physical and intellectual capacities".

To demonstrate whether a machine could be considered "intelligent" Turing proposed a test inspired by the "Imitation Game". The Turing test, developed by Alan Turing in 1950, is a test of a machine's ability to exhibit intelligent behavior equivalent to, or indistinguishable from, that of a human. Turing proposed that a human evaluator would judge natural language conversations between a human and a machine designed to generate human-like responses. The evaluator would be aware that one of the two partners in conversation is a machine, and all participants would be separated from one another. The conversation would be limited to a text-only channel such as a computer keyboard and screen so the result would not depend on the machine's ability to render words as speech. If the evaluator cannot reliably tell the machine from the human, the machine is said to have passed the test. The test results do not depend on the machine's ability to give correct answers to questions, only how closely its answers resemble those a human would give.

We ask ourselves the question, "What would happen if a machine takes the role of A in this game? Would the interrogator be so frequently mistaken in this new version of the game than when it was played by a man and a woman? These questions replace the original question, Can machines think?"

Later in the text a similar version was proposed in which a judge conversed with a computer and a man. Although none of the proposed versions are the same as the one we know today, Turing proposed a third option, which he discussed on a BBC radio broadcast, where a jury asks questions to a computer and the purpose of the machine is to deceive the majority of the jury into believing it is a human.

The power and appeal of the Turing test derived from its simplicity. Philosophy of mind, psychology and modern neuroscience have been unable to provide definitions for "intelligence" and "thought" that are precise and general enough to be applied to machines. Without these definitions, the main unknowns of the philosophy of Artificial Intelligence cannot be answered. Turing's test, though imperfect, at least provided something that could be measured and, as such, was a pragmatic solution to a difficult philosophical question. In the course of the following years several attempts have been made to pass the Turing test with remarkable results although **the time has not yet come for its complete and strong acceptance.**

To commemorate the 60th anniversary of Alan Turing's death (June 7, 1954) two audacious programmers set out to create a conversational robot or chat bot to pass the famous Turing test. **Vladimir Veselov, a Russian computer scientist living in the United States, and Eugene Demchenko**, a young Ukrainian resident in Russia, took on the task of applying their computer skills to produce the program that would give the computer "intelligence" to pass the Turing test. They named the bot Eugene Goostman and to make the project more real, the two computer geniuses decided to give Eugene Goostman the personality of a 13-year-old "know-it-all" boy. When interviewed about their creation they said "Eugene was born in the Ukraine in 2001 and, although he presumes to know everything, it is perfectly reasonable that at his age he still has things to learn. We spent a lot of time building his personality, and we have managed to improve the dialogue controller in the last year, to give a more human touch to his answers. In the future we plan to make him smarter and continue improving his conversation logic."

After several attempts at its presentations, the AI program was able to convince 33% of the judges who participated in the test at the Royal Society in London that they were really chatting with a 13-year-old Ukrainian boy, answering questions about his childhood in Odessa, revealing his disdain for Star Wars or his passion for Eminem songs, especially Stan and The Real Slim Shady.

The announcement of the success was celebrated by Kevin Warwick, professor of Cybernetics at the University of Reading, who threw the bells into the air: "In the field of Artificial Intelligence, there is no milestone more iconic and controversial than the Turing test and that milestone has been reached at the Royal Society, which is home to British science and the scene of great advances over the centuries."

Other scientists refused to accept the success on the grounds that if the bot could well start a conversation, it did not have the capacity to think. Something similar happened when a computer managed to beat a Chess champion. However, each step brings the human being closer to Strong Artificial Intelligence.

Dartmouth College

Dartmouth College is a private university located in Hanover, New Hampshire. It was founded by the British clergyman Eleazar Wheelock with funds obtained by the preacher Samson Occom. On December 13, 1769, King George III of the United Kingdom approved the establishment of the academic institution by naming it Dartmouth College in memory of his friend William Legge, second Earl of Dartmouth. The initial mission of the university was to provide education and at the same time Christianize Native Americans. After a long period of political and financial struggle, Dartmouth emerged from relative obscurity in the late 19th century as one of the best universities in the United States and the world.

By the second half of the twentieth century the idea of building a computer that would have the ability to think was present at some universities in the United States. In the summer of 1956 a group of Dartmouth College students decided to organize a conference to analyze the possibility of producing software to make a computer react intelligently. In a paper presented to the Rockefeller Foundation to obtain the financial backing it needed, the group set the goal of the conference with these words: "The study is based on the idea that learning and any other characteristic of intelligence can be described so precisely that a machine can simulate them."

The Dartmouth College conference allowed for close relationships in the group of enthusiastic students who attended. Of the 10 organizers, four of them, in their professional life, continued to permanently work in research in the field of Artificial Intelligence and founded some of the most important institutions for research and development of AI. John McCarthy organized the Artificial Intelligence Laboratory at the Massachusetts Institute of Technology (MIT) in 1957 and in 1963 founded the AI Research Center at Stanford University in California. Marvin Minsky took over the direction of the AI laboratory at Carnegie Melon University in Pittsburgh.

The student environment allowed for a fresh and informal air that contributed to the free expression of ideas. The computer scene had been dominated by the great masters John von Neumann and Alan Turing, so the young students gave new life to thinking and drove software development.

The objective of the conference was to demonstrate that the computer was not just a crunching numbers machine, but could also be used to execute logical processes of information and, to some extent, **to make the machine take some decisions without the intervention of the programmer. This remains the central idea of the principle of Artificial Intelligence.** Arthur Samuel presented a program to play checkers; Alex Bernstein demonstrated that the computer could play Chess; Nathan Rochester wrote an interesting program to simulate a network of the nervous system with the computer and Marvin Minsky demonstrated the possibility of applying the computer in the solution of Euclid's theorems.

One of the most interesting programs was written by Allen Newell and Herbert Simon to demonstrate theorems taken from the work Principia Mathematica by Bertrand Russell, a remarkable English philosopher and mathematician. The program had registered the basic rules of operation, which were a list of axioms and demonstrations of theorems in such a way that the program could receive a new expression and execute its demonstration. Here the important thing is that the computer executed a procedure without the intervention of the programmer to study the problem, took alternatives, looked for the solution and printed the result. The demonstration of the program was a great success. Of the 52 theorems of chapter II of the Principia the computer managed to demonstrate 34 theorems and one of them with such elegance that it surpassed the quality of Russell and Whitehead. Herbert Simon, one of the authors of the program, informed Bertrand Russell about this event and the mathematician was surprised that a machine could perform a procedure that required a sophisticated logical treatment. All these programs meant an important step toward considering the machine as an intelligent entity.

One of the most enthusiastic students during the conference was John McCarthy, who made a contribution that has been one of the cornerstones of this new field of research: **McCarthy coined and defined the concept of Artificial Intelligence.**

John Patrick McCarthy was born in Boston, Massachusetts, on September 4, 1927, and died in Stanford, California on October 24, 2011. He was from an Irish immigrant and Lithuanian Jewish immigrant family. They were obliged to relocate frequently during the Great Depression, until McCarthy's father found work as an organizer for the Amalgamated Clothing Workers in Los Angeles, California. In 1948 the young McCarthy graduated in Mathematics from the California Institute of Technology and received his Ph.D. in the same discipline in 1951 from Princeton University. After short stays at Princeton, Stanford, Dartmouth and MIT, he became a full-time professor at Stanford University in 1962, where he remained as a teacher and researcher until his retirement in late 2000. After his retirement he was appointed Professor Emeritus of Stanford University.

Visionary is the qualification that would best define McCarthy. His mind was that of a mathematician and he believed that this was an essential discipline to develop Artificial Intelligence. In a document published in 2007 by Stanford University he explained that he understood **Artificial Intelligence to mean "the science and engineering of creating intelligent machines, especially intelligent computer programs. It is related to the similar task of using** computers to understand human intelligence, but AI is not limited to methods that are biologically observable." McCarthy's main contributions are the LISP language that he designed with the development of Artificial Intelligence in mind; he introduced the concept of cloud computing with the idea of computing as a public service by stating that "One day computing may be organized as a public service. Another important contribution was the concept of time-sharing in computers that allows the execution of several programs at the same time."

Innovation and Artificial Intelligence

In 2016 the development of Artificial Intelligence received an important boost from the government of **president Barack Obama** of the United States. For this reason, The American Institute of Artificial Intelligence considers that president Obama should be recognized as the founder of the Artificial Intelligence (AI) Revolution: "For providing unprecedented leadership in advancing the big data and artificial intelligence technologies, for creating the opportunity for a great future for human civilization, for making sure that the perils are understood and addressed before it is too late, and for advancing science and technology during extremely challenging times for our country, we nominate president Obama as the Founder of the Artificial Intelligence Revolution. Wherever this revolution takes us, we will find out in two or three decades, but it will always be remembered that it was in the time period between 2009-2016 when the winter of Artificial Intelligence ended permanently and the revolution began." (https://bit.ly/2AHUVoO)

Companies, universities, research centers, governments and even ordinary people are increasingly interested in Artificial Intelligence. This growing interest generates a virtuous circle that drives the development of AI and its acceptance in society. **The concept of Artificial Intelligence is associated with research, technological innovation, creativity and even progress and the opportunity to invest in this field to make good business and prosperous companies.** Large companies are allocating more and more resources of all kinds to Artificial Intelligence research and its application in different fields. One would say that the hallmark of a company's growth perspective is the degree to which AI is used and applied to revolutionize traditional products or create new products for a market eager to receive them and pay more for them. To understand this new wave that drives AI we will go over the actions that have taken place in companies, universities and governments and that together create the conditions for Artificial Intelligence to advance at a frantic pace.

Innovation is generated as an idea that produces a change whose effect is a new product, service or procedure that finds a successful application and conquers the market through wide dissemination. The American Heritage Dictionary defines innovation as the creation or modification of a product and its introduction in a market. In this way, an essential condition of innovation is its successful application at a commercial level, because not only is it worth inventing something, but also what is important or "sine qua non" condition is to introduce it satisfactorily and with repercussion in the market so that people know it and then adopt it to take advantage of it or enjoy it to the full. A clear example is the cell phone.

Artificial Intelligence has registered an important advance thanks to the innovation that has been generated in products based on the microprocessor, software and the Internet. Innovation is one of the driving powers behind it. Later we will review the applications of Artificial Intelligence. Now we will focus on the development of innovation worldwide.

Bloomberg publishes annually a list of countries classified by their degree of innovation taking into account the following factors: Research and Development Intensity (R&D), Value Added Manufacturing, Productivity, High Technology, Tertiary Efficiency, Research Concentration and Patent Activity. The top ten countries (2018) are: South Korea, Sweden, Singapore, Germany, Switzerland, Japan, Finland, Denmark, France and Israel. The Strong number of countries listed is 50, with the United States ranked 11th and Russia 26th. Only two Latin American countries are on the list: Brazil 46th and Argentina 49th.

South Korea remained at the top of the ranking in terms of research and development intensity, value-added manufacturing and patent activity, thanks in large part to Samsung. Even though it dropped a little in productivity, it remained the leader of the group. Sweden, a silver medalist, owes most of its rise to an improvement in value-added manufacturing, while neighboring Finland climbed two places largely due to an increase in high-tech firms in the country. The United States dropped this year to rank eleventh. However, the efforts and large investments that are being made in the field of Artificial Intelligence predict that it will rise in the future.

Esko Tapani Aho (May 20, 1954, Politician and former prime minister of Finland) defines **research as the procedure of investing money to obtain knowledge**, while **innovation consists of investing knowledge to obtain money**. This expresses very well the phenomenon of feedback that occurs with an RDI strategy (Research plus Development plus Innovation). Although it is a definition that could be described as bold, or even materialistic, it correctly describes the engines that drive research and innovation as well as the objectives that both activities pursue. The investment of money allows us to obtain knowledge and the investment of knowledge leads us to obtain money to close a virtuous circle. Consequently, in order to obtain knowledge and reach innovation, money is required as a fundamental ingredient according to Esko Tapani.

This scheme has been well understood by companies that spend a substantial part of their budget on research to obtain knowledge that they then turn into money. It has also been understood by the universities that obtain funds to dedicate them to research and then transform it into knowledge that they sell to large companies that partner with universities to transform knowledge into money. It is these virtuous circles that drive research and innovation that have fostered the development of Artificial Intelligence. It is not surprising, then, that the most important advances in this field can be found in the most prosperous and developed nations that have large companies with enormous capital resources and universities with extensive resources devoted to research. **The link between universities and business is a key factor in fostering innovation.**

If the development of Artificial Intelligence is based on research and innovation, then Artificial Intelligence requires money for its development. In the most developed countries it is the big companies and the universities that provide the resources. In developing countries, an external source is required to finance research. This source could be the government if it decided to invest 1% of GDP in the promotion of science and technology with a long-term vision. However, the attention of developing country governments is focused on other objectives. In order to promote technology and in particular Artificial Intelligence, it is necessary to provide broad and decisive financial support to the institutions that promote science, technology and innovation.

Partnership on AI

Convinced of the importance of Artificial Intelligence, in September 2016 some of the leading technology companies in the United States decided to join forces to create a consortium to use an open standard license for all content published in the field of Artificial Intelligence, including reports focused on areas such as ethics or privacy. The objective of the group is to create the first consortium that will also include non-profit academic researchers to guide efforts to ensure the reliability of Artificial Intelligence and lead research toward technologies that are ethical, secure and reliable; technologies that help and do not harm, while dispelling fears and misunderstandings about them. The official name of the consortium is "Partnership on Artificial Intelligence to Benefit People and Society". It was originally integrated by Google (with its subsidiary DeepMind), Amazon, Facebook, Microsoft and IBM. At the end of January 2017 Apple joined the Consortium. It is currently integrated by more than 50 companies and non-profit organizations established in nine countries. Other technology companies are expected to join in the near future.

This is the statement of principles of the Partnership:

- "To ensure that Artificial Intelligence technologies benefit and strengthen as many people as possible.
- Listen to and educate people and actively involve stakeholders to receive their feedback on our approach, inform them of our work and answer their questions.
- Establish a commitment to research and dialogue on the ethical, social, economic and legal implications of Artificial Intelligence.
- We believe that Artificial Intelligence research and the effort to develop it should be actively integrated with a wide range of interested people.
- We will integrate with and have stakeholder representation from the business community to ensure that points of interest and opportunities are understood and taken into account.
- We will work to maximize the benefits and respond to the potential challenges of Artificial Intelligence by protecting the privacy and security of individuals, striving to understand and respect the interests of all parties that may be impacted by Artificial Intelligence.

- We will work to ensure that Artificial Intelligence and technology communities maintain a social responsibility, sensitivity and commitment to the influence that Artificial Intelligence may have on society as a whole.
- Ensure that Artificial Intelligence technology is robust, reliable and operates within a margin of safety.
- Oppose the development and use of Artificial Intelligence technologies that may violate international treaties or human rights and promote harmless safeguards and technologies.
- We believe it is important for the functioning of Artificial Intelligence systems that can be understood and interpreted by people so that the technology can be explained and understood.
- We will strive to create a culture of cooperation, trust and openness about Artificial Intelligence to scientists and engineers so that it can help us achieve the goals we have set for ourselves."

For a better understanding we can group the objectives of the Consortium in two main aspects: 1). To promote the development of Artificial Intelligence through the use of an open standard license for all the contents that are published, attracting in this way more programmers and users who would handle a standard that would facilitate the production and commercialization of applications 2). Produce reports focused on areas such as ethics or privacy in a highly promising segment but that would be watched closely because Artificial Intelligence applications point to fields where they could turn against their creators and whose study would be an important topic later in this essay on Artificial Intelligence.

Panorama of AI in the world

Artificial Intelligence is the main theme in the development of science and technology. Investment in innovation is mainly oriented to Artificial Intelligence projects. The most important companies in the world are making large investments to conquer or maintain a leadership position based on AI technology and this happens not only in the cyber industry but covers virtually all sectors including military, banking, finance, commerce, education, games, health and all economic, political and social activity. **Artificial Intelligence is a horizontal technology that can cross all sciences and be present in all activities**. This fact is very important for its development.

The governments of the nations are focusing on Artificial Intelligence as the main axis to promote its development. Investment in AI will be fundamental to ensure the international competitiveness of large companies and will be the main engine of economic growth. In this way a virtuous circle is created where AI becomes the engine of economic development.

The United States remains at the forefront of global investment, research and results production. High-tech companies are spending a significant portion of their R&D budget in the field of AI. Google, Amazon, Facebook, Microsoft, Apple, and IBM are examples of large companies that have their sights set on AI to consolidate their leadership. In Silicon Valley, the heart of technology in the United States, new companies are often created with young people who have high hopes in technological entrepreneurship to succeed in this competitive field. The participation of universities is crucial as research centers and seedbeds where ideas are incubated that will later become prosperous companies. Between 2012 and 2016, the United States made an investment of 17.9 billion dollars in AI followed at a distance by China, with 2.6 billion. The other countries are at remote distances: the United Kingdom invested 800 million, Canada 640 million and Germany 600 million. The number of companies involved in AI also makes a difference: **the United States remains ahead followed by China.**

But China, the world's second largest economy, wants to become a leader in Artificial Intelligence by 2030, according to a decision by the State Council that has proposed a three-stage plan to achieve its goal: keep up with AI's leading technology by 2020, achieve breakthroughs by 2025, and be the world leader five years later. Among the businessmen who are driving the development of AI in China most strongly are Jack Ma, founder of the Alibaba consortium of companies; Robin Li, founder and current director of Baidu, China's largest Internet search engine; Lei Jun, director of Xiaomi, the smartphone manufacturer; and Sheng Yue Gui, founder of Geely Automobile. They have all submitted motions and proposals for the government to take the initiative for Chinese companies to collaborate in AI research and facilitate technology.

Robin Li believes that China is in a position to lead technological change with strong investments coupled with a large number of Chinese mathematical talents to close the gap and surpass the United States. And he states that the restrictive migration policy imposed by Donald Trump, president of the United States, will produce a decrease in the entry of talents to America and this could be taken advantage of by China for the development of Artificial Intelligence. For his part, China's Minister of Science and Technology, Wan Gang, said during the country's parliamentary meeting **that public finances will lead the way in AI research**, including the development of supercomputers, high-performance semiconductor chips, software and the hiring of key talent to conduct Artificial Intelligence research.

In Hangzhou, capital of China's Zhejiang province and home to the offices of Alibaba, the giant of online commerce, an important space has been set aside to house the latest achievements of Artificial Intelligence. The city attracted more than 15 AI platforms and 90 innovative projects. In this unusual place you can see cooking, dancing and talking robots, virtual reality technologies, gaming platforms and various research devices. Project participants point out that the city has a perfect atmosphere for innovative research and at the same time represents an advantageous financial asset. "We believe it is a good place to attract young talent and incubate businesses. We hope that our technologies will enable the entire industry to progress," said Ha Aimin, the project's deputy director.

The United States and China are the world's most advanced powers in research and development. China is the second largest producer of AI-related patents surpassed only by the United States. In China, universities, research centers and students publish more documents than their US counterparts. This is because people in China use local electronic consumer services, whose data must be stored and processed locally. For its part, the United States is a leader in technology: its companies and universities developed 75 percent of all patents in the field of Artificial Intelligence from 2000 to 2016. IBM, Microsoft, Facebook and Qualcomm have been the most active companies in this technological field. The United States is home to 42 percent of the world's AI companies. **Artificial Intelligence is a benchmark for measuring the leadership of nations.**

Artificial Intelligence in Latin America

The development of AI in Latin America lags far behind Europe, the United States and leading Asian countries. In order to know with more accuracy the situation of AI in Latin

America, as well as its characteristics and the challenges it faces, we have taken as a reference the excellent study on "The impact of Artificial Intelligence on entrepreneurship" elaborated by Endeavor in collaboration with everis. (The company writes this as **everis**, with lower case) This is an extract of its results. For those who are interested in more comprehensive and timely information, we encourage you to consult the full text of the study that gathers information on the current state, the main challenges, and the future of the more than 240 companies that have participated. Through surveys and interviews, the report gathers quality information from 70 entrepreneurial projects in Argentina, Brazil, Chile, Colombia, Mexico and Peru. Endeavor and everis deserve praise for conducting this study, which must be taken into account by Latin American companies and governments in the preparation of their development plans.

"Today, thousands of organizations use AI techniques as a key to their business or as a complement to it. In any continent there is a boom of entrepreneurship around AI, in which proposals of all kinds are intended to help other businesses or change them completely. We currently have a lot of information about this phenomenon from the US, Europe and lately China, but unfortunately the data are very scarce when we focus on Latin America. That's why everis and Endeavor conducted this study, in order to shed some light on the AI entrepreneurship ecosystem in major Latin American countries.

Our research gathers information on the current state, the main challenges, and the future of the more than 240 companies that have participated. Through surveys and interviews we have collected quality information from 70 entrepreneurship projects in Argentina, Brazil, Chile, Colombia, Mexico and Peru. We hope that this effort will be of interest to you, and above all will contribute to the development of AI entrepreneurship in Latin America.

One of the main results of the study is that the situation of AI-based entrepreneurship in Latin America is in early stages. Our AI Innovation and Growth Level Index, calculated from variables such as the year of foundation of the companies, investment received, AI techniques used, among others, is 32%. Thus, for example, most companies are young (63% were founded less than 6 years ago) and small (50% of them have between 1 and 10 direct employees). Despite its size, the expected percentage growth in revenue generation is significant. In 2017, the average AI Company in Latin America sold 1.1 million USD, and plans to end 2018 with a turnover of 1.64 million USD.

The sectors in which the activity of companies with a high level of specialization in AI in Latin America is concentrated are the provision of software and services to companies, although there are a variety of firms dedicated to education, mining, marketing, logistics chain, retail, etc. In order to develop their activity in these markets, 60% of the companies represented in the study have received external financing from one or several sources (33% seed capital, 29% private capital, 21% in series A or B financing rounds, and 17% angel investors).

AI is undoubtedly very important for the group of companies studied, 65% state that this type of technique is part of their core business and the intellectual property they have generated constitutes a competitive advantage. In this respect, in 87% of cases the technological developments are supported by third party frameworks, the most popular being Google Tensorflow, Microsoft Cognitive Toolkit and Amazon MXNet. Likewise, there is also a group of companies that base the use of AI on the consumption of third-party products such as Microsoft AI Cognitive Services, Google Cloud AI or IBM Watson.

Currently an important group of entrepreneurs (30%), focuses on the development of chatbots, due to the demand and acceptance in the market of this kind of applications. A widespread use of techniques such as natural language processing (53% of cases) and text-to-speech conversion (21%) is notorious, but other techniques such as classification and prediction (59%) or pattern recognition (39%) are also widely used.

The main challenges identified by companies based on the use of Artificial Intelligence in Latin America are the following:

- **Shortage of talent specializing in AI.** The job market lacks professionals with the kind of technical knowledge needed to develop these solutions.
- **Lack of data to train AI.** Given that many of the techniques most used today in AI require information to carry out learning, entrepreneurs require a greater volume of data with which to carry out such learning.
- **Lack of knowledge of AI on the part of clients.** Another of the problems faced by AI entrepreneurs is that their clients (both business and residential) do not know this type of solution, generating a certain mistrust regarding the products and services proposed.

- **Difficulty in finding funds.** Most respondents have stated that in Latin America finding funds to finance their AI project is too complicated compared to the ease of obtaining financing in the United States.

Despite the challenges mentioned above, and the difficulties inherent in any venture, the application of AI in Latin America is in crescendo, with dozens of companies expanding their operations.

At everis and Endeavor we believe that it is necessary to carry out actions from the governments, universities, companies and civil society to support and accelerate the use of AI in Latin America.

From our point of view, four of the areas in which we should all work, related to the challenges that entrepreneurs transmit to us are:

- **Talent.** Universities and companies should focus on generating the necessary skills to create AI solutions, promoting diversity from a knowledge point of view (we lack engineers, programmers, but also specialists in user experience, linguists, etc.).
- **Data.** The private sector, and especially public administrations, should make public more data sets in areas such as health or education, in order to make learning possible and therefore the generation of new solutions based on AI in these fields.
- **Dissemination.** Civil society, the business sector, and public administrations in Latin America should disseminate and support AI, eliminating adoption barriers and introducing complex issues such as the impact on work activity or data privacy.
- **Financing.** Latin America must continue to develop its ecosystem of economic investment in AI ventures. We must aspire not only to have the financial and legal mechanisms to facilitate investment in the venture, but also to have an adequate focus on AI through specialized funds, public-private initiatives and specific awards.

In general, companies in the six countries selected in the study (Argentina, Brazil, Chile, Colombia, Mexico and Peru) have seen increases in their sales. AI companies in Argentina and Brazil are above the Latin American average. Despite all the work that remains to be done, AI-based entrepreneurship in Latin America has clear potential for the future. We expect companies like Aivo (Argentina), Arara (Chile), Beepharma (Colombia), Direct One (Brazil), Nimblr (Mexico) and Xertica (Peru) will have the success they deserve."

Everis is a multinational consulting firm of Spanish origin that works on business development projects, business strategy, maintenance of technological applications and outsourcing. The business group covers the sectors of telecommunications, financial institutions, industry, utilities and energy, banking, insurance, public administration and health. It was founded in Madrid in 1996 as the Spanish subsidiary of DMR Consulting. In 2006, after the executives purchased 100% of the company's capital from Fujitsu, the name was changed to everis. Today everis operates in fifteen countries around the world and employs around 18,000 people.

Endeavor leads the High Impact entrepreneurship movement globally and promotes economic growth and job creation by selecting, mentoring and accelerating the best high-impact entrepreneurs in the world. Established in 1997, Endeavor has evaluated more than 50,000 entrepreneurs and selected more than 1,500 individuals who lead more than 900 high-growth companies. Supported by Endeavor's global network of mentors, these high-impact entrepreneurs have created more than 650,000 jobs, generated more than $10 billion in revenue in 2016 and inspired future generations to innovate and take risks. Headquartered in New York City, Endeavor operates in 30 countries around the world.

The case of Nimblr

One of the entrepreneurial projects that have stood out in Mexico in the field of Artificial Intelligence is Nimblr, a company created by Juan Vera, Andrés Rodríguez, David Jiménez and Silvana Valencia whose objective is to help improve medical care. Nimblr's mission is to improve the doctors' office, to make it more efficient and innovative. The AI system allows conversations with patients via text messages (e.g. SMS) and voice (e.g. Amazon Alexa) to confirm and reschedule appointments, create waiting lists and provide patients with spaces available for last-minute cancellations. To learn more about Nimblr we reproduce below an excerpt from the interview that AMEXCAP (Mexican Association of Private Capital) did with Juan Vera, co-founder and CEO of Nimblr: (https://bit.ly/2naopsg)

What does Nimblr.ai do?

Nimblr.ai is an Artificial Intelligence communication platform where we created a virtual assistant called "Holly". Holly is an assistant who specializes in managing the entire life cycle of medical appointments; the way she works is very similar to a human assistant where she connects to or reads an appointment calendar such as Google Calendar or another medical scheduling system. From recorded appointments, Holly establishes text conversations with patients in natural language, as if she were a person.

Holly is able to make an appointment and follow-up confirmation, cancellation, and rescheduling. She also recovers patients who do not keep appointments and asks for feedback in the event of abandonment of treatment. We add value to medical practices by improving communication with patients by updating all activities on their medical agenda online. The importance of what Holly does is that appointments in the health industry represent the source of income of the system and due to lack of communication many appointments are missed, either because the patient forgets or needs to reschedule or the contrary, the doctor has an emergency that modifies his schedule. This lack of communication generates huge losses to the industry and is a problem that we are solving by automating the process. We maximize the income of the medical offices by generating more occupation and improve the patient experience by providing an easy and friendly service, where they can control and manage their appointments through text messages.

Could you tell us how the idea of creating Nimblr.ai was born?

Two years ago, the same group of Nimblr founders worked on Blue Messaging which is a chatbot platform. Trying to expand the business to the USA we worked on a project with MIT to investigate which were the most attractive market niches to apply our technology. The result was that the Healthcare industry in the United States was under transformation and had very important areas of opportunity in their communication with patients.

How is your founding team made up?

We are four co-founders, two hackers and two on the business side who have been working together for more than six years. The company's CTO is Andres Rodriguez, he is a Stanford University researcher who worked for more than 10 years in the Artificial Intelligence department of SIRI. The VP of Engineering is David Jiménez. The VP of LATAM is Silvana Valencia and I am the CEO of the company.

When did you decide to look for a fund to support Nimblr.ai?

We realized that we had a short window of opportunity to penetrate, with our technology, the healthcare space in the United States and Latin America and that we would need sufficient resources to penetrate it quickly and have a margin for error. Since the company was created it was designed to attract investors.

What have been the key moves to develop your business?

There are several aspects, the first being strategic. You must be very clear about the market where you want to work and what you need to win in that area. In our case, we decided that we wanted to participate in the health industry, even though there are other interesting industries. The second is the focus on product and technology.

How long did it take you to get close to the fund and, for the fund, to decide to participate in your company?

The complete cycle was between five and six months. We initially worked with On Ventures who later supported us leading the round with the other funds.

What are the key aspects of you and your company that you think convinced the fund to invest in you?

I think this is more a question for them, but if I think like an investor, I see that we are a team of founders who have a track record of executing several successful companies. We participate in a large scale and fragmented market where we are as competitive as healthcare is in the United States and Latin America. And we have a disruptive product that solves a relevant problem such as medical appointments.

What are the actions taken by the fund that you feel have most supported the company's growth?

The funds have a more holistic view of the market: competition, trends and synergies with other companies, etc. than the one you have as an entrepreneur. I have three funds that are On Ventures, Ideas and Capital and Innova Salud and all three add high strategic value to me, each with different emphasis. On the other hand, when you have institutional investors, they set you even more ambitious corporate goals than you would have as a person.

So far, what has been the most important achievement of your company?

To operate from the beginning in the USA and Latin America. We are a startup that has teams in both countries. We started the sales stage just five months ago, but the fact that we already have customers and participation in both markets seems to us a very relevant achievement.

What is the long-term vision for your company?

We want to transform the communication between patients and health professionals making Holly the best assistant for medical practices. Our goal is to be a company that in the next five years sells more than 100 million dollars and has more than 150 thousand customers.

From the study carried out by everis and the interview with Nimblr, it is evident that **Artificial Intelligence represents an important opportunity for software developers,** AI companies and users of Artificial Intelligence systems, such as banking, the medical sector, commerce, customer service, stock market operators, the army and many other activities. It also represents an opportunity for universities and research centers. And, of course, for countries that have set their sights on Artificial Intelligence.

–5–

TECHNIQUES OF AI

A technique (from the Greek, τέχνη tékhnē 'art, technique, craft') is a procedure or set of rules, norms or protocols that aims to obtain a certain and effective result, whether in the field of science, technology, art, sport, education or any other activity. It is also a set of activities based on the practical application of methods and knowledge relating to the various sciences, especially when it involves the use of machines or the application of specific methods.

Artificial Intelligence has been nourished by different techniques that have strengthened its development. These techniques are used individually to build a system or are integrated into a more complex system. **Below we will study the most important techniques that support AI and are laying the foundation for Strong Artificial Intelligence.**

Machine learning

One of the most powerful techniques of Artificial Intelligence is machine learning which has a wide range of applications in search engines, medical diagnostics, credit card fraud detection, stock market analysis, DNA sequence classification, speech and written language recognition, games, robotics and many more. Machine learning is a data analysis technique that teaches computers to do what is natural for people and animals. That is, **learn from experience**. Automated learning algorithms employ calculation methods to "learn" information directly from data without relying on a predetermined equation as a model. Algorithms improve their performance adaptively as the number of samples available for learning increases.

The goal of automatic learning is to develop procedures that allow computers to learn on their own. More specifically, it is about creating programs capable of generalizing behaviors from information provided in the form of examples. It is, therefore, a process of induction of knowledge. In many cases, the field of action of automatic learning overlaps with that of computational statistics, since both disciplines are based on data analysis. However, automatic learning also focuses on studying the computational complexity of problems. Many problems are NP-hard class, so much of the research done in machine learning focuses on designing workable solutions to these problems. Machine learning can be seen as an attempt to automate some parts of the scientific method through mathematical methods.

In computational complexity theory, NP (nondeterministic polynomial time) is a complexity class used to classify decision problems. NP is the set of decision problems for which the problem instances, where the answer is "yes", have proofs verifiable in polynomial time. An equivalent definition of NP is the set of decision problems solvable in polynomial time by a non-deterministic Turing machine. This definition is the basis for the abbreviation NP; "nondeterministic, polynomial time." These two definitions are equivalent because the algorithm based on the Turing machine consists of two phases, the first consists of a guess about the solution, which is generated in a non-deterministic way, while the second phase consists of a deterministic algorithm that verifies if the guess is a solution to the problem.

The human being performs the automatic learning in a natural way from the moment of his birth and maybe even before he is born. It does so without the need for awareness. From birth to death it carries out different processes to acquire knowledge, to analyze and evaluate through methods and techniques as well as through own experience. However, machines must be told how to learn, because if a machine is not able to develop its skills, the learning process will not be carried out, but will only be a repetitive sequence. We must also bear in mind that having knowledge or the fact of performing the automatic learning process well does not imply that one knows how to use it. It is necessary to know how to apply it in everyday activities. Learning also implies knowing how and when to use our knowledge.

Automatic learning is one of the main foundations that support the great structure of AI. It is based on a set of algorithms grouped into a taxonomy or classification according to their output function.

> **An algorithm** (from Greek and Latin, dixit algorithmus and perhaps also influenced by the name of the Persian mathematician **Al-Juarismi**) is a prescribed set of well-defined, ordered and finite instructions or rules that allows an activity to be carried out by successive steps that do not generate doubts for whoever has to do this activity, be it a human being or a machine.

These are some types of algorithms:

Supervised learning. The algorithm produces a function that establishes a correspondence between the desired inputs and outputs of the system. An example of this type of algorithm is the classification problem, where the learning system tries to label (classify) a series of vectors using one among several categories or classes. The knowledge base of the system is formed by examples of previous tagging. This type of learning can become very useful in problems of biological research, computational biology and bioinformatics.

Unsupervised learning. The whole modeling process is carried out on a set of examples formed only by inputs to the system. There is no information on the categories of these examples. Therefore, in this case, the system has to be able to recognize patterns in order to label the new entries.

Semi-supervised learning. This type of algorithm combines the two previous algorithms in order to classify properly. Marked and unmarked data are taken into account.

Reinforcement learning. The algorithm learns by observing the world around it. Its input information is the feedback it gets from the outside world in response to its actions. Therefore, the system learns on a trial-and-error basis. Reinforcement learning is the most general of the three categories. Instead of an instructor telling the agent what to do, the intelligent agent must learn how the environment behaves through rewards (reinforcements) or punishments, derived from success or failure respectively. The main objective is to learn the value function that helps the intelligent agent to maximize the reward signal and thus optimize his policies in such a way that he can understand the behavior of the environment and make good decisions for the achievement of its formal objectives.

Transduction. Similar to supervised learning, but does not explicitly construct a function. Tries to predict the categories of future examples based on the input examples, their respective categories and the new examples in the system.

Multi-task learning. Learning methods that use knowledge previously learned by the system in order to face problems similar to those already seen.

With the increase of available information, automatic learning has become a key technique to solve problems in areas such as:

- **Computational Finance**: for credit rating and algorithmic trading
- **Image processing** and machine vision: for facial recognition, motion detection and object detection
- **Computational biology**: for tumor detection, drug discovery, and DNA sequencing
- **Energy production**: for forecasting load and price
- **Automotive,** aerospace and manufacturing: for predictive maintenance

Big data

Big data is generally used to describe the processing of massive or large-scale data. It is a concept that refers to a set of data so large that traditional computer data processing applications are not sufficient to deal with them and the procedures used to find repetitive patterns within that data. Although the size used to determine whether a given data set is considered big data is not firmly defined and continues to change over time, most analysts and professionals currently refer to data sets ranging from 30-50 terabytes to several petabytes.

Terabyte (TB) is a multiple of the unit byte for digital information. The prefix tera represents the fourth power of 1000, and means 10*12 in the International System of Units (SI), and therefore one terabyte is one trillion bytes.

1 TB = 1 000 000 000 000 bytes

Petabyte (PB) is a storage unit of information equivalent to 10*15 bytes. The prefix peta comes from the Greek πέντε, which means five, as it is equivalent to 1000*5 or 10*15. It is also based on the tera model, from the Greek "monster".

1 PB = 1 000 000 000 000 000 bytes.

What makes big data so useful for many companies is the fact that it provides answers to many questions that companies did not even know they had. In other words, it provides a point of reference. With such a large amount of information, the data can be molded or tested in any way the company deems appropriate. By doing so, organizations are able to identify problems in a more understandable and accurate way.

Big data allows Artificial Intelligence to no longer be science fiction as the processing of large volumes of data allows for accurate decision making. Collecting large amounts of data and searching for trends within the data allows companies to move much faster, smoothly and efficiently. Big data analysis helps organizations leverage their data and use it to identify new opportunities. That, in turn, leads to smarter business, more efficient operations, higher profits and happier customers.

- Companies that have been most successful with big data get value in the following ways:
- **Cost reduction**. Large data technologies such as Hadoop and cloud-based analysis bring significant cost advantages when it comes to storing large amounts of data, as well as identifying more efficient ways of doing business.
- **Faster, better decision making.** With Hadoop's speed and in-memory analytics, combined with the ability to analyze new data sources, companies can immediately analyze information and make decisions based on what they've learned.
- **New products and services**. With the ability to measure customer needs and satisfaction through analysis comes the power to give customers what they want. With big data analytics, more companies are creating new products to more accurately meet and customize customer needs.

There are several tools for processing big data. Examples include Hadoop, NoSQL, Cassandra, MapReduce, business intelligence and automatic learning. These tools deal with three types of big data:

- **Structured data:** data that is well defined in length and format, such as dates, numbers, or character strings. They are stored in tables. Examples are relational databases and data banks.

- **Unstructured data**: data in the format in which they were collected; they lack a specific format. They cannot be stored within a table as their information cannot be disaggregated to basic types of data. Some examples are pdf´s, multimedia documents, e-mails or text documents.

- **Semi-structured data**: data that is not limited to particular fields, but contains markers to separate the different elements. This information is not regular enough to be managed in a standard way. These data have their own semi-structured metadata describing the objects and the relationships between them, and may end up being accepted by convention. Examples are spreadsheet, HTML, XML or JSON files.

What is the source of all this data? Human beings generate it every day and it is also produced by any type of device that has the capacity to generate, store and communicate information. An iPhone today has more computing capacity than NASA when man reached the Moon, so that the amount of data generated per person every hour is very large. We catalog the origin of the data according to the following categories:

- **Generated by people**: sending e-mails or messages by WhatsApp, publishing a status on Facebook, tweeting content or responding to a street survey are things we do every day and create new data that can be analyzed. It is estimated that every minute 24/7 more than 200 million emails are sent, more than 700,000 pieces of content are shared on Facebook, two million Google searches are conducted, or 48 hours of video are edited on YouTube. On the other hand, traces of use in an ERP system, including records in a database or entering information into a spreadsheet are other ways of generating this data.

- **Data transactions**: billing, calls or transactions between accounts generate information that can generate relevant data. A clearer example is found in banking transactions: a deposit of money in the bank account means more money for the account holder but the AI system will interpret it as an action carried out at a specific date and time, in a specific place, between registered users, and more metadata.

- **Electronic and web marketing**: a large amount of data is generated when surfing the Internet. With web 2.0 the webmaster-content-reader paradigm has been broken and the users themselves become content creators thanks to their interaction with the site. There are many tracking tools used mostly for marketing and business analysis purposes. Mouse movements are recorded on heat maps and there is a record of how much time we spend on each page and when we visit them. Facebook recently admitted that it records and processes mouse movements on its pages.

- **Machine to machine** (**M2M**): these are the technologies that share data with devices: meters, sensors of temperature, light, height, pressure, sound, etc. that transform physical or chemical magnitudes and convert them into data. They have existed for decades, but the advent of AI systems and wireless communications (Wi-Fi, Bluetooth, and RFID) has revolutionized the world of sensors. Some examples are GPS in the automobile or sensors of vital signs in medicine.

- **Biometrics**: the set of data coming from security, defense and intelligence services. It is data generated by biometric readers such as retina scanners, fingerprint scanners or DNA string readers. The purpose of these data is to provide security mechanisms. They are usually guarded by the ministries of defense and intelligence. An example of an application is the DNA cross between a crime sample and a sample in our database.

The next goal is to have the data collected in one place and formatted. This is where the platforms for extracting, transforming and loading (ETL) come into play. Their purpose is to extract data from different sources and systems, then make transformations (data conversions, dirty data cleansing, format changes) and finally load the data into the specified database. An additional difficulty is ensuring that the data being uploaded is relatively consistent. Multiple source databases have different update cycles (some may be updated every few minutes, while others may take days or weeks). In an ETL system it will be necessary that certain data can be stopped until all sources are synchronized. Similarly, when a database has to be updated with the contents in a source system, it is necessary to establish synchronization and update points.

ETL stands for Extract, Transform and Load. It is the process that allows organizations to move data from multiple sources, reformat it, clean it and load it into another database for analysis or, in another operational system, to support a business process.

The next step is analysis to turn the data into information. This analysis is so important that it has led to the birth of a **special tool called analytics** that combines methods of statistics, research, machine learning and some disciplines such as psychology. The ideas provide information for organization and decision making. By contrast, the traditional concept of business intelligence tends to refer to information extraction, reporting, and the provision of alerts in connection with the applied problem of interest. In the area of political analysis, the data have led to technological and scientific development.

Deep learning

It is a set of class algorithms belonging to automatic learning that attempts to model high-level abstractions in data using architectures composed of multiple nonlinear transformations. **Deep learning is part of a broader set of automated learning methods based on assimilating representations of data.** Observation of something, for example, an image, can be represented in many forms (such as a pixel vector), but some representations make it easier to learn tasks of interest (e.g., "Is this image a human face?") on the basis of examples, and research in this area attempts to define which representations are best and how to create models to recognize these representations. Several deep learning architectures, such as deep neural networks, deep convolutional neural networks, and deep belief networks, have been applied to fields such as computer vision, automatic speech recognition, and recognition of audio and music signals, and have been shown to produce cutting-edge results in various tasks.

The "deep" in "deep learning" refers to the number of layers through which the data is transformed. More precisely, deep learning systems have a substantial credit assignment path (CAP) depth. The CAP is the chain of transformations from input to output. CAPs describe potentially causal connections between input and output. For a feedforward neural network, the depth of the CAPs is that of the network and is the number of hidden layers plus one, as the output layer is also parameterized. For recurrent neural networks, in which a signal may propagate through a layer more than once, the CAP depth is potentially unlimited. No universally agreed upon threshold of depth divides shallow learning from deep learning, but **most researchers agree that deep learning involves CAP depth > 2.** CAP of depth 2 has been shown to be a universal approximator in the sense that it can emulate any function. Deep models (CAP > 2) are able to extract better features than shallow models and hence extra layers help in learning features.

Deep learning is a difficult concept to understand when explained in terms that are too scientific, so it is best to approach an expert in this field, ask him and thank him for defining it in more accessible words.

Augusto Vega, from Argentina, is a permanent researcher at IBM T. J. Watson Laboratories in New York and an expert in systems architectures for deep learning and Artificial Intelligence applications: "Deep learning is a field belonging to Artificial Intelligence whose objective is the study and construction of computer systems capable of learning from experience, slightly inspired by some principles of the functioning of the animal brain. In general, these systems must be trained from known examples, in a similar way in which a small child is taught to recognize objects or sounds around him (pointing to a tree and being told "that's a tree"; or listening to the noise of a train and being told "that's a train"). This type of auto learning is called "deep" because it has a hierarchical structure that extracts different levels of detail from the data in question. For example, during image recognition, edges are extracted that, combined, allow us to detect contours, which in turn allow us to recognize different parts of the object, in order to finally determine its identity." (https://bit.ly/2VqCbUB)

While traditional automatic learning algorithms are linear, deep learning algorithms are stacked in a hierarchy of increasing complexity and abstraction. To understand deep learning imagine a child whose first word is "dog". The child learns what a dog is (and is not) by pointing at objects and saying the word "dog". The parent says "Yes, that's a dog" or "No, that's not a dog". As the child continues to point to objects, he becomes more aware of the characteristics of all dogs. What the child does, without knowing it, is to clarify a complex abstraction (the concept of dog) by constructing a hierarchy in which each level of abstraction is created with the knowledge obtained from the preceding layer of the hierarchy.

Computer programs that use deep learning go through the same process. Each algorithm in the hierarchy applies a non-linear transformation to its input and uses what it learns to create a statistical model as an output. Iterations continue until the output has reached an acceptable level of accuracy. The number of processing layers through which the data must pass is what inspired the "deep" label.

Deep learning is based on a class of algorithms devised for automatic learning. From this point, different publications focus on different characteristics, for example:

- **Use a cascade of layers** with non-linear processing units to extract and transform variables. Each layer uses the output of the previous layer as input. Algorithms can use supervised learning or unsupervised learning and applications include data modeling and pattern recognition.

- **Be based on learning multiple levels** of data features or representations. Higher-level characteristics are derived from lower-level characteristics to form a hierarchical representation.

- **Learn multiple levels of representation** corresponding to different levels of abstraction. These levels form a hierarchy of concepts.

All of these ways of defining deep learning have in common multiple layers of nonlinear processing and supervised or unsupervised learning of feature representations at each layer. Layers form a hierarchy of characteristics from a lower to a higher level of abstraction. Deep learning algorithms contrast with shallow learning algorithms by the number of transformations applied to the signal as it propagates from the input layer to the output layer. Each of these transformations includes parameters that can be trained such as weights and thresholds. As we said, there is no de facto standard for the number of transformations (or layers) that makes an algorithm deep, but most researchers in the field believe that deep learning involves more than two intermediate transformations.

Deep learning is present very broadly (and in some cases, unimaginable) in our daily lives. Predictors of words on mobile phones, virtual assistants such as Apple Siri, translation of text between different languages, and automatic recognition of objects and people in photographs on social networks are some well-known examples but there are many more that are hidden in the algorithms of Artificial Intelligence.

A big advantage with deep learning is that it's powered by massive amounts of data. The "big data era" of technology will provide huge amounts of opportunities for new innovations in deep learning. The rocket engine is the deep learning model and the fuel is the huge amount of data we can feed to these AI algorithms.

Artificial neural networks

Its name is impressive and its objective also because it essentially originates in the idea of imitating the functioning of the neural networks of living organisms. That is, a set of neurons connected to each other and working together, without there being a specific task for each one. With experience, neurons create and reinforce certain connections in order to "learn" something that remains fixed in the tissue.

Neurons (from the Greek νεῦρον neûron, 'string', 'nerve') are a type of nervous system cells whose main function is the electrical excitability of their plasma membrane. They specialize in the reception of stimuli and conduction of nerve impulses (in the form of action potential) between them or with other types of cells such as the muscle fibers of the motor plaque. Most neurons do not divide once they reach maturity, although it has been proven that some of them do.

By 1943, **Warren McCulloch and Walter Pitts** created a computer model for neural networks based on mathematics and algorithms called threshold logic. This model pointed the way for neural network research to be divided into two distinct approaches. One approach focused on biological processes in the brain and the other focused on the application of neural networks for Artificial Intelligence.

The human brain has some 8.6 x 10^{10} (eighty six billion) neurons. Each neuron has on average 7,000 synaptic connections to other neurons. It has been estimated that the brain of a three-year-old child has about 10^{15} synapses (1 quadrillion). This number declines with age, stabilizing by adulthood. Estimates vary for an adult, ranging from 10^{14} to 5 x 10^{14} synapses (100 to 500 trillion).

Neurons communicate with each another via synapses, where either the axon terminal of one cell contacts another neuron's dendrite, soma or, less commonly, axon. Neurons such as Purkinje cells in the cerebellum can have over 1,000 dendritic branches, making connections with tens of thousands of other cells; other neurons, such as the magnocellular neurons of the supraoptic nucleus, have only one or two dendrites, each of which receives thousands of synapses.

Synapses can be excitatory or inhibitory, either increasing or decreasing activity in the target neuron, respectively. Some neurons also communicate via electrical synapses, which are direct, electrically conductive junctions between cells.

When an action potential reaches the axon terminal, it opens voltage-gated calcium channels, allowing calcium ions to enter the terminal. Calcium causes synaptic vesicles filled with neurotransmitter molecules to fuse with the membrane, releasing their contents into the synaptic cleft. The neurotransmitters diffuse across the synaptic cleft and activate receptors on the postsynaptic neuron. High cytosolic calcium in the axon terminal triggers mitochondrial calcium uptake, which, in turn, activates mitochondrial energy metabolism to produce ATP to support continuous neurotransmission. An autapse is a synapse in which a neuron's axon connects to its own dendrites.

Neural networks or connection systems are a computational model based on a large set of simple neuronal units (artificial neurons), approximately analogous to the behavior observed in the axons of neurons in biological brains. Each neuronal unit is connected to many others and the links between them can increase or inhibit the activation state of adjacent neurons. Each neuronal unit, individually, operates using addition functions. There may be a limiting function or threshold in each connection and in the unit itself, so that the signal must exceed a limit before propagating to another neuron. These systems learn and form themselves, rather than being explicitly programmed, and excel in areas where the detection of solutions or characteristics is difficult to express with conventional programming. They usually consist of several layers or a cube design, and the signal path goes from front to back. Backward propagation is where forward or "front" stimulation is used to restore the weights of the neural units and this is sometimes done in combination with a formation in which the correct result is known. Modern neural networks are a little freer in the sense that they flow in terms of stimulation and inhibition with connections that interact in a much more chaotic and complex way.

Dynamic neural networks are the most advanced way in which new connections and even new neural units can be dynamically formed. Their function is to solve problems in the same way as the human brain, although neural networks are more abstract. Modern neural network projects usually work from a few thousand to a few million neuronal units and millions of connections which, although there are many orders, are still of a magnitude less complex than that of the human brain, rather close to the computational power of a worm. **However, their rapid development has allowed artificial neural networks to reach greater power.** With time, one would expect a capacity similar to that of a vertebrate and much later imitate the human being. **Neural networks and deep learning could become the most important techniques in the future to support Strong Artificial Intelligence.**

New brain research often stimulates new patterns in neural networks. A new approach is using connections that extend far beyond and link processing layers rather than always being located in adjacent neurons. Other research is studying the different types of signal at the time axons propagate, such as deep learning, which interpolates greater complexity than a set of Boolean variables that have only two states: on or off.

Neural networks are based on real numbers, with the value of the nucleus and axon typically being a representation between 0 and 1. An interesting aspect of these systems is that they are unpredictable in their success with self-learning. After training, some become great problem solvers and others don't work as well. In order to train them, several thousand iteration cycles are needed. Neural networks have been used to solve a wide variety of tasks, such as computer vision and speech recognition, that are difficult to solve using ordinary rule-based programming. Historically, the use of neural network models marked a shift in direction, in the late 1980s, to a higher level characterized by expert systems with knowledge built into itself.

There are several types of neural networks depending on their architecture and way of learning. One of the most used is the network based on several layers of perceptron neurons, trained by the backpropagation technique. The network connections are randomly initialized and progressively self-adjust as they are trained with the available data, so that it learns to gradually recognize all the cases of the data set used for its training. The learning ends when, after a variable number of iterations, 100% of the cases are correctly classified, or a maximum value of hits is reached that does not increase with more iterations. In this way, we achieve that the network learns to recognize patterns with all kinds of forms which increases and improves its classification potential.

> **Perceptron** refers to the artificial neuron or basic unit of inference in the form of a linear discriminator from which an algorithm is developed capable of generating a criterion for selecting a subgroup from a larger group of components. The limitation of this algorithm is that if we draw these elements in a graph, we must be able to separate with a hyperplane only the "desired" elements, discriminating (separating) them from the "undesired" ones. Perceptron can be used with other types of perceptron or artificial neuron to form a more complex artificial neural network.

One example that best illustrates the idea behind multilayered perceptrons is the recognition of isolated objects in an image. A very typical but difficult problem is to create a neural network capable of distinguishing a dog from a cat and vice versa. In this case, and taking into account the previous scheme, the neural network inputs would be all those data taken from the image that could help us to identify whether it is a dog or a cat: length of legs or tail, shape of ears, color, and so on. Based on these data, each cell would decide if the data it processes is specific to a dog or a cat (with data it has stored and that it has learned previously). These data and decisions would travel along the neuronal layers and would deliver to the exit the data that we want, if the animal is a dog or a cat.

Apple's personal assistant, Siri speech recognition service, also features neural networks to provide the end user with the best possible quality of service. This application uses natural language processing to answer questions, make recommendations, and take action by delegating requests to a set of web services that has grown over time. When this speech recognition is used, the data collected by the microphone is sent to the servers and processed over a large neural network. This neural network is able to identify what is requested and acts showing the relevant results. In this case the same thing happens as with Google Photos. **The more people use Siri, the better the quality of the service as it learns from all voices.**

Neural networks are also present in Bixby, Samsung's assistant. Bixby understands English, Spanish and other languages and the AI team of the company working in C-Lab report that they are working on a project called Aurora that consists of a virtual assistant that is shown as a hologram and that aims to offer a closer interaction with users. **Aurora is not**

only thought of as an assistant but as a colleague capable of encouraging you, helping you when you go shopping or waking you up in the morning. A virtual friend!

Fuzzy logic

The term fuzzy logic was introduced with the 1965 proposal of fuzzy set theory by Lotfi Zadeh. Fuzzy logic had however been studied since the 1920s, as infinite-valued logic—notably by Łukasiewicz and Tarski. Fuzzy logic is a form of many-valued logic in which the truth values of variables may be any real number between 0 and 1 inclusive. It is employed to handle the concept of partial truth, where the truth value may range between completely true and completely false. By contrast, in Boolean logic, the truth values of variables may only be the integer values 0 or 1.

Fuzzy logic has found a wide field of action in the study of very complex or disordered processes. This is because conventional algorithms only resolve orderly processes, leaving behind complex and chaotic contexts. If we take into account that unpredictable phenomena are present in the human mind, in society and in nature, we will be able to warn that this technique is of fundamental importance to reinforce Artificial Intelligence and **increase the possibilities that a machine or computer system can understand and even emulate human thought**.

The capacity of fuzzy logic to solve indeterminate and hyper complex situations has focused it in fields that require decision making and pattern recognition. Using this technique, the computer can analyze real-world information on a scale between the false and the true, manipulate vague concepts such as "hot" or "wet," and allow engineers to build devices that judge information difficult to define. It began being used in Expert Systems but thanks to its characteristics it is used to solve a wide variety of problems, mainly those related to the control of complex industrial processes, the resolution and compression of data and decision systems in general. Fuzzy logic systems are also widespread in everyday technology, e.g. digital cameras, air conditioning, washing machines, etc. Systems based on fuzzy logic mimic the way humans make decisions, with the advantage of being much faster. These systems are generally robust and tolerant to inaccuracies and noise in input data. Some logical programming languages that have incorporated Fuzzy logic would be for example the various implementations of Fuzzy PROLOG.

To illustrate the functioning of Fuzzy logic we will take the example used in air conditioners. Let's see what terms the average person uses to describe temperature:

- Too cold
- Cold
- Warm
- Hot
- Very hot

All these terms are relative. That is, there is no convention of how many degrees it is correct to say that the environment is hot, so we must seek to give a numerical value to these "imprecise quantifiers". To do this it is necessary to start with the determination of some reference points expressed in quantitative form and thus we would have the following:

- A horizontal axis ranging from -10 °C to 40 °C
- Temperatures below zero are very cold
- Temperatures above 40 °C are very hot

Very cold and very hot conditions extend to the left and right of the horizontal axis respectively.

The remaining three states (cold, warm and hot) can be modeled as trapezoidal membership functions of equal dimensions:

- Major base: 10 °C interval
- Lower base: 5 °C range

In this way, we can assign numerical values to certain degrees of temperature expressed with the words too Cold, Cold, Warm, Hot and Very Hot. The next step would be to write a program for the computer (In the case of an air conditioning equipment it would be a small microprocessor integrated into the apparatus) that would take this form:

IF (temperature is cold OR too cold) AND (objective is warm) THEN GO TO heat.

With this simple example you can get an idea of the purpose of fuzzy logic. Of course, the real world presents much more complex conditions that require a modeling of conditions also more complicated and a broader programming and at the same time more precise to cover all conditions. Imagine all the variables that must be taken into account to calculate the direction, speed and intensity of the winds of a tornado. Or imagine all the factors that must be taken into account to trace the algorithm of a financial system to calculate the movements of the stock market. There are so many conditions and factors that intervene that the human mind simply cannot consider and process them in the time necessary to make the right decision. However, the computer can do it and in fact already does it with great success. Fuzzy logic is applied with great benefits in Internet search engines, wastewater treatment plants or intelligent control of automobile engines. However, what made fuzzy logic particularly famous was its contribution to the improvement of techniques in the driving of metros and railways. The best known example is the Sendai train in Japan.

A higher or more complex level of fuzzy logic technique has been developed in **Compensatory fuzzy logic** (CFL). CFL is a multivalent logic model that allows simultaneous modeling of deductive and decision making processes. The use of CFL in mathematical models allows the use of concepts related to reality following behavior patterns similar to human thought. The most important characteristics of these models are flexibility, tolerance with imprecision, and the ability to mold non-linear problems and their foundation in common sense language. On this basis, it is specifically studied how to condition the model without conditioning reality. The CFL uses the FL scale, which can vary from 0 to 1 to measure the degree of truth or falsity of its propositions, where propositions can be expressed through predicates. A predicate is a function of the X Universe in the interval [0, 1], and the operations of conjunction, disjunction, negation and implication are defined in such a way that, restricted to the domain [0, 1], Boolean logic is obtained.

The different ways of defining operations and their properties determine different multivalent logics that are part of the fuzzy logic paradigm. Multivalent logics are those that allow intermediate values between the absolute truth and the strong falsehood of an expression. Then 0 and 1 are both associated with the certainty and accuracy of what is affirmed or denied and 0.5 with the maximum vagueness and uncertainty. In decision-making processes, exchange with experts leads to complex and subtle formulations requiring compound predicates. The truth values obtained on these composite predicates must be sensitive to changes in the truth values of the basic predicates.

This need is satisfied by the use of CFL, which renounces compliance with the classical properties of conjunction and disjunction, opposing to these the idea that the increase or decrease of the truth value of the conjunction or disjunction caused by the change of the truth value of one of its components, can be "compensated" with the corresponding decrease or increase of the other. These properties make possible, in a natural way, the work of translation from natural language to that of logic, including extensive predicates if these arise from the process of modeling. Fuzzy logic has an enormous future in the development of Artificial Intelligence.

Expert systems

The human being is stubborn in transferring his knowledge to a machine so that later the machine can solve by itself the problems that the human being presents to the computer. This desire has led him to develop the technique of expert systems that are the cornerstone on which Artificial Intelligence is developed. **An expert system is a computer system that emulates the process of learning, memorization, reasoning, communication and action of a human expert in any branch of science and technology.** These characteristics allow it to store data and knowledge, draw logical conclusions, make decisions, learn from experience, communicate with human experts and perform actions as a result of all of the above.

In 1957 Herbert Simon, J.C. Shaw, and Allen Newell designed and programmed a system that would serve as the basis for building a machine capable of solving general problems. Their ambition was so great that they gave it the name General Problem Solver (GPS). Its goal was to solve any formal symbolic problems such as testing theorems, solving geometric problems, working with propositional logic and playing Chess. It was based on Simon and Newell's previous theoretical work on logic machines. GPS was able to solve simple problems, such as the Hanoi Towers, which could be expressed in a sufficiently formalized way, but could not solve real-world problems. The user defined the objects and the operations that could be done with and on the objects and the GPS generated heuristics through an analysis of the means and objectives, in order to solve the problems. To do this, it focused on available operations, finding out which inputs were acceptable and what results were generated. Sub-objectives were then created to get closer to the previously defined goal. The GPS paradigm evolved into the SOAR (State Operator and Result) symbolic-cognitive architecture.

Expert systems have evolved significantly and now have practical applications that turn them into valuable tools to increase human productivity. In the design of an expert system several functional characteristics must be taken into account. The most important is the one that separates the stored knowledge (Knowledge Base) from the program that controls it (Inference Engine). This is a fundamental characteristic that has defined computational systems since their origins.

These are the characteristics that an expert system must have:

- **Ability** to acquire knowledge.
- **Reliability** to be able to trust in its results or appreciations.
- **Strength** of knowledge
- Ability to solve problems.

Other desirable characteristics:

- **Competence in its field**: Solve problems with efficiency and quality comparable to those of a human expert
- **Reduced domain**: A reduced domain is a requirement to reach competence.
- **Ability to explain**: The ability to explain how the problem has been solved, what method has been applied and why it has been applied.
- **Treatment of uncertainty**: This is a requirement that derives from the complexity of the problems addressed by expert systems.
- **Flexibility in dialogue**: It is desirable that expert systems have this capacity, reaching as far as possible to communicate (understand and express themselves) in natural language as a human expert.
- **Explicit representation of knowledge**: It is necessary to consider that a system is based on knowledge.

An expert system must execute a set of tasks to achieve its objectives. These are the most important:

Monitoring. It is a particular case of interpretation and consists of the continuous comparison of the values of input signals or data and the values that act as criteria of normality or standards. In the field of predictive maintenance, expert systems are mainly used as diagnostic tools. The objective is for the program to be able to determine the operating status of complex systems at any given time, anticipating possible incidents that may occur. Thus, using a computational model of a human expert's reasoning, it provides the same results as the expert would achieve.

Design. It is the process of specifying a description of an artifact that satisfies several characteristics from a number of knowledge sources. Design is conceived in two basic ways: 1) Engineering design is the use of scientific principles, technical information and imagination in the definition of a mechanical structure, machine or system that performs specific functions with maximum economy and efficiency. 2) Industrial design seeks to rectify engineering omissions. It is a conscious attempt to bring form and visual order to hardware engineering where technology does not provide these characteristics.

Planning. It is the realization of plans or sequences of actions and is a particular case of simulation. It is composed of a simulator and a control system. The final effect is the arrangement of a set of actions in order to achieve a global objective.

Control. A control system participates in the performance of interpretation, diagnosis and repair tasks sequentially. In this way, a process or system can be led or guided. Control systems are complex due to the number of functions they must handle and the large number of factors they must consider; this growing complexity is another reason that points to the use of knowledge and therefore of expert systems.

Simulation. It is a technique that consists of creating models based on facts, observations and interpretations on the computer, in order to study their behavior by observing the exits for a set of inputs. Traditional simulation techniques require mathematical and logical models that describe the behavior of the system under study.

Instruction. An instructional system will track the learning process. The system detects errors and identifies the appropriate remedy. In other words, it develops a teaching plan that facilitates the learning process and the correction of errors.

Information retrieval. The expert systems, with their capacity to combine information and rules of action, have been seen as one of the possible solutions to the treatment and recovery of information, not only documentation. The 1980s were full of research and publications on experiments of this order, an interest that continues today. What differentiates these systems from a traditional information retrieval system is that the latter are only capable of retrieving what explicitly exists, while an expert system must be capable of generating non-explicit information, reasoning with the elements it is given.

But the capacity of the expert systems in the field of information retrieval is not limited to retrieval. They can be used to help the user in the selection of information resources, in the filtering of responses, etc. An expert system can act as an intelligent intermediary that guides and supports the work of the end user.

Several expert systems have been developed over the last five decades. Some of them have achieved fame and their name has been recorded in the history of computing. **These are some of the best known expert systems:**

MYCIN: It is the first expert system that ever worked with the same quality as a human expert. It is a highly specialized medical diagnostic and prescription system designed to help physicians treat meningitis and bacteremia infections. A series of tests have shown that MYCIN works just as well as a doctor.

TROPICAID: Provides additional information on the most commonly used medications. It selects a set of possible diagnoses from the analysis of the medical picture and proposes an optimal treatment for the specific case.

LABEIN: The Industrial Testing and Research Laboratory based in Spain developed a system for the design of electric motors by applying the classic technologies of expert systems to the CAD/CAE systems of design and analysis.

DELTA: Assistance to mechanics in the diagnosis and repair of diesel and electric locomotives. This system not only gives expert advice, but also presents information via a video player.

GUIDON: Used by the faculties of medical schools to train doctors to carry out consultations. GUIDON is a reorganization of MYCIN with educational intentions, in such a way that it has the additional advantage of having the whole knowledge base of MYCIN in addition to accumulated experience.

CASHVALUE: Evaluates investment projects.

COACH (Cognitive Adaptive Computer Help): Design custom help for the user

Expert systems offer great advantages for solving problems in specific areas. Perhaps the most important is that it allows the valuable knowledge of an expert to be retained as it can be permanently stored for later use, transferred and even combined with the knowledge of other experts. In expert systems the essence of the problems that are being solved is stored and how to apply the knowledge for their resolution is programmed. Expert systems emerged as one of the first manifestations of Artificial Intelligence and there are those who think that this technique will be surpassed by new technologies. However, as other Artificial Intelligence techniques such as automatic learning, deep learning and neural networks advance, expert systems will become more consistent, accurate and reliable.

Natural language processing

Natural language processing (NLP) is an Artificial Intelligence technique that, essentially, aims to make a machine understand what a person expresses through the use of a natural language (English, Spanish, Chinese, etc.). Natural languages can be expressed orally (by voice), written (a text) or by signs. Obviously, written expression is much more documented and easier to achieve and deal with than oral or sign language. Therefore, natural language processing is much more advanced in the processing of human-produced written texts.

NLP is concerned with the formulation and research of computationally effective mechanisms for communication between people and machines by means of natural languages. NLP is not about communication through natural languages in an abstract way, but about designing mechanisms to communicate that are computationally effective. The applied models focus not only on the comprehension of language per se, but also on general human cognitive aspects and the organization of memory. Natural language serves only as a means to study these phenomena. Until the 1980s, most NLP systems were based on a complex set of handmade rules. In the late 1980s there was a revolution in NLP with the introduction of automatic learning algorithms.

The development of NLP began around 1950, although some work in computer science has served as a precedent. As we have seen, Alan Turing published "Computing Machinery and Intelligence" in which he proposed what we now call the Turing test as an intelligence test. An experiment conducted by Georgetown University and IBM in 1954 involved automatic translation of more than sixty sentences from Russian into English. The authors argued that in three or five years machine translation would be a solved problem. However, real progress in machine translation was slower and after the ALPAC (Automatic Language Processing Advisory Committee) report in 1996 it was shown that the research had performed poorly. Later research conducted in the late 1980s, when the first statistical machine translation systems were developed, demonstrated important advances in machine translation. This was due to the constant increase in computational power resulting from Moore's Law and the application of the first automated learning algorithms used, such as decision trees and systems produced by sentences if-then similar to handwritten rules. Since then, machine translation has made important advances and is frequently used by search engines such as Google.

Moore's law states that approximately every two years the number of transistors in a microprocessor doubles. Although the law was originally formulated to establish that duplication would occur every year, Moore later redefined his law and extended the period to two years. It is an empirical law, formulated by the co-founder of Intel, Gordon E. Moore, on April 19, 1965.

Some companies have developed translation systems with surprising results. One of them is DeepL with better translation than Google and Microsoft. DeepL is an online machine translation service of DeepL GmbH, launched on August 28, 2017 by the founding team of Linguee. The service allows the translation of 9 languages in 72 language combinations (Dutch, English, French, German, Italian, Polish, Portuguese, Russian, and Spanish). Several tests at the time of publication indicated that DeepL would outperform its competitors, including Google's translator, Bing Translator and Facebook. Try it. www.DeepL.com/Translator

In order for a machine to communicate with a human being through a natural language, it is necessary to give a computational treatment to the language. That is, transforming natural language into a language based on bits and bytes so that the computer can understand it. This requires the joint work of the computer expert and the computational linguists who are in charge of preparing the model for computer engineers to implement.

In order to achieve the objective of understanding natural language by the computer, it is necessary to overcome some difficulties, among which we can mention **ambiguity as the most important**. If we take into account that natural language is inherently ambiguous we would have different levels:

- **At a lexical level**. The same word can have several meanings and the selection of the most appropriate one must be deduced from the oral context or basic knowledge. Many investigations in the field of natural language processing have studied methods of solving lexical ambiguities through dictionaries, grammars, knowledge bases and statistical correlations.

- **At the referential level**. The resolution of anaphora and cataphora implies determining the previous or subsequent linguistic entity to which they refer.

> In linguistics, **anaphora** is the use of an expression whose interpretation depends upon another expression in context (its antecedent or postcedent). In a narrower sense, anaphora is the use of an expression that depends specifically upon an antecedent expression and thus is contrasted with **cataphora**, which is the use of an expression that depends upon a postcedent expression.

- **At a structural level**. Semantics is required to disambiguate the dependence on prepositional syntagmas that lead to the construction of different syntactic trees. (Syntagma: Word or group of words that constitute a syntactic unit).

- **On a pragmatic level**. A sentence often does not mean what is really being said. Elements such as irony play an important role in the interpretation of the message.

Other difficulties that arise are the detection of separation between words and the imperfect reception of data. This is what computer scientists and linguists are working on, and judging from the progress they have made, it can be said that their work has been successful and that it will soon be normal for a human being to communicate with the computer and vice versa without being able to distinguish the source from which the words come.

Voice assistants from large technology companies have made great strides in recent years and competition is strong. **Roberto Adeva** writes for the Smart Life section of the newspaper El País: "Neither Siri nor Google Now, the best voice assistant is **Hound**. After several years of development a new voice-activated digital assistant has emerged that comes from the hand of one of the most famous song recognition applications to tackle Google Now, Siri and Cortana."

Microsoft had lagged a bit behind Google and Apple, but recently acquired a leading company in natural language processing technology to regain ground and keep up with leaders in the field. This fact reflects the importance attached to the technique of recognizing the human voice and the possibility of engaging in peer-to-peer conversation between man and machine.

With the title "Microsoft also wants Cortana to be able to converse like a human" a note was published in the media to highlight the importance that large computer companies assign to natural language processing.

"Artificial Intelligence continues to advance by leaps and bounds and Microsoft is betting strongly on this trend. Following in the footsteps of Google and the new skills of its Assistant, the technology giant announced the acquisition of Semantic Machines, a company focused on the development of conversational technology based on Artificial Intelligence."

The company previously worked with major technology firms, leading the automatic development of speech recognition for Apple's Siri. In essence, Semantic employs Automated Learning to provide context to chatbots' conversations, making dialogue more natural and fluid, a measure that could help give Cortana the edge it needs over its competitors.

Quantum computing

Quantum computing is not really an Artificial Intelligence technique. It is a paradigm of classical computing that supports the AI Revolution. Quantum computers belong to a later development than traditional computers and their technology promises to improve computing by employing quantum mechanics to process and solve problems millions of times faster than current devices.

In a "classic" computer the unit of information is called a "bit", which can have a value of 1 or 0. Its quantum equivalent operates with "qubits" or quantum bits. **Qubits can have the whole combination of values**: 0 0, 0 1, 1 0 and 1 1. Like a bit, a qubit represents a basic unit of information, but a quantum information unit is governed by the rules of quantum physics. Qubits can be in a 1 or 0 quantum state. **But they can also be in a superposition of the 1 and 0 states.** However, when qubits are measured the result is always either a 0 or a 1; the probabilities of the two outcomes depends on the quantum state they were in.

This property opens the way for doing multiple calculations simultaneously. Instead of doing a calculation following a linear progression as in a traditional digital computer - where the answers are yes or no, on or off, 1 or 0 - the quantum system has the ability to execute the operations simultaneously and deliver the results in a shorter time. We could say that quantum performs them simultaneously achieving an effect closer to the way the brain works.

Large computer companies are already competing to produce the highest capacity quantum computer. IBM was at the forefront but recently Google's Quantum AI lab has made the announcement of its Bristlecone computer to position itself as a leader in quantum computing.

Julian Kelly, Research Scientist at Quantum AI Lab comments on the Google AI blog the main features of the Bristlecone project (Monday, March 5, 2018): "The goal of the Google Quantum AI lab is to build a quantum computer that can be used to solve real-world problems. Our strategy is to explore near-term applications using systems that are forward compatible to a large-scale universal error-corrected quantum computer. In order for a quantum processor to be able to run algorithms beyond the scope of classical simulations, it requires not only a large number of qubits. Crucially, the processor must also have low error rates on readout and logical operations, such as single and two-qubit gates.

Today we presented Bristlecone, our new quantum processor, at the annual American Physical Society meeting in Los Angeles. The purpose of this gate-based superconducting system is to provide a testbed for research into system error rates and scalability of our qubit technology, as well as applications in quantum simulation, optimization, and machine learning.

The guiding design principle for this device is to preserve the underlying physics of our previous 9-qubit linear array technology which demonstrated low error rates for readout (1%), single-qubit gates (0.1%) and most importantly two-qubit gates (0.6%) as our best result. This device uses the same scheme for coupling, control, and readout, but is scaled to a square array of 72 qubits. We chose a device of this size to be able to demonstrate quantum supremacy in the future, investigate first and second order error-correction using the surface code, and to facilitate quantum algorithm development on actual hardware."

Julian Kelly concludes his comment with an optimistic message: "We are looking to achieve similar performance to the best error rates of the 9-qubit device, but now across all 72 qubits of Bristlecone. We believe Bristlecone would then be a compelling proof-of-principle for building larger scale quantum computers. Operating a device such as Bristlecone at low system error requires harmony between a full stack of technology ranging from software and control electronics to the processor itself. Getting this right requires careful systems engineering over several iterations. We are cautiously optimistic that quantum supremacy can be achieved with Bristlecone, and feel that learning to build and operate devices at this level of performance is an exciting challenge! We look forward to sharing the results and allowing collaborators to run experiments in the future." (https://bit.ly/2KweJSF).

Quantum computing is based on quantum mechanics which is one of the last branches to be born from the leafy tree of physics. Even though quantum computing has accelerated its pace in this century, quantum mechanics begins in the early 20th century when the Law of Universal Gravitation and Classical Electromagnetic Theory, two of the theories that attempted to explain the Universe around us, became insufficient to explain certain phenomena. The electromagnetic theory generated a problem when it tried to explain the emission of radiation from any object in equilibrium, called thermal radiation, which is the one that comes from the microscopic vibration of the particles that compose it. With the equations of classical electrodynamics, the energy emitted by this thermal radiation gave Infinity if all the frequencies emitted by the object were added together with an illogical result for physicists.

The physicist **Max Planck came up with a mathematical trick**: if, in the arithmetic process, the integral of those frequencies was replaced by a non-continuous sum, an infinite was not obtained as a result, thus eliminating the problem and, in addition, the result obtained agreed with what was later measured. With this base he enunciated the hypothesis that the electromagnetic radiation is absorbed and emitted by the matter in the form of Quanta of light or Photons of energy by means of a statistical constant that was denominated Planck Constant. Its history belongs to the XX Century, since the first quantum formulation of a phenomenon was made known on December 14, 1900 in a session of the Physical Society of the

Academy of Sciences of Berlin by the German scientist Max Planck.

> **Max Karl Ludwig Planck** was a German physicist and mathematician considered the founder of quantum theory who received the Nobel Prize in Physics in 1918. He was born on April 23, 1858 in Kiel and died in Göttingen, Germany in 1947.

Planck's idea would have remained for many years only as a hypothesis if Albert Einstein had not taken it up again proposing that light, in certain circumstances, behaves as independent energy particles (the Light Quanta or Photons). It was Albert Einstein who in 1905 completed the corresponding laws of motion with what is known as the Theory of Relativity, demonstrating that electromagnetism was essentially a non-mechanical theory. Thus culminated what has been called Classical Physics. That is, non-quantum physics. He used this point of view, called by him "heuristic", to develop his theory of the photoelectric effect, publishing this hypothesis in 1905, which earned him the Nobel Prize in 1921.

One of the greatest challenges for quantum computing is controlling or removing quantum decoherence. This usually means isolating the system from its environment as interactions with the external world cause the system to decoherence. However, other sources of decoherence also exist. Examples include the quantum gates, and the lattice vibrations and background thermonuclear spin of the physical system used to implement the qubits. Decoherence is irreversible, as it is effectively non-unitary, and is usually something that should be highly controlled, if not avoided.

> **Quantum decoherence** is the loss of quantum coherence. In quantum mechanics, particles such as electrons are described by a wave function, a mathematical representation of the quantum state of a system; a probabilistic interpretation of the wave function is used to explain various quantum effects. As long as there exists a definite phase relation between different states, the system is said to be coherent. Coherence is preserved under the laws of quantum physics, and this is necessary for the functioning of quantum computers.

Decoherence times for candidate systems, in particular the transverse relaxation time T2 (for NMR and MRI technology, also called the dephasing time), typically range between nanoseconds and seconds at low temperature. Currently, some quantum computers require their qubits to be cooled to 20 millikelvins in order to prevent significant decoherence.

NMR Nuclear magnetic resonance is a physical observation in which nuclei in a strong constant magnetic field are perturbed by a weak oscillating magnetic field (in the near field and therefore not involving electromagnetic waves and respond by producing an electromagnetic signal with a frequency characteristic of the magnetic field at the nucleus. MRI Magnetic resonance imaging is a test that uses powerful magnets, radio waves, and a computer to make detailed pictures.

As a result, time-consuming tasks may render some quantum algorithms inoperable, as maintaining the state of qubits for a long enough duration will eventually corrupt the superpositions. Error rates are typically proportional to the ratio of operating time to decoherence time, hence any operation must be completed much more quickly than decoherence time.

The kelvin is the base unit of temperature in the International System of Units. One kelvin is equal to a change in the thermodynamic temperature that results in a change of thermal energy.

Quantum supremacy is the potential ability of quantum computing devices to solve problems that classical computers practically cannot. Quantum advantage is the potential to solve problems faster. In computational-complexity-theoretic terms, this generally means providing a superpolynomial speedup over the best known or possible classical algorithm. The term was originally popularized by John Preskill but the concept of a quantum computational advantage, specifically for simulating quantum systems, dates back to Yuri Manin's (1980) and Richard Feynman's (1981) proposals of quantum computing. The quantum supremacy concept is taking more space in the media of technology.

For the time being, classical technology can manage any task thrown at a quantum computer. Quantum supremacy describes the ability of a quantum computer to outperform their classical counterparts. Some companies, such as IBM and Google, claim we might be close, as they continue to cram more qubits together and build more accurate devices.

The convergence of AI and quantum computing can solve complex artificial intelligence problems and obtain multiple solutions to complex problems simultaneously. This will enhance Artificial Intelligence more efficiently performing complex tasks in human-like ways. Similarly, robots can optimize decisions in a real-world scenario, which will be possible once quantum computers based on artificial intelligence are deployed. **The key is the convergence.**

-6-

APPLICATIONS

Artificial intelligence has become a crucial part of our daily lives. When you use your mobile phone to ask about the status of a purchase order, consult about the appropriate medicine to cure a disease, prepare a recipe at home, ask the best way to get to the place of your business appointment or what is the best alternative to make an investment in the stock market, you will receive the answer from a system with Artificial Intelligence integrated in an App on your mobile. No human being will have intervened to receive your question and answer it immediately and accurately. All the information was processed by an App with AI.

> **Application software (app for short)** is software designed to perform a group of coordinated functions, tasks, or activities for the benefit of the user. Examples of an application include a word processor, a spreadsheet, an accounting application, a web browser, an email client, a media player, a file viewer, a console game or a photo editor. Applications may be bundled with the computer and its system software or published separately. Apps built for mobile platforms are called mobile apps. In recent years, the shortened term "app" has become popular to refer to applications for mobile devices such as smartphones and tablets, the shortened form matching their typically smaller scope compared to applications on personal computers.

Artificial Intelligence applications have left the field of science fiction to become part of everyday reality. Without realizing it, we have AI applications at hand to help us in our daily activities, solve problems, give us some advice or simply make our lives more enjoyable. Some applications have been developed for mobiles and others to run on a computer, a car, an airplane or a robot. When we use a cell phone, which is no longer just a phone, but an entire communication and information processing center, we have a whole host of applications at our disposal. Many of them have been developed with AI techniques and their performance is sensational. Some take advantage of automatic learning and little by little they learn our tastes and preferences to such an extent that sometimes we are surprised to see that they anticipate our desires to please us before we give an order.

The influence of Artificial Intelligence on mobile phones is so strong that the Honor View10 incorporates an independent neural network processing unit (NPU). This means that the equipment has an additional processor that optimizes the tasks associated with AI. In this way, multiple Artificial Intelligence applications are enhanced so that the user can perform different tasks. An imperceptible point at first sight for the user is that the mobile optimizes its performance by learning the behavior of the person and the tasks it performs habitually to respond more efficiently.

The speed with which the applications developed with Artificial Intelligence techniques are produced makes it difficult to mention, and qualify all of them. Next we will study some in different fields of application, for mobiles, computers or robots, but perhaps **the most important thing for now is to become aware of their presence, their ability to interact as intelligent entities and glimpse how far they can go** if they are integrated into a Strong Artificial Intelligence system.

Applications in Medicine.

Artificial Intelligence has gone beyond science fiction in the health sector. It is currently a very broad and constantly changing field of study. The applications that have been developed are extensive. Here we will review only a few of them, aware that new ones often appear that cause surprise and astonishment even to medical professionals themselves.

For the first time in its history, **the US FDA has approved six AI-based programs** to aid diagnosis after having proven their effectiveness in clinical trials. They are systems that help predict the onset of stroke and diabetic retinopathy, among other diseases. In the case of diabetes detection, it is a program with an AI algorithm that allows the analysis of images of the eye uploaded to a server and offer a recommendation to the doctor. According to the FDA, "it is one of the first devices authorized for commercialization that provides a detection decision without the need for a physician to also interpret the image or the results. Another authorized program analyzes computed tomography (CT) results to warn of a possible stroke."

The diagnosis and treatment of diseases is a branch of medicine that has been studied extensively and with the help of robotics has obtained great results that help in the care and treatment of patients.

Robots are able to perform repetitive tasks faster, cheaper, and more accurately than humans. The first real trial of a robot capable of operating on human eyes took place in June 2018 and was a great success.

Several teams of scientists are trying to create systems that fight against the large number of geriatric diseases that cause memory loss. Assisted cognition systems combine software with Artificial Intelligence, GPS technology, sensor networks and infrared identification plates that accompany patients at all times. With assisted cognition systems, the elderly will be able to stay at home longer and take care of themselves on their own.

Scientists at the Human Genome Research Institute in the United States and Lund University in Sweden have developed a technique that applies Artificial Intelligence to biochips used for genetic analysis. These make it possible to quickly distinguish between various types of cancer.

The Website for medical consultations on the Internet evolved to become one of the most used applications in the medical field. They added some functions and a touch of Artificial Intelligence. Now **WebMD** is one of the most famous symptom-checkers on the net. It is used by millions of people every day and now has an app to further extend its reach. The app, unlike its online checker, includes medication reminders, habit and fitness tracking, first aid tips, a drug database, as well as other educational content. Users can also use the application to help them find and arrange an appointment with a nearby physician.

Pattern recognition technology taken to a higher level with Artificial Intelligence to interpret images and make decisions has led to an important application **to detect cancer based on the analysis of photographs.** The Japanese technology company Kyocera and the University of Tsukuba have developed a system to detect skin cancer in its earliest stages, based on the analysis of photographs of patients using Artificial Intelligence. The method, still in its experimental phase, has achieved 90 percent diagnostic accuracy in 4,000 analyzed snapshots of patients' skin, according to the Japanese business newspaper Nikkei.

Nils Strodthoff, researcher at the Fraunhofer Institute Heinrich Hertz (Germany) and Claas Strodthoff, from the Schleswig-Holstein University Medical Center (Germany) have developed a neural network that can detect signs of myocardial infarction and claim that the machine matches and can surpass the performance of human cardiologists. A standard electrocardiograph records the electrical signal through 12 different wires connected to different parts of the patient's body. These signals denote the electrical behavior of the heart in different ways. However, interpreting the data is difficult. The approach developed by both Strodthoffs is generically applicable to any classification problem such as ECGs and electroencephalography (EEG) problems that abound in medicine, which opens up an extensive panorama for their health use.

Stock market

On August 8, 2010 an interesting news story was published that would change the execution of financial operations with stocks, bonds, commodities, futures and any financial market. An IBM computer competed with stockbrokers to invest in the buying and selling of commodities and gold to determine who could obtain better results. The computer won by a margin of 7% against seasoned stock market investors. Since then better and more sophisticated Artificial Intelligence systems have been used that regularly execute financial operations handling billions of dollars every day. **One advantage of Artificial Intelligence systems is that they do not mix emotions**, fears, greed or moods that interfere with the numbers and facts that determine the behavior of the financial market. This is a decisive advantage, although in certain cases it represents a danger since it does not apply the "common sense" that on many occasions warns of something out of the ordinary but that must be taken into account in making a decision.

In April 2017, JP Morgan's Chief Operating Officer, Matt Zames, explained in a letter to his shareholders the strategic direction the company was taking with the aim of making AI an important pillar in the investment bank's financial operations: "Last year we introduced machine learning technology for banking investments. We launched the Emerging Opportunity Capital Markets Engine that allows us to identify the best investment offerings for each client, offering personalized recommendations through automated analysis of current financial positions, market conditions and historical data. Given the initial success of the Emerging Opportunity Engine in Capital Markets, we are expanding it to other areas such as Debt Capital Markets, similarly basing predictions on client financial data, issuance history and market activity."

The Financial Times, one of the most authoritative publications in the world of finance speculates in an interesting article on the future of Artificial Intelligence in the stock market:

"The gigantic advances in information technology have revolutionized practically every facet of modern life, and the financial markets are no exception. The world's most successful hedge funds are currently looking for computer scientists, not economists or investment bankers with MBAs. Even the investment funds that manage the savings of the baby-boom generation and oil-rich states employ the "quantitative" techniques made possible by modern computer science and complex mathematical models. The next frontier in this technological scale is Artificial Intelligence. Advances in research have generated enormous interest in the industry, where some believe that a thinking computer capable of learning and trading will make even today's high-speed, complex investment algorithms look archaic - and possibly make the figure of the human fund manager unnecessary." Could the next Warren Buffett be an AI algorithm?

The cover of the prestigious magazine The Economist of October 3, 2019 is entitled "Masters of the Universe. The rise of the financial machines. How machines are taking over Wall Street" and is presented with this text: "This week our cover looks at how machines are taking control of financial markets—not just the humdrum buying and selling of securities, but also the commanding heights of monitoring the economy and allocating capital. Funds run by computers that follow rules set by humans account for 35% of America's stock market, 60% of institutional equity assets and 60% of trading activity. New artificial-intelligence programs are also writing their own investing rules, in ways their human masters only partly understand. Industries from pizza-delivery to Hollywood are being changed by technology, but finance is unique because it can exert voting power over firms, redistribute wealth and cause mayhem in the economy." (https://econ.st/30G4kYJ)

The challenge facing the investment world is that the human mind has not improved over 100 years ago and for someone using traditional methods it is very difficult to assimilate in their head all the information from the global economy. David Siegel, co-chairman of Two Sigma, said at a conference last year: "There will come a day when no human investment manager will be able to outperform the computer."

Customer service

The development of technology that has the ability to recognize natural language and answer in a language understandable to humans has allowed the advancement of Artificial Intelligence systems to provide customer service. Large companies have invested in systems that are installed in huge call centers with answering machines to serve customers.

Marín Frascaroli, Director and founder of AIVO, a company in charge of developing customer service software based on Artificial Intelligence said: "The main objective of the companies in terms of customer service must be focused on solving the needs of the consumer immediately to achieve their loyalty. However, what is the key to achieving this goal? The main thing is to build a new experience of interaction between them and their customers. Today's consumer is more informed, is in constant communication and is self-sufficient, and this has been a great challenge for companies, as there is constant doubt about how to satisfy a customer with this profile. This is where the role of Artificial Intelligence comes in, an excellent tool that provides the brand with virtual agents focused on fast customer service."

Using solutions to optimize the use of human resources and at the same time solve customer needs without waiting from the first interaction is crucial to create loyalty among today's consumers. Artificial Intelligence allows you to create models of relationships similar to those that a human would do to find information, emulate their way of thinking and dialogue in a natural way, so you can serve a user in the same way that a human being would. This allows the company to be available 24 hours a day, seven days a week, have the ability to make content suggestions if it does not have the requested information. **Now it is not just a question of having the best tool, the personality of the tool is also important**. A virtual assistant must be empathetic to transmit the values of the company when communicating with the clients and understand what it is that the client needs to solve. Its knowledge about the company and its products must be deep and must be integrated to the smallest detail for the customers, so the company must have a comprehensive, constantly up-dated database.

To the extent that the requirements indicated by Marín Frascaroli are met, customer service systems based on Artificial Intelligence will prevail. And for this there is not much time left.

Games

The application of Artificial Intelligence in games can be traced to the year 1956 when a group of students from Darmouth College organized a conference to demonstrate that the computer could perform intelligent functions. Arthur Samuel presented a program to play checkers and Alex Bernstein to play Chess. Since then there have been more surprising games that leave little doubt that computers have intelligence similar to that of a human being. Their ability to react, their ability to make good decisions and even their ability to learn from experience is fascinating.

Artificial Intelligence is one of the most important points when studying and criticizing a video game and, while there have been advances in recent years, it seems that it has reached a peak and the true intelligence of our allies and virtual enemies has stagnated. Why? Well, if you buy a new game and started playing, would you enjoy being completely destroyed over and over again? Or would you rather be paired against someone/something more on your level so that you could learn and improve over time? The vast majority of players would likely choose the later. But what about the future? Will we have more astute enemies, capable of tracking our steps? And what about allies that cover our backs at the right time?

One of the first games to surprise us with its players' AI was Half-Life where our enemies were so cunning that they could flank us and combine grenades with rifles to immobilize us in a matter of seconds. It was a real challenge for those of us who were used to more passive enemies.

After Half-Life, games like Thief, where the experience was more about stealth and defensive attitude, showed that the AI, besides knowing how to attack, could recognize alterations in the scenario and alert by noises, both from our character and of any other element. Other examples of AI progress were shooters such as Unreal Tournament and Halo. In this period of time shooter and action games where active enemies were the main part of the adventure grew and grew steadily. On the other hand, games like the classic Tycoon Sim Theme Park or Theme Hospital style used Artificial Intelligence based on basic protocols where a character style always reacted in the same way, something very far from real AI.

From that moment until now many games have given a good sample of what Artificial Intelligence can achieve. However, we are still much closer to the word "artificial" than "intelligence".

New technologies and higher capacity devices have allowed developers to create more powerful engines for non-player characters and with this, improved Artificial Intelligence. However, the advance has been more horizontal than vertical, it is not so much that the intelligences have improved but now you can create more characters simultaneously and more diversity of actions for them.

One case of this is Far Cry 3 where the animals have a very advanced Artificial Intelligence and where not only do they move from one place to another, but also hunt, hide, flee, and change attitude depending on their environment. Beyond this, while it may seem very good for animals, it does not seem so incredible when adapted to a human character, which in real life could present many more variables and actions.

The fact is that progress has been made, but not in terms of options because in FPS games (First Person Shooter) the enemies have a limited number of positions. For example, they can be alert, calm, defensive or attack. In the game it doesn't really matter if the enemy is hungry or sleepy. However, progress has been made in a process that allows these enemies to collect information and, in relation to this, change their attitude a priori.

New technologies allow more information and speed to process this Artificial Intelligence, but programmers need to work more on developing these intelligences to improve the AI games. It seems that it is no longer a matter of hardware that limits them but of rethinking of how Artificial Intelligence should work. On the other hand the AI used in strategy games like Crusader King present different attitudes to those of a FPS and some developers claim that it has already reached the limit of its capacity.

In this way we can continue adding actions to the characters, we can make them run, scratch, look and touch something, and interact with each other, but getting these characters to make intelligent decisions based on "artificial mental process" is another major task. It will depend on the developers and their ability to create processes that emulate reality for this to improve.

Autonomous vehicles

The automobile was invented more than 100 years ago. In all that time its mechanical performance has improved. The comfort of its interior, the efficient use of fuel, the ease of driving and the safety of passengers have also improved. But no change is as important as the production of the autonomous vehicle thanks to Artificial Intelligence. Already in the experimental phase is a versatile and powerful software to make the autonomous car without a driver a reality. It will be guided by cameras, sensors, GPS and radar that will generate a large amount of data that will be processed by software that must use Artificial Intelligence to be able to make decisions.

Several companies dedicated to Information Technology and the automotive industry already contemplate in their expansion plans the commercial production of autonomous vehicles. Google is one of the pioneering companies in this field. Its vehicles can already be seen on streets and roads undergoing experimentation. Automotive companies such as BMW, Mercedes Benz, Audi, Honda, Nissan, Toyota, General Motors and Ford are already dedicated to the research of autonomous vehicles. In this field the quality of Artificial Intelligence software will be the key to success in the automotive market. **And when it comes to developing a project with software, Google is the leading company.**

Google's interest in autonomous cars dates back to 2005 when the team, led by Sebastian Thrun, professor at Stanford and founder of Google X, won, with a car called Stanley, the DARPA Grand Challenge autonomous vehicle race promoted by the US Department of Defense. Years later, supported by its enormous technological capacity, Google initiated plans for the production of an autonomous car at the dawn of the decade of 2010. Shortly thereafter it had a first prototype circulating around the company and five years later obtained, from the California Department of Motor Vehicles, a permit for its autonomous cars driven with Artificial Intelligence software to circulate on state streets and highways. In 2016 Alphabet, Google's parent company, took a new step in the development of the autonomous car by announcing that this project would operate under a completely independent company in its corporate structure. The new subsidiary was called Waymo. The name of this Alphabet Company says a lot: Mobile Way or a new way in mobility. John Krafcik, the director of the autonomous automobile program, says that the decision to separate it into an independent company is "an indication of the maturity" that its technology has already reached.

IBM, the pioneer in the production of computers and now mainly dedicated to the production of software, has also entered into the production of autonomous cars with Artificial Intelligence. Olli, an autonomous vehicle with capacity for 12 people is IBM's first incursion in this field. Olli is an automobile for driving in confined spaces and at low speed. It is designed to serve within the campus of a university, a company, an amusement park or as a tourist vehicle in a city. Thanks to its Artificial Intelligence system, it can answer questions from its passengers. For example, Olli can tell which places of interest, restaurants or museums are close to your route.

The Ford automotive company has taken an important step to fully engage in the production of autonomous vehicles with Artificial Intelligence and intends to enter the market before 2021. In order to achieve its objective, it has made an investment of 1,000 million dollars to acquire a firm in the Artificial Intelligence segment. In this way Ford will have majority control of Argo AI, a Pittsburgh-based company recently started by former Google and Uber employees specializing in autonomous cars. This alliance will allow Ford to have engineers and robotics experts to develop a "virtual driver" that, according to Ford, will be the "brain" of the future car. Argo AI employees will have a minority stake in the company and Ford executives said they are confident that the most important projects of the autonomous car will be driven by Argo

Tesla's automotive strategy is not limited to the production of electric cars. The company led by Elon Musk also wants to be a leader in the manufacture and sale of autonomous cars with Artificial Intelligence. **Elon Musk has said: "I believe that all cars will run completely autonomously in the long term. In 15 or 20 years it will be quite rare to see cars that do not have full autonomy**. And in the case of Tesla it will happen much earlier. In fact, I think cars that don't have full range will have a negative value. It will be like owning a horse, only for sentimental reasons." In a bold statement on the future of Tesla cars, Elon Musk has stated that electric cars, that have caused a sensation, may be 100% autonomous by the end of 2019. This has made its competitors rush not to stay out of the market.

It is true that the first accidents with self-driving cars have already been recorded, but this has not stopped the progress of the application of Artificial Intelligence and surely in the near future we will see more cars circulating without drivers. **So don't be surprised if you find one as you drive along.**

Military

The army has stood out for being an important driver of technology for military use. Ballistic calculations, deciphering enemy codes and the production of increasingly sophisticated weaponry have led the military to invest large sums of money and technological resources to stay at the forefront of innovation. Let us remember that the Colossus computer was built in England precisely to decipher the communication codes of the German army and in the United States the first computers were produced for the army. The Internet was born under the auspices of the Department of Defense in the United States working in liaison with several universities.

Artificial Intelligence is a very attractive field for the military and they currently work closely with research and development centers to stay at the forefront of innovation. Not surprisingly, the US military maintains an office in Silicon Valley to liaise with researchers and businesses to learn first-hand about advances in the field.

Artificial Intelligence facilitates the possibility of accessing massive amounts of data and processing them faster in order to discover relationships between them, detect patterns and make inferences and learning through probabilistic models to apply them in the construction of increasingly sophisticated and lethal equipment and weaponry.

In the same way that an autonomous automobile with the capacity to make decisions has been produced, experimentation is also be done in **the production of autonomous armament with the capacity of decision** to fire against a target when the Artificial Intelligence system with which it has been programmed decides it. This is one of the situations in which Artificial Intelligence could represent a fatal risk for humanity.

An example of autonomous armament production can be found in the company Kratos Defense & Security Solutions with offices in San Diego, California that actively works in the production of combat drones to minimize casualties in air combat. The Washington Post reports on experimentation with UTAP-22 Mako and XQ-222 Valkyrie drones, the latter very different from what is normally understood to be a drone and closer to a human-piloted fighter, with an autonomy of close to 6,000 kilometers. According to the Washington Post, its characteristics make it a vehicle capable of accompanying the F-16 or F-35 in flight as ideal combat companions to distract the attention of the enemy without risking the lives of human beings.

For its part, **Russia does not want to fall behind in the military race with AI** and is developing new missiles and unmanned aerial vehicles that will use Artificial Intelligence to make decisions for themselves, according to arms manufacturers and defense officials, in an attempt to equalize military might against the United States and China. Boris Obnosov, chief executive officer of the Tactical Missiles Corporation, said the new weapon would be available in the coming years. Speaking at Zhukovsky's annual MosAeroShow (MAKS- 2017), Obnosov told attendees that he studied the US use of the Raytheon Block IV Tomahawk cruise missile against Russia's allies in Syria and sought to emulate its advanced technology, such as the ability to change targets in mid-flight, in an upcoming weapon. "This is a very serious field where fundamental research is required and there are some successes available today, but we will still have to work for several years to achieve specific results," Obnosov said, according to the state news agency TASS Russian. Although technically any AI-enabled military attack system is capable of making its own decisions based on various sensors and instruments, the concept of giving a weapon the power to choose its targets and decide when and how to fire at them has been a much more recent and controversial innovation.

Russian firm Kalashnikov, creator of the AK-47 known as the goat horn, recently introduced its new line of autonomous combat robots controlled by an Artificial Intelligence system. These robots would be able to open fire automatically when they detect an intruder, **all without the need for human intervention.**

Concerned about the misuse of Artificial Intelligence in the production of military weapons, more than a thousand technology experts, scientists and philosophers signed a letter against the development of Artificial Intelligence weapons that was presented at the International Conference on Artificial Intelligence held in Buenos Aires in July 2015. The scientists signed a text that warned about the application of Artificial Intelligence in the development of weapons at a global level, since it is "feasible" that in a matter of "years, not decades" we will find teams capable of selecting, setting and attacking objectives without any human intervention. Experts stress the risk of this technology ending up in the hands of terrorists. "If any major military power pushes towards the development of Artificial Intelligence weapons, a global arms race is virtually inevitable and the end of this technological trajectory is obvious: autonomous weapons will become the Kalashnikovs of tomorrow," the letter states. The United States, Russia and China, in that order, are considered the main military powers of the world and they bear this great responsibility.

Education

The production of software dedicated to education began with the large computer and gained a renewed boom with the personal computer. Important companies dedicated entirely to the production of educational software emerged. Spinnaker is one of the best examples of these new software companies. They conducted a careful market study and concluded that it would be more opportune to focus on the production of educational software and towards that field they focused their batteries. Some universities have reinforced their study programs with Artificial Intelligence and have achieved success and recognition with their educational programs on the Internet such as the University of Phoenix, the Distance University of Madrid and even the large and recognized universities that have opened their online education programs such as Harvard and the Massachusetts Institute of Technology (MIT).

Artificial Intelligence is entering education with great power. There are several fields of application and here are five ways that AI can support education:

- **Educational programs adapted to students**. An example of education tailored to the needs of students is the tool developed by McGraw-Hill Textbook Publishing. The online platform, which uses AI, reacts to each student's progress and designs courses focused on their weak points. This means that there will be a specific program taught using the limitations and advantages of each student rather than general models for all students. The tool is also useful for teachers as it allows them to track each student and respond according to their needs.

- **Offer multi-channel teaching**. The integration of AI in education would produce a decentralization of educational spaces. Through the implementation of these systems, students will be able to learn no matter where they are. Technologies such as augmented reality and the Internet of things will contribute to Artificial Intelligence to offer a more comprehensive, attractive and profound educational experience. The student will acquire basic knowledge, and as these are perfected, services will become increasingly complex and refined in distance education and continuing education.

- **Help the teacher qualify.** If applied widely, Artificial Intelligence would perform educational functions such as grading, which would give the teacher the time needed to improve their knowledge base or dedicate to students the extra attention that they might need. Teaching, like many other professions, is a career in which the professional must keep up-to-date because knowledge is renewed with amazing speed, so that this type of tool would be an invaluable support.

- **New learning tools**. The development of AI will lead to the creation of new teaching tools, for example, IBM's Artificial Intelligence system, Watson. Its Teacher Advisor tool allows primary school teachers to be guided and provides them with learning tools for students, personalized according to subject, grade level and type of activities. The great differentiator of Watson's Teacher Advisor is that, being driven by Artificial Intelligence, its search engine is refined with each use, offering increasingly accurate and relevant results. Another teacher support tool is Google's G Suite for Education, which takes advantage of AI to create more complete and efficient educational experiences. It currently consists of tools already known to Google as Docs, Drive, Gmail and Calendar, but designed with intelligent features that facilitate the link with students and teachers.

- **Teaching without barriers.** Learning can sometimes be an intimidating experience that can cause students to slow down their learning process for fear of making a mistake. Artificial Intelligence would offer students an alternative to experiment and learn without fear of being judged or becoming the object of ridicule; Artificial Intelligence, like students, perfects and refines its knowledge when it learns from its mistakes. While we probably won't see a major change in AI technologies in the next five years, it is important to note the speed with which this technology is being developed that is increasingly integrated into different aspects of our lives.

Steve Wozniak, Apple´s co-founder, is convinced that the future for students and teachers lies in the application of Artificial Intelligence systems in Education combined with virtual reality applications that would give a 180-degree turn to the learning experience. Wozniak says, "If a computer were like a human being and knew everything we like, every student could have a teacher who would lead them from a very young age to what they are passionate about and what they could really be good at."

Virtual assistant with voice

A virtual assistant with voice is a computer program or software endowed with a certain degree of Artificial Intelligence that helps users of computer systems by automating and performing tasks with minimal human-machine interaction. The interaction between a virtual assistant and a person is done through the voice of the human being and the imitation of the voice by the assistant (a mobile or a computer). The interaction must be natural: the person uses his voice to communicate and the virtual assistant processes, interprets and responds.

The large computer and communications companies have developed their own virtual assistant with voice to integrate it to their smart phones, computers, search engines or user help systems and so we have Siri, Cortana, Google Assistant, Bixby, Alexa, Silvia, Alice, Sherpa, and so on.

Some perform really sophisticated tasks to communicate and help the user. To illustrate their operation and capabilities we will take **Siri, Apple's assistant**, as an example. Siri has been an integral part of the iOS operating system since the launch of iOS 5 in 2011. It started with basic concepts such as climate and messaging, but has expanded significantly since then to support more integration and functions. Now it can be asked to call people, send messages, schedule meetings, start applications and games, play music, answer questions, set reminders, and provide weather forecasts. Siri can also integrate with third-party applications and understand follow-up queries. That's a big change in Apple's strategy.

The advancement of technology will enable the voice assistants now installed and operating on digital phones to become personal assistants at home. This will allow an assistant inside your home to help you control the operation of electrical appliances including the television, refrigerator, washing machine and, of course, the telephone.

It is estimated that **by the year 2025 it will be common to have an in-home assistant** connected to Google to perform searches for information, recipes, weather, news and everything that is needed for daily activity. Of course, your assistant will bring you the agenda and you can even establish a conversation to make the day more enjoyable. As Artificial Intelligence advances, your assistant will increase your level of intelligence to the point of not distinguishing between a human being and a digital assistant with voice. **At that point the Turing test will be completed and the era of Strong Artificial Intelligence will be on its way.**

-7-

PASSION FOR TECHNOLOGY

Human beings are passionate about technology. From the Homo habilis who took a stick to use it as a weapon or tool, man has based his development on technology. Over the centuries there have been alternating periods of great brilliance with others of opacity. We are currently living in a frenzy of information and communication technologies that are accelerating the pace to reach the Fifth Wave in the evolution of humankind. These are some technologies that have stood out:

- Biotechnology
- Robotics
- 3D printing
- New materials
- Internet of Things (IoT)
- Virtual Reality
- Alternative energy sources
- Blockchain
- Augmented Reality

Due to their importance not only in the industrial process but also in people's daily lives, we will study in the following sections the most important features of each of these **technologies that pave the path to Strong Artificial Intelligence**.

Biotechnology

The Organization for Economic Co-operation and Development (OECD) defines biotechnology as the "application of scientific and engineering principles for the treatment of organic and inorganic materials by biological systems to produce goods and services". Its bases are engineering, physics, chemistry, biology, medicine and veterinary medicine. The field of this science has great repercussions in pharmacy, medicine, food science, solid, liquid and gaseous waste treatment, industry and agriculture.

The name is derived from the Greek βίος [bios], "life", τέχνη [-tecne-], "dexterity" and -λογία [-logía], "treaty, study, science"). It refers to any technological application that uses biological systems and living organisms or their derivatives for the creation or modification of products or processes for specific uses. Such organisms may or may not be genetically modified, so biotechnology should not be confused with genetic engineering. The term was probably coined by the Hungarian engineer Károly Ereki in 1919, when he introduced it in his book "Biotechnology in the meat and dairy production of a large farm".

Biotechnology comprises basic and applied research that integrates different approaches derived from technology and the application of biological sciences such as cell biology, molecular biology, bioinformatics and applied marine microbiology. It includes research and development of bioactive substances and functional foods for the well-being of aquatic organisms, cellular and molecular diagnosis, and management of aquaculture-related diseases, environmental toxicology and genomics, environmental management and biosafety associated with the cultivation and processing of marine and freshwater organisms, biofuels, and laboratory quality control and management.

The **Cartagena Protocol on Biosafety** to the Convention on Biological Diversity defines modern biotechnology as the application of:

-In vitro nucleic acid techniques, including recombinant deoxyribonucleic acid (DNA) and direct injection of nucleic acid into cells or organelles.

-Fusion of cells beyond the taxonomic family, which overcome the natural physiological barriers of reproduction or recombination and which are not techniques used in traditional breeding and selection.

Recent experience has shown that non-reproducible random results can be obtained with a low probability in the gene modification process, so that the scientific community is postulating for the specific classification of this type of product and the creation of a protocol that ensures the safety of all supposedly unexpected probable results.

Artificial Intelligence, big data analytics and deep learning are converging on health care in a big way. Such convergence of biology and technology should bring about a complete transformation of medical care.

Chris Coburn, chief innovation officer at Partners HealthCare says: "My personal perspective would be in three to five years, the huge majority of patients will be touched in one way or another with some AI-related system, whether they know it or not. **We're on a path to turning the lights on** and revealing what works for whom, and by getting at the underlying mechanisms of these diseases, we can now stop the guesswork. That's what's really exciting for me." (https://bit.ly/2mjmfpH)

Robotics

Robotics is a branch that emerges from the lush tree of mechanical, electrical, electronic, biomedical engineering, and very importantly of computer science, communications and Artificial Intelligence. It deals with the design, construction, operation, structure, manufacture, and application of robots. Other important areas in robotics are algebra, programmable automatons, animatronics, mechatronic and state machines.

The term robot became popular with the success of the book R.U.R. (Rossum Universal Robots), written by **Karel Capek** in 1920. In the English translation of this work the Czech word robota, meaning forced labor or simply labor, was translated into English as robot.

A robot is a virtual or artificial mechanical entity. Because of its appearance or its movements, it offers the sensation of having a purpose of its own. The independence created in its movements makes its actions the reason for a reasonable and deep study in the area of science and technology. The word robot can refer to both physical mechanisms and virtual software systems, although the term bots usually refers to the latter.

There is no consensus on which machines can be considered robots, but there is general agreement among experts and the public that robots tend to do part or all of the following: move, operate a mechanical arm, feel and manipulate their environment and display intelligent behavior, especially if that behavior mimics that of humans or other animals. Currently, a robot could be considered to be a computer with the capacity and purpose of movement that in general is capable of carrying out multiple tasks in a flexible way according to its programming; so it could be differentiated from a specific appliance.

Today commercial and industrial robots are widely used and perform tasks more accurately or cheaper than humans. They are also used in jobs that are too dirty, dangerous or tedious. Robots are used in manufacturing, assembly and packaging plants, transport, explorations on Earth and in space, surgery, armament, laboratory research and in the mass production of industrial or consumer goods. Other applications include toxic waste clearance, mining, people search and rescue, and landmine location. In addition to the fields mentioned above, there are models working in the education sector, services and search and rescue tasks. There is great hope, especially in Japan, that home care for the elderly can be performed by robots. Robot caregivers are saving the elderly from lives of loneliness.

The future of robots could be the convergence of the robot with the human. This is an exciting topic that we will develop in more detail towards the end of the book in the Man-Machine symbiosis section.

Nanotechnology

Nanotechnology is the manipulation of matter at a nanoscale. It integrates the study, design, creation, synthesis, manipulation and application of materials, apparatus and functional systems through the control of matter at the nanoscale and the exploitation of phenomena and properties of matter also at the nanoscale. When matter is manipulated at such a minuscule scale it presents totally new phenomena and properties. Scientists therefore use nanotechnology to create novel and inexpensive materials, devices and systems with unique properties. Nanoscience is a discipline dedicated to the study of physical, chemical and biological phenomena occurring at the nanoscale. Today there are many instruments and devices of nanometric dimensions and precision that facilitate this process.

> **Nanometer** is the unit of length of the International System of Units that is equivalent to one billionth of a meter (1 nm = 10-9 m) or one millionth of a millimeter. The nanometer symbol is nm.

The winner of the 1965 Nobel Prize in Physics, **Richard Feynman, was the first to highlight the properties of**

nanoscience and nanotechnology in a speech he gave at Caltech (California Institute of Technology) on December 29, 1959, entitled "There's Plenty of Room at the Bottom", in which he describes the possibility of synthesis via direct manipulation of atoms.

Inspired by the concepts of Feynman, independently **Kim Eric Drexler** used the term "nanotechnology" in his 1986 book "Engines of Creation: The Coming Era of Nanotechnology" in which he proposed the idea of a nanoscale "assembler" that would be able to construct a copy of himself and other elements of arbitrary complexity with a level of atomic control. Also in 1986, Drexler co-founded The Foresight Institute to help increase public awareness and understanding of nanotechnology concepts and their implications. (https://amzn.to/2mqsqbq)

Thus, the emergence of nanotechnology as a field of study in the 1980s occurred because of the convergence of the theoretical and public work of Drexler, who developed and popularized a conceptual framework for nanotechnology, and high-visibility experimental advances that attracted additional attention on a large scale to the prospects of atomic control of matter.

For example, the invention of the tunnel-effect microscope in 1981 provided unprecedented visualization of individual atoms and links, and was successfully used to manipulate individual atoms in 1989. Microscope developers Gerd Binnig and Heinrich Rohrer of the IBM Zurich Research Laboratory received a Nobel Prize in Physics in 1986. Binnig, Quate and Gerber also invented the analog atomic force microscope that same year.

In the early 2000s, nanotechnology garnered increased scientific, political and commercial interest that led to both controversy and progress. Controversies arose over the definitions and potential implications of nanotechnologies. The challenges arose from the feasibility of applications imagined by proponents of molecular nanotechnology, which culminated in a public debate between Drexler and Smalley in 2001 and 2003.

Meanwhile, commercialization of products based on advances in nanoscale technologies began to emerge. These products are limited to bulk applications of nanomaterials and do not involve atomic control of matter. Examples include the Nano Silver platform that uses silver nanoparticles as an antibacterial agent, transparent sunscreens based on nanoparticles, and carbon nanotubes for stain-resistant fabrics.

Governments moved to the promotion and funding of nanotechnology research starting with the United States with its National Nanotechnology Initiative, which formalized the definition of nanotechnology based on size and created a fund for nanoscale research.

Today, medicine has more interest in research in the microscopic world, since it possibly contains the structural alterations caused by diseases. The branches of medicine that have benefited the most are microbiology, immunology and physiology. New sciences have also emerged such as genetic engineering, which has generated controversy over the repercussions of processes such as cloning or eugenics.

Human cloning is the creation of a genetically identical copy (or clone) of a human. The term is generally used to refer to artificial human cloning, which is the reproduction of human cells and tissue.

Eugenics is a set of beliefs and practices that aim to improve the genetic quality of a human population by excluding (through a variety of morally criticized means) certain genetic groups judged to be inferior, and promoting other genetic groups judged to be superior.

The development of nanoscience and nanotechnology in Latin America is relatively recent compared to what has happened globally. Countries such as Mexico, Costa Rica, Argentina, Venezuela, Colombia, Brazil and Chile contribute worldwide with research in different areas of nanoscience and nanotechnology. In addition, some of these countries also have educational programs at the bachelor's, master's, postgraduate and specialization levels in the area.

Traditional industries will be able to benefit from nanotechnology to improve their competitiveness in common sectors such as textiles, food, footwear, automotive, construction and health. The aim is for companies belonging to traditional sectors to incorporate and apply nanotechnology in their processes in order to contribute to the sustainability of employment.

The adoption of AI with nanotechnology has not been as widespread as other scientific industries but is growing. **AI can help with the future of nano computing**, that is, computation which is performed through nanoscale devices. There are currently many ways that these devices can perform a function, and these range from the physical operations to computational approaches. Because of a lot of these devices rely on complex physical systems to enable complex computational algorithms to be performed, machine learning methods can be employed to provide novel data representations for a wide range of applications.

Liam Critchley, writer and journalist who specializes in nanotechnology, writes about the convergence of AI and nanotechnology: "Artificial Intelligence (AI) has been an increasingly growing area for many years now; not just within itself, where the areas of machine learning, deep learning and artificial neural networks (ANNs) are now powerful methods in their own right, but also in the amount of areas and industries that they are now prevalent in....AI can also help with the future of nanocomputing, that is, computation which is performed through nanoscale devices. There are currently many ways that these devices can perform a function, and these range from the physical operations to computational approaches. Because of a lot of these devices rely on complex physical systems (e.g. plasmons) to enable complex computational algorithms to be performed, machine learning methods can be employed to provide novel data representations for a wide range of applications." (https://bit.ly/2mhD6ZU)

3D printing

Three-dimensional printing is revolutionizing the production of all types of objects and is projected as one of the technologies of greatest application in the near future.

Although several ideas on 3D printing were generated in previous years, **Charles Hull is considered the inventor of stereo lithography,** a printing process that allows a 3D object to be created from digital data. The technology is used to create a 3D model from an image and allows users to test a design before investing in manufacturing the final model. Charles Hull founded the company 3D Systems in Rock Hill, South Carolina in 1986 to manufacture and sell 3D printers and systems.

The basic idea originated in inkjet printers. Instead of using an inkjet, plastic materials are used to print one layer on top of another according to the design of the computer until the desired object is produced. Various materials are currently used in addition to plastic: powders, resins, metal, carbon fiber, graphite and paper.

Depending on the printer used, the plastic or bonding material is deposited on the construction bed layer by layer until the layering material/binder is completed and the final 3D model is "printed". A standard data interface between CAD software and machine software is the STL (STereo Lithography) file format. It is a computer-aided design file format that defines geometry of 3D objects, excluding information such as color, textures, or physical properties. An STL file approximates the shape of a part or assembly using triangular facets. Smaller facets produce a higher quality surface. CAPA is an input file format analyzer used as input for 3D printing technologies that are capable of printing in full color.

When they appeared a few years ago, they began to be used to build models and small objects at an industrial level, but over time their technology has been improved and thanks to this, as well as to the ingenuity of many people, their use has been increasing. The variety of things that can be made with a 3D printer is very wide since it is possible to create small tools, toys or even jewelry. Its versatility is very wide, and one could say that its possibilities in the future are infinite. One of the great hopes lies in the ability to make advances in the field of medicine to produce organs such as a heart or kidney and graft them into a human body. Musical instruments, drones, automobiles, houses and weapons have been printed. The latter has alerted the authorities to the danger they represent and although they do not always work, the most skilled have managed to create relatively reliable weapons.

Tim Weingärtner, professor, Lucerne University of Applied Sciences and Arts, sees a convergence between Artificial Intelligence, **3D printing,** IoT and other technologies. "The amount of digital data available in the world, he said, is growing exponentially, and with it we are seeing the growth of a new digital realm in parallel to the physical world. In this digital realm we will have IoT to gather data ("see" and "feel"), AI to analyze data and make decisions ("think"), agents like robots, **3D printers,** etc. to carry out actions in the physical world ("act"), For its part, blockchain can play a crucial role by allowing us to create "digital twins", unique, non-counterfeit able digital representations of the physical world – be they of people, organizations or objects – and to provide trust in data, allowing us among other things to transact in a fully digital, trustworthy way." (https://bit.ly/2mhE5JA)

New materials

The world is surprised by the new materials used for the production of clothing, household goods, house building, automobiles, airplanes, boats, kitchen utensils, containers, furniture, etc. The production of all these new materials is one of the technologies that drives AI Revolution.

The activity to produce new materials is so intense that it has given rise to the birth of a science and formal studies in several universities. **Materials science** is the scientific field responsible for investigating the relationship between the structure and properties of materials. It is a multidisciplinary field that studies the fundamental knowledge about the macroscopic physical properties of materials and applies them in various areas of science and engineering, so that they can be used in various works, machines and tools, or turn them into products necessary or required by society. It includes elements of chemistry and physics, as well as chemical, mechanical, civil and electrical engineering, medicine, biology and environmental sciences. With the focus on nanoscience and nanotechnology in recent years, materials science has been promoted in many universities.

Radical advances in materials technology may lead to the creation of new products or the flourishing of new industries, but today's industries in turn need materials scientists to increase improvements and locate possible breakdowns of materials in use. Industrial applications of materials science include material choice, material cost benefit, processing techniques and analysis techniques.

In addition to the characterization of the material, the material scientist or engineer must also deal with the extraction and its subsequent conversion into useful materials. Ingots molding, melting techniques, blast furnace extraction, electrolytic extraction, etc., are part of the knowledge required in a metallurgical engineer or an industrial engineer to assess the capabilities of that material.

In materials science, metals, ceramics and polymers are recognized as categories, and any material can be included in one of these categories. Semiconductors belong to ceramic materials and composite materials are only mixtures of materials belonging to the main categories. The science of new materials is very important and both companies and countries compete for a leading position.

Steve Bednarczyk writes: "The convergence of mind and matter, of digital and physical technologies lies at the heart of the Fourth Industrial Revolution. The marriage of Artificial Intelligence (A.I.) and materials science represents one of the clearest examples. Pure digital innovation has attracted the greatest attention—and a large share of financial investment—over the last several years. But we live in a material world, where the quality of our lives depends on improvements in physical products and services: food and shelter, health care, transportation, energy. True, we spend a lot more time in our online virtual worlds; but this is mirrored by a growing number of Amazon packages at our doorsteps. Our ability to discover and master new materials has defined successive stages of economic development: wood and clay; bronze and steel; paper; glass; plastics; semiconductors. It is our mastery of silicone that allowed the digital revolution to unfold. Now we can harness the power of digital technologies to accelerate the discovery of new materials, by marrying A.I. and materials science. The Canadian Institute for Advanced Research reported earlier this year that leveraging A.I. could cut the average time needed to develop a new material to one-two years from the current 10-20 years. A.I. often conjures dystopian images of mass unemployment; but this is instead another example of the power of human-machine collaboration." (https://bit.ly/2kLhG6Y)

Pure digital innovation has attracted the greatest attention—and a large share of financial investment—over the last several years. But we live in a material world, where the quality of our lives depends on improvements in physical products and services: food and shelter, health care, transportation, energy. Our ability to discover and master new materials has defined successive stages of economic development: wood and clay; bronze and steel; paper; glass; plastics; semiconductors. It is our mastery of silicone that allowed the digital revolution to unfold.

Now we can harness the power of digital technologies to accelerate the discovery of new materials, by marrying AI and materials science. **The Canadian Institute for Advanced Research** reported earlier this year that leveraging AI could cut the average time needed to develop a new material to one-two years from the current 10-20 years.

In a recent interview, **Greg Mulholland,** founder and CEO of Citrine Informatics, stresses that the role of AI in materials science is to enable scientists to formulate better hypotheses at a faster pace, and test them more rapidly. Human expertise remains crucial; **AI helps material scientists identify and compare a much wider range of options.**

Manufacturing today benefits from three waves of innovation: new production techniques (like 3-D printing), new design methods (like generative design, also driven by AI) and new materials. These three waves of innovation are interdependent and mutually reinforcing: 3-D printing allows us to manufacture components with different geometries, yielding greater resistance, lighter weight and better performance; finding new geometries requires a different approach to design, where AI helps us break free from the mental constraints acquired through decades of traditional manufacturing methods; new materials can in turn broaden the range of possible design solutions.

Each of these trends is powerful in itself, but bringing them together compounds their transformational potential, for example by co-optimizing new geometries and new materials. Going forward, we are likely to see the powerful impact of new materials across a range of sectors: more efficient batteries for electric vehicles, more environmentally-friendly plastics and dyes, new 3-D printed artificial organs and other medical implants.

Companies operating in the materials space will have to adapt. While past phases of economic development have been characterized by one or a few dominant materials, the future will shift towards greater specialization, towards a wider range of new materials individually suited to specific applications. For companies in the materials space, success will hinge on the ability to quickly identify, design and develop the new materials that can best meet the shifting priorities of their customers. Companies will need a different set of skills, bringing together material scientists and data scientists and, increasingly, experts conversant in both data and materials science. **The coming together of AI and materials science** can help boost manufacturing productivity; and innovations in tangible reality might prove as exciting as those of virtual and augmented reality.

Internet of Things (IoT)

Internet speed and advances in information technology are driving the Internet of Things better known by its abbreviation IoT to be considered one of the most important technologies of AI Revolution. IoT is a concept that refers to a digital interconnection of everyday objects with Internet. It is the Internet connection with objects rather than people. It is also often referred to as the Internet of all things. If the objects of everyday life had built-in radio tags, they could be identified and managed by other teams in the same way as if they were by human beings.

The concept of the Internet of things was proposed in 1999 by **Kevin Ashton** at MIT's Auto-ID Center, where research was being conducted in the field of networked radio frequency identification (RFID) and sensor technologies. For example, if books, thermostats, refrigerators, packaging, lamps, first aid kits, automotive parts, among others, were connected to the Internet and equipped with identification devices, there would theoretically be no out-of-stock items or expired medicines. We would know exactly the location, how they are consumed in the world and loss would become a thing of the past. We would know what is on and what is off at all times.

The IoT could theoretically encode 50 to 100 billion objects and track the movement of these. **It is estimated that every human being is surrounded, at least, by a total of approximately 1,000 to 5,000 objects.** According to Gartner, in 2020 there will be in the world approximately 26 billion devices with an Internet connection system of things. Abi Research states that for the same year there will be 30 billion wireless devices connected to the Internet.

The US company Cisco, which supports the Internet of things initiative, has created a dynamic "connection counter" that allows it to estimate the number of "things" connected from July 2013 to 2020. Connecting devices to the network through low-power radio signals is the Internet's most active field of study of things.

Applications for Internet-connected devices are broad. Multiple categories have been suggested, but most agree to separate applications into three main branches of use: consumer, business, and infrastructure. George Osborne, a former finance cabinet member, proposes that IoT is the next stage in the information revolution, referring to the interconnectivity of everything from urban transport to medical devices to household appliances.

The ability to connect embedded devices with limited CPU, memory and power capabilities means IoT can have applications in almost any area. These systems could be responsible for collecting information in different environments: from natural ecosystems to buildings and factories, so they could be used for environmental monitoring and urban planning.

Smart shopping systems, for example, could follow the buying habits of a specific user by tracking their mobile phone. These users could be guided to the location of the items they need to buy. These items would be on a list automatically created by your smart refrigerator on your mobile phone. More cases of use can be found in applications that deal with heating, water supply, electricity, energy management, and even intelligent transportation systems that assist the driver. Other applications that the Internet can provide of things are adding security features and home automation. The concept of an **"Internet of living things"** has been proposed, describing networks of biological sensors that could use cloud-based analysis to allow users to study DNA and other molecules.

An increasing percentage of IoT devices are created for consumption. Examples of consumer applications include connected automobiles, entertainment, home automation, clothing, health and household appliances such as washing machines, dryers, robotic vacuum cleaners, air purifiers, ovens and refrigerators that use Wi-Fi for remote monitoring.

IoT devices can be used for remote patient tracking and emergency notification systems. These devices can range from blood pressure and pulse monitoring to devices capable of tracking specialized implants such as pacemakers, electronic bracelets or sophisticated hearing aids. Some hospitals have begun to use "smart beds" that detect when they are occupied and when a patient tries to get up. It can also be automatically adjusted to ensure that the patient has adequate support without nurse interaction.

Specialized sensors can be installed in living spaces **to monitor the health and overall well-being of older people.** Other consumer IoT devices encourage healthy living, e.g. connected scales or portable heart monitors. More comprehensive tracking IoT platforms are appearing for prenatal and chronic patients that help track of vital signs and administer necessary medication. According to the latest research, the US Department of Health plans to save up to 300 billion in the national budget due to medical innovations.

Joseph Zulick, manager at MRO Electric and Supply says: "Even though the full capability of AI and IoT are still in their relative infancy, these two technology superpowers are now being combined across every industry in scenarios where information and problem-solving can improve outcomes for all stakeholders. The last great convergence of this magnitude occurred in the late 1990's as mobile phones and the internet were on a collision course that has changed the course of human history in a significant manner. Most people now hold more computing power in the palm of their hand than was required to put a man on the Moon in 1969. The convergence of AI and IoT is about to do the same thing on an even greater scale." (https://bit.ly/2XaJeVy)

Virtual Reality

Virtual reality (VR) is the use of computer technology to create a simulated environment. Unlike traditional user interfaces, VR places the user inside an experience. Instead of viewing a screen in front of them, **users are immersed and able to interact with 3D worlds.** Simulating as many senses as possible such as vision, hearing, touch, even smell, the computer is transformed into a gatekeeper to this artificial world. This environment is contemplated by the user through a device known as **virtual reality glasses or helmet.** This can be accompanied by other devices, such as gloves or special suits, which allow greater interaction with the environment as well as the perception of different stimuli that intensify the sensation of reality.

The term virtual reality (VR) became popular in the late 1980s by **Jaron Lanier**, one of the pioneers of the field. The Encyclopedia Britannica describes virtual reality as "The use of computer modeling and simulation that allows a person to interact with an artificial three-dimensional (3D) sensory environment or other sensory environment." In addition, it states that "virtual reality applications immerse the user in a computer-generated environment that simulates reality through the use of interactive devices that send and receive information and are used as glasses, headphones, gloves or body suits." For example, a user using a head-mounted screen with a stereoscopic projection system can see animated images of a virtual environment. An important term is presence or telepresence, which can be described as an illusion of being there.

Presence is defined as "the fact or condition of being present; the state of being with or in the same place as a person or thing; attendance, company, society or association", although presence also has different meanings. In the early 1990s, the term presence was increasingly used to describe the subjective experience of participants in a virtual environment.

These types of definitions follow a transport metaphor, as the user perceives himself to be in a different place. In addition to considering presence as transport, the concept can be defined as social wealth when used for human interaction in organizations as the degree of realism of the environment shown or as the degree of immersion. In trying to find a common denominator for all these definitions, a general definition of presence as a **"perceptual illusion of non-mediation"** was suggested.

In contrast to presence, immersion is generally defined as a quantifiable feature of the system, which describes the ability of a system to display an artificially generated environment in a manner that approximates actual experience. The characteristics of highly immersive systems are real-time interaction, stereoscopic vision, high frame rate and resolution, and multiple displays (visual, auditory and haptic).

Non-immersive systems have gained popularity due to their lower cost, ease of use and ease of installation. They are sometimes called **desktop-based virtual reality systems;** the most representative examples are video games. The good combination of interactivity, ease of use, attractive graphics and sound can generate a high level of user interest and participation in the simulation. Few virtual reality systems can compete with a good video game in terms of psychologically isolating the user from the world and producing strong emotional responses.

The psychological aspects of the virtual reality experience are an area of active research. It is not entirely clear what factors in a simulation can produce specific user reactions in terms of emotional response, participation, and degree of interest. One of the most important concepts that helps us understand the psychology of the virtual reality experience is the **"sense of presence"**.

The use of the virtual reality helmet allows users to perceive stereoscopic 3D images and determine the spatial position in the visual environment through movement tracking sensors in the helmet. Meanwhile, users can listen to sounds through headphones and interact with virtual objects using input devices such as joysticks, rods and data gloves. As a result, users feel they can look around and move through the simulated environment.

Virtual reality applies to various areas, including adult industry, art, education, entertainment and video games as well as interactive storytelling, militia, education and medicine. Due to its dizzying growth it is predicted that it will cover other industries.

John DeCleene, global citizen and VR expert writes: "When we talk about modern innovation, two technologies stand out – Virtual Reality (VR) and Artificial Intelligence (AI). While one aims to create an alternate reality for us, the other tries to equip computers with perception and insight of a sentient being. In recent years, we've taken huge steps toward refining both and one can't shrug the idea of combining both to unravel infinite possibilities. Merging AI and VR can lead to creation of some mind-bending environments." (https://bit.ly/2kNdpQj)

Alternative energy sources

In the first stage of the Industrial Revolution the most important source of energy was coal that later became steam to power the locomotive and other engines in both industry and transportation. In the second stage electricity appears that gives a renewed impulse to industrialization to boost the motors of industries and to illuminate work centers, homes and the streets of the nascent cities.

Alternative energy sources are those energy sources proposed as an alternative to the traditional ones. However, there is no consensus regarding which technologies are included in this concept, and the definition of "alternative energy" differs according to different authors: in the most restrictive definitions, alternative energy would be equivalent to the concept of renewable energy or green energy, while broader definitions consider alternative energy as all energy sources that do not involve the burning of fossil fuels (coal, gas and oil); in these definitions, in addition to renewable energy, nuclear energy or even hydroelectric energy are included.

Fossil fuels have been the source of energy used during the Industrial Revolution, but at present there are basically two problems: they are finite resources, and the depletion of reserves (especially oil) is predicted in a near term, depending on the different studies published. On the other hand, the burning of these fuels releases large quantities of CO_2 into the atmosphere, which has been blamed of **being the main cause of global warming**. For these reasons, different options are being studied to replace the burning of fossil fuels with other energy sources that do not have these problems.

Alternative energies are divided into two main groups:

- **Renewable energy sources** (wind, solar, biomass, tidal, etc.).
- Nuclear energy

Not everyone agrees in classifying nuclear energy as an alternative energy, since, like fossil fuels, it is a finite resource and also presents important environmental problems, such as the management of radioactive waste or the possibility of a nuclear accident. However, the reduced CO_2 emission from this technology, and the still insufficient capacity of renewable energies to completely replace fossil fuels, make nuclear energy an alternative subject to strong controversy.

With better computer technology AI has scaled new heights in utility and application, exceeding all initial expectations. Currently, the global energy market is undergoing a massive shift with the emergence of decarbonization, decentralization, and new technologies. Utilities, independent power producers (IPPs), and other energy companies are exploring effective ways to manage the imbalance in supply and demand caused by the growing use of unpredictable renewable energy sources (RES) in power generation. Therefore, utilities, energy companies, and grid operators are exploring ways to employ AI technologies to improve the accessibility and efficiency of renewable energy technologies. Despite its nascence, AI possesses tremendous potential to transform the energy & utilities sector. In combination with other technologies like big data and IoT, it can aid the active management of electricity grids by balancing supply and demand.

Blockchain

Speculation with Bitcoin and its dizzying rise in the stock market contributed significantly to putting the blockchain technology in the media. The blockchain concept was first implemented in 2009 as part of Bitcoin. However, crypto currencies are not the only application. Blockchain has several interesting applications in industry, banking and other fields.

Blockchain was invented by a person (or group of people) using the name Satoshi Nakamoto in 2008 to serve as the public transaction ledger of the cryptocurrency bitcoin. The identity of Satoshi Nakamoto is unknown. The invention of the blockchain for bitcoin made it the first digital currency to solve the double-spending problem without the need of a trusted authority or central server.

Blockchain or string of blocks is a data structure in which the information contained is grouped into sets (blocks) to which metainformation are added relative to another block of the previous string in a timeline, so that thanks to cryptographic techniques, the information contained in a block can only be repudiated or edited by modifying all subsequent blocks. This property allows its application in a distributed environment so that the blockchain data structure can act as a non-relational public database containing an irrefutable history of information. In practice it has allowed, thanks to asymmetric cryptography and summary or hash functions, the implementation of a distributed accounting record (ledger) that supports and guarantees the security of digital money. By following an appropriate protocol for all operations carried out on the blockchain it is possible to reach a consensus on the integrity of their data by all network participants without the need to resort to a trusted entity that centralizes the information.

This is why it is considered a technology in which the "truth" (reliable state of the system) is built, reached and strengthened by the members themselves; even in an environment in which there is a minority of nodes in the network with malicious behavior (Sybil nodes) since, in theory, to compromise the data, an attacker would require more computing power and presence in the network than the resultant of the sum of all the other nodes combined. For the above reasons, blockchain technology is especially suitable for scenarios in which it is required to store increasingly ordered data over time, without the possibility of modification or revision and whose confidence is intended to be distributed instead of residing in a certifier entity. This approach has different aspects:

- **Data storage**: achieved by replicating information from the blockchain

- **Data transmission**: this is achieved through peer-to-peer networks.

- **Data confirmation**: this is achieved through a consensus process among the participating nodes. The most commonly used type of algorithm is the working test in which there is an open competitive and transparent process of validation of new entries called mining.

Mining, in the context of blockchain technology, is the process of adding transactions to the large distributed public ledger of existing transactions, known as the blockchain. The term is best known for its association with bitcoin, though other technologies using the blockchain employ mining. Bitcoin mining rewards people who run mining operations with more bitcoins. Mining is intentionally designed to be resource-intensive and difficult so that the number of blocks found each day by miners remains steady. Individual blocks must contain a proof of work to be considered valid. This proof of work is verified by other Bitcoin nodes each time they receive a block. Bitcoin uses the hash cash proof-of-work function. The primary purpose of mining is to set the history of transactions in a way that is computationally impractical to modify by any one entity. By downloading and verifying the blockchain, bitcoin nodes are able to reach consensus about the ordering of events in bitcoin.

The data stored in the blockchain is usually financial transactions. However, they do not need to be. We could really consider that what is recorded are atomic changes in the state of the system. For example, a chain of blocks can be used to encrypt documents and secure them against alterations.

Strings of blocks can be classified based on access to the data stored in them:

- **Public blockchain**: it is the one in which there are no restrictions either to read the data of the blockchain (which may have been encrypted) or to send transactions to be included in the blockchain. They are easy to enter and exit, they are transparent, are built with a caution for operation in an unreliable environment and are ideal for use in fully decentralized applications such as the Internet.

- **Private blockchain**: it is the one in which both the accesses to the data of the blockchain and the sending of included transactions are limited to a predefined list of entities.

Both types of strings must be considered as extreme cases and there may be intermediate cases.

Strings of blocks can be classified based on the permissions to generate blocks:

Blockchain without permissions: it is the one in which there are no restrictions for entities to process transactions and create blocks. These types of blockchain need native tokens to provide incentives for users to maintain the system. Examples of native tokens are the new bitcoins that are obtained when building a block and the commissions of the transactions. The amount rewarded for creating new blocks is a good measure of the security of a chain of blocks without permissions.

Blockchain with permissions: it is the one in which the processing of transactions is developed by a predefined list of subjects with known identities. For this reason they generally do not need native tokens. Native tokens are necessary to provide incentives for transaction processors. For this reason it is typical that they use as a consensus protocol proof of participation.

The use of a chain of blocks has made possible to solve two problems related to the exchange of assets without a trusted certifier body. In addition, trust is another intrinsic feature of the system. From the legal point of view, Bitcoin would be a patrimonial, private, incorporeal, digital asset, in the form of a unit of account, created through a computer system and used as a common measure of value by agreement of the users of the system. Its future looks promising.

Jean-Charles Cabelguen, executive of the high-tech company iExec sees a convergence between Artificial Intelligence and blockchain. "When talking about AI, he said, you need to differentiate between soft AI, which is trained on datasets, and strong AI, which learns by itself from its environment. The latter is still in the R&D phase. Another important trend is edge computing, in which a certain degree of data processing is carried out on the device, not in the data center in the cloud. This can improve efficiency and speed. AI and blockchain are transversal technologies, he added, to be used for industrial purposes: they do not exist in vacuums. We are already seeing a convergence of AI and blockchain teams within big companies. This is an important indication of the ultimate convergence and integration of these technologies. Blockchain can help AI in terms of scaling data aggregation (allowing for multiple data sets and the renting of data), managing the sharing of computer resources, and in creating a more transparent and trustworthy data economy."

Augmented Reality

Augmented reality (AR) is the union of the real and virtual world to create new conditions for the image, where physical and digital objects coexist and interact in real time. This means projecting a layer of digital information about reality that can include audio, images and graphics, as well as text-based information. It is a set of technologies that allow a user to visualize part of the real world through a technological device with graphic information added by the software. This device adds virtual information to the already existing physical information; that is to say, a virtual synthetic part to the real one. In this way, tangible physical elements are combined with virtual elements to create an augmented reality in real time.

In 1992 Tom Caudell coined the term augmented reality, followed by definitions related to it in the media. One of them was given by Ronald Azuma (1997). Azuma's definition says augmented reality:

- combines real and virtual elements.
- is interactive in real time.
- is registered in 3D.

Augmented reality is totally different from virtual reality. On the material reality of the physical world it mounts a visual reality generated by technology, in which the user perceives a mixture of the two realities; in virtual reality the user isolates himself from the material reality of the physical world, to submerge himself in a totally virtual scenario or environment.

Augmented reality allows the creation of a virtual world through 3D graphic design. It is a world in which there are no limits and where you can see, create and do multiple things. While it is true that the experience is increasingly realistic, the basis on which this world is based is fantasy.

Augmented reality is becoming as one of the most promising technologies of the moment. Since the smartphone revolution, virtually everyone uses one continuously in their day-to-day life. These devices have a processor, GPS, screen, camera, microphone, etc., everything you need to have AR experiences. AR developers have been taking advantage of this for the last few years, focusing mainly on the creation and development of applications (apps). Because of this, among other things, AR technology is continuously growing and capturing the attention of a multitude of users around the world. In fact, you may have been experimenting with AR yourself in the last few days without realizing it. Social networks like Snapchat and Instagram have filters and effects that can be used in your stories, and that are actually AR technology that we use in our everyday life.

Due to the great advance and benefits that this new technology provides, we can also affirm that it is the favorite within the scope of the military. The US military wants to "improve the lethality" of its soldiers by improving their ability to detect, decide and confront the enemy. How, exactly? With the help of AR and helmets developed by companies such as Magic Leap or Microsoft, able to create a simulation as interesting as if it were a video game

The ultimate goal of this new technology is that during training, soldiers wear augmented reality devices and simulate attacks with chemical weapons or ambushes. The practices would be recorded from all angles and analyzed later for the repetition of the exercise and the improvement of the given response. In its final version, they want the device used by these soldiers to have integrated communications, thermal and night vision and a system for monitoring vital signs and breathing.

With AR it is possible to identify, locate, obtain, store, organize and analyze digital information, evaluating its purpose and relevance. It is defined as an efficient resource to share through open resources, such as communities and networks, allowing teachers to create new digital content. Through AR, learning can be developed faster and more efficiently by enabling enriched interaction with knowledge associated with increased student motivation.

Its application in kindergarten and elementary education is done through books with AR that allows contributing to the creation of experiences of enriched reading by incorporating an immersive component that structures the content in an innovative way. The dynamics of these new technologies have great novelties and surprises prepared daily. Augmented reality has entered a number of areas of our daily work becoming part of our real world and its environment.

Bas Grasmayer, product director at IDAGIO writes about trends and innovation in tech and says: "In order to understand the significance of a lot of today's hype-surrounded topics, you have to link them. Artificial intelligence, smart homes, IoT and augmented reality will all click together seamlessly a decade from now. And that shift is already well underway.

In recent years, there have been big advances in Artificial Intelligence. This has a lot to do with the availability of large data sets that can be used to train AI. A connected world is a quantified world and data sets are continuously updated. This is useful for training algorithms that are capable of learning.

This is also what has given rise to the whole chatbot explosion right now. Our user interfaces are changing: instead of doing things ourselves, explicitly, AI can be trained to interpret our requests or even predict and anticipate them.

Conversational interfaces sucked 15 years ago. They came with a booklet. You had to memorize all the voice commands. You had to train the interface to get used to your voice... Why not just use a remote control? Or a mouse and keyboard? But in the future, getting things done by tapping on our screens may look as archaic as it would be to do everything from a command-line interface

You've probably already been using AR. Two current examples of popular augmented reality apps: Snapchat and Pokémon Go. The latter is a great example of how you can design a virtual interaction layer for the physical world.

So the context in which you have to imagine augmented reality reaching maturity is a world in which our environments are smart and understand our intentions... in some cases predicting them before we even become aware of them.

Our smart environments will interact with our AR device to pull up HUDs when we most need them. So we won't have to do awkward voice commands, because a lot of the time, it will already be taken care of.

This means we don't actually have to wear computers on our heads. Meaning that the future of augmented reality can come through contact lenses, rather than headsets.

But who actually wants to bother with that, right? What's the point if you can already do everything you need right now? Perhaps you're too young to remember, but that's exactly what people said about mobile phones years ago. Even without contact lenses, all of these trends are underway now.

Augmented reality is an audiovisual medium, so if you want to prepare, spend some time learning about video game design, conversational interfaces, and get used to sticking your head in front of a camera.

There will be so many opportunities emerging on the way there, from experts on privacy and security (even political movements), to designing the experiences, to new personalities... because AR will have its own PewDiePie.

It's why I just bought a mic and am figuring out a way to add audiovisual content to the mix of what I produce for MUSIC x TECH x FUTURE. Not to be the next PewDiePie, but to be able to embrace mediums that will extend into trends that will shape our digital landscapes for the next 20 years." (https://bit.ly/2kNv76f)

-8-

THE US-CHINA TECHNOLOGY WAR

The First Industrial Revolution was born in England without competition with any other nation. England was the Master of the Seas and the great empire on Planet Earth in the 18th century. The United Kingdom had the optimal conditions for industrial take-off as it had iron and coal as essential raw materials for industry, adequate transportation to distribute goods and the maritime domain to control the routes and provide themselves with the raw materials they needed from America.

The Second Industrial Revolution also found fertile soil in England, but the competition from the US and other European countries was already beginning. In the third stage of the Industrial Revolution the United States showed great strength and took the lead. In the fourth stage Germany was placed at the head of the industrialized countries of Europe but the United States kept the world leadership. However, at this stage China occupies a predominant place followed by Japan and South Korea. Geopolitical conditions indicate that there will be a great battle between the United States and China to conquer technological supremacy. That battle is currently being waged in the form of a trade war, but under the table there is a fierce battle for technological mastery. **The hill that both countries dispute is Artificial Intelligence**. The victorious country will dominate the world.

Trade war

President Donald Trump signed a memorandum on March 22, 2018 under Section 301 of the Trade Act of 1974, ordering the United States Trade Representative (USTR) to apply tariffs of 50 billion to Chinese products. In a formal statement, as required by law, Trump said the proposed tariffs were "a response to China's unfair trade practices over the years," including the theft of intellectual property.

On April 2, China's Ministry of Commerce imposed tariffs on 128 US products, including aluminum scrap, airplanes, automobiles, pork products and soybeans (which have a 25% tariff), as well as fruit, nuts and steel pipes (15%). The next day, the USTR published a list of more than 1,300 categories of Chinese imports worth 50 billion that were expected to establish tariffs, including aircraft parts, batteries, flat-screen televisions, medical devices, satellites and weapons.

In retaliation for that announcement, China imposed an additional 25% tax on aircraft, automobiles and soybeans, which is the main US agricultural export to China. On April 5, Trump ordered the USTR to consider additional tariffs of 100 billion.

In May, China cancelled US soybean orders. On May 20, Treasury Secretary Steven Mnuchin, in an interview with Fox News, said that "we are putting the trade war on hold." The BBC reported June 3 that China had "warned that all trade negotiations between Beijing and Washington will be void if the United States establishes trade sanctions."

On June 15 Trump confirmed the imposition of a 25% tariff on 50 billion Chinese exports, of which 34 billion would be taxed on July 6, while the remaining 16 billion would be taxed at a later date. China's Commerce Minister accused the United States of initiating a trade war and said China would respond with similar tariffs to US imports. Three days later, the White House declared that the United States would establish additional tariffs of 10 percent to another 200 billion Chinese imports if China responded to US measures. China replied almost immediately by threatening tariffs on 50 billion US goods and reaffirming the "start of a trade war" by the United States. On August 8, the USTR published the final list of 279 Chinese goods, worth 16 billion, that would be subject to 25% tariffs.

China initiated World Trade Organization (WTO) dispute settlement proceedings concerning United States tariffs on imports of crystalline silicon photovoltaic products and measures related to renewable energy. US Treasury under Secretary for International Affairs David Malpass and China's Deputy Commerce Minister Wang Shouwen met in Washington DC on August 22 in an attempt to restart negotiations. The next day, August 23, tariffs imposed on

Chinese goods worth 16 billion began. Thus, on August 27, China initiated a new WTO proceeding.

On December 1, during the G-20 meeting in Argentina, the presidents of both countries agreed to postpone the imposition of new trade tariffs for 90 days to allow negotiations to resume.

Negotiations continued in an atmosphere of tension and calm.

But announcing a truce does not mean that the trade war is over. Tariffs valued in billions of dollars that were imposed on the import of goods are still in force. And both sides have many issues to agree on.

Washington wants Beijing, in essence, to change the way China's economy has grown over the past four decades, eliminate subsidies to state-owned enterprises, open its domestic market and, more importantly, wants it to be held accountable if it fails to meet any of these commitments. But Beijing has already said publicly that it will not give in on matters of principle or give in to pressure from the United States.

The commercial war with China can escalate and become a financial war. Ray Dalio, founder of the world's largest hedge fund, co-chief investment officer and co-chairman of Bridgewater Associates, said "reports of the US limiting capital flows to China may just be the start." Dalio notes in a post to LinkedIn that the US president can unilaterally cut off capital flows to China, freeze payments on the debts owed to China and use sanctions to inhibit non-American financial transactions with China. (https://bit.ly/2okAECZ)

"There is a rising power (China) challenging the existing world power (the US), which will probably lead to more conflicts between them about many different issues. History has shown that this situation has led to the increased risk of wars that typically come in four forms: trade wars, capital wars, technology wars, and geopolitical wars. As far as the trade wars go, you can see them for yourself (so I won't delve into them) and probably have yourself drawn comparisons with the Smoot-Hawley Tariffs in 1930 and with various tariffs in several countries during the 1930s. Regarding the capital and currency wars, the ability of the US president to unilaterally cut off capital flows to China and also freeze payments on the debts owed to China and also use sanctions to inhibit non-American financial transactions with China must be considered as possibilities. That's why the proposed step of limiting American portfolio investments in China makes me both think about the implications of this step and wonder if it is an inching toward bigger moves." Ray Dalio said.

The tension surrounding current US-China relations goes far beyond a trade war. Tariffs are discussed on the table, but below the table the war is for technological supremacy and specifically for the domain of Artificial Intelligence.

Technology war

The US-China trade war is, at its core, a battle for technological supremacy and the enormous economic, commercial, and national security advantages that go with it.

China's bold plan under president Xi Jinping to dominate in the field of technology led US companies operating in China to complain for years about forced transfers of technology and theft of intellectual property. As tensions mount after Huawei Technologies was blacklisted in the United States, the ghost of a technological cold war is materializing.

The United States has created the world's most valuable technology companies and major players in software, smartphones, e-commerce, search engines, and social networks. Today Microsoft, Amazon, Apple, Google and Facebook are the most capital-valued companies in the world and the most influential in their technology sector. However, China's technology sector has skyrocketed in the past five years with Alibaba, Tencent, Huawei, Baidu, Xiaomi and others making their way to the top of the global companies. Capitalization is not only a measure of how the market values these companies, it also shows how much financial capital they have to make acquisitions, hire talent, raise capital and invest in new technologies.

The United States was for a long time the world's largest and most important Internet market, but China surpassed the United States because of the size of its population. The Asian giant now has four times as many mobile users as the United States, providing opportunities for domestic companies in everything from e-commerce, search engines, e-mail, gaming and digital payments.

While China has the advantage in number of users, US consumers have much more purchasing power, generating nearly seven times per capita GDP of their Chinese counterparts. That gives US technology companies an environment to generate revenue, whether it's for use in developing the next big high-tech product or simply for profit.

US introduced the idea of venture capital and used the private equity model to create many of the world's most powerful technology companies. For its part, China has closed the money gap with backing capital provided by the central government. This has led to an increase in the number of one billion capital new companies in China, with as many unicorns created as there are in the US

A **unicorn** is a privately held startup company valued at over 1 billion. The term was coined in 2013 by venture capitalist Aileen Lee, choosing the mythical animal to represent the statistical rarity of such successful ventures. Decacorn is a word used for those companies over 10 billion.

Semiconductors are the raw material that brings power to the heart of the technological revolution. US companies have the advantage now, controlling most intellectual property and dwarfing Chinese competitors in production. Huawei's chip unit, HI Silicon, China's largest semiconductor company, had revenues of 7.6 billion last year (2018). That's about a tenth of the revenue of Intel, the chip giant of the United States. Chinese semiconductor companies also require software from Cadence and Synopsys for design and equipment from Applied Materials and Lam Research to manufacture semiconductors.

When it comes to the most sought-after Artificial Intelligence experts, China continues to catch up. At the end of 2017, the United States led the world with more than 28,000 people educated in AI compared to about 18,000 in China, according to estimates from Tsinghua University's School of Public Policy and Management. But the gap may be closing. The World Economic Forum said in a report that China had 4.7 million recent graduates in science, technology, engineering and mathematics (STEM) in 2016, while the United States had only 568,000. A good part of these technology graduates will be professionals in Artificial Intelligence and some will be brilliant scientists who will contribute knowledge to drive the 4.0 Industry in China.

Fred Dunkley writes in an article published on the Safe haven website: "American education continues to fall behind China...While China is making moves to bolster STEM education as much as possible, the United States seems to have grown complacent on education, and STEM exists, but is hardly thriving. China's political leadership understands that STEM leadership means power...China is turning out STEM students at a ratio of 1: 293, compared to America's ratio of 1: 573...**The US won't be winning at global leadership in tech awards in the future at this rate.**" (https://bit.ly/2kMg3Ga)

Over the past two decades Apple and other leading US technology companies have shifted production to traditional Chinese manufacturers. Foxconn Technology Group, the leading manufacturer of iPhone employs one million workers in the peak season. US workers are more productive by the hour and continue to handle sensitive technologies such as aerospace products. But even taking into account the value added during manufacturing, China has far surpassed the United States.

China's technology companies are advancing rapidly, and some have displaced their counterparts from the United States in China's territory. This is a very important aspect of the technology war between the two powers because it impedes US advancement in the world's most populous country and strengthens China's businesses. In this battle the government of Xi Jinping plays an important role in that it supports the development of technology of Chinese companies as well as the nationalist spirit of the population that prefers to use the commercial services of Alibaba instead of Amazon or Baidu instead of Google and make their payments online with Alipay instead of Paypal.

The escalating trade war is starting to damage Apple's brand in China, according to a new survey of Chinese consumer trends. The brand consultancy Prophet surveyed 13,500 Chinese consumers and discovered that a wave of nationalism is sweeping across the country, deterring many from using US brands.

Apple plunged in the company's latest brand-relevance index, published on 18 September 2019, which asked respondents which brands they liked the most. Apple crashed to No.24 in the index, falling from No. 11 last year. Before the trade war began, Apple was No. 5. Rivals like Huawei soared in the index to the No. 2 spot, just behind Chinese payment service Alipay.

The survey suggests that increasing nationalism in China could kill US brands, especially if the trade war continues into the early 2020s. Calls for boycotting US brands have already circulated onto social media platforms in China, reaching millions of consumers who believe that it's their patriotic duty in this economic war to buy Chinese, not US.

Above the table, the United States and China negotiate a new trade agreement. Underneath the table both are waging a terrible technological war.

On October 7, 2019 the US blacklisted several companies **engaged in Artificial Intelligence** in China under the pretext that their technology is being used to attack the Muslim minority living in China.

Reuters publishes the news under this heading: "US widens blacklist to include China's top AI startups ahead of trade talks."

Reuters reports: "The U.S. government expanded its trade blacklist to include **some of China's top artificial intelligence startups,** punishing Beijing for its treatment of Muslim minorities and ratcheting up tensions ahead of high-level trade talks in Washington this week... The action bars the firms from buying components from U.S. companies without U.S. government approval - a potentially crippling move. It follows the same blueprint used by Washington in its attempt to limit the influence of Huawei Technologies Co Ltd for what it says are national security reasons."

Technology warfare occurs between technology companies supported by the governments of their respective countries. To better understand the technology war between China and the United States, we will briefly study the confrontation between their leading tech companies.

Amazon vs. Alibaba

Amazon.com, Inc. is a US-based e-commerce and cloud computing company headquartered in Seattle, Washington. Amazon was one of the first companies to sell goods over the Internet. Amazon also owns Alexa Internet, a9.com, Shopbop, Internet Movie Database, Zappos.com, DPreview.com and Twitch in Ireland, Canada, Australia, Germany, Austria, France, China, Japan, Italy, Spain, Brazil, Netherlands, India and Mexico to offer products from those countries. It is currently fully diversified into different product lines, offering software, video games, electronics, clothing, furniture, food, books, etc. It is the most valuable retail brand in the world according to the BrandZ index. The company was founded in 1994 by Jeff Bezos. In that year Bezos left his job as vice president of D. E. Shaw & Co., and moved to Seattle, where he began working on a business plan for what would eventually become Amazon.com. Bezos selected Amazon's name by looking at the dictionary. He chose the name Amazon because the Amazon River is an "exotic and different" place just as he planned for his store. The Amazon River is the "largest" in the world and he was planning to turn his store into the largest in the world. Market value: 960B (July 2019).

Alibaba Group is a Chinese consortium with 18 subsidiaries headquartered in Hangzhou, China dedicated to e-commerce on the Internet, including business-to-business, retail, and consumer-to-consumer portals. It also offers online payment services, a price comparison search engine and cloud data storage services. In 2012 two of Alibaba's portals together handled a trillion yuan (170 billion USD) in sales more than eBay and Amazon.com combined. The company operates mainly in the People's Republic of China. The consortium began operations in 1999, when Jack Ma founded the Alibaba.com website. The Alibaba.com portal has become the world's best-known platform for companies in any industry to find manufacturers of products not only from China, but from anywhere in the world, so it functions as a business-to-business portal. The Taobao portal, owned by Alibaba, is similar to eBay and has about a billion products and is one of the 20 most visited websites worldwide. Alibaba Group's sites handle more than 60% of the packages delivered in China. Alipay, Alibaba's online payment service, accounts for about half of all online payment transactions in China. Alibaba went public on Wall Street in 2014 becoming the largest IPO in history and raising some 25 billion. Market value: 450B (July 2019).

Google vs. Baidu

Google is a subsidiary of Alphabet Inc., a US-based multinational that specializes in products and services related to the Internet, software, electronic devices and other technologies. Google was founded by Larry Page and Sergey Brin who started Google as a university project in January 1996 when they were both graduate students in computer science at Stanford University. It is headquartered in Mountain View, California. On August 10, 2015 Google became the principal subsidiary of Alphabet Inc., a company created to better manage all of Google's products and services that operated primarily for research and development of new products and technologies. Google's main product is the Internet search engine, although it also offers other products and services such as Gmail, its map services Google Maps,

Google Street View and Google Earth, the YouTube video website and other web utilities such as Google Books, Google News and Google Chrome. Google leads the development of the Android operating system based on Linux aimed at smartphones, tablets, television and cars, as well as augmented reality glasses, Google Glass. With thousands of servers and data centers around the world, Google is capable of processing more than 5.6 billion searches per day (which translates into at least 2 trillion searches per year, 228 million searches per hour, 3.8 million searches per minute) and its search engine is the most visited website worldwide. Market value: 850B (July 2019).

Baidu (in Chinese, 百度; pinyin, Bǎidù; literally, "a hundred times") is a Beijing-based Chinese search engine founded in late 1999 by Robin Li and Eric Xu. Its design is similar to that of Google and includes the ability to search for news, images and songs, among other functions. Its name comes from a classic Chinese poem by the poet Xin Qiji, during the Song Dynasty, about a man who sought the love of his life. In February 2018 it was the fourth most visited Internet site in the world. Baidu's most popular feature, which other search engines such as Google do not offer, is the ability to search for audio files (MP3, WMA/SWF). This option is mainly used for searching Chinese pop music and the search results are surprisingly accurate. Baidu can perform these searches because the laws of the People's Republic of China do not prohibit putting music on the Internet and Baidu is under Chinese jurisdiction. Baidu.com made its public offering on August 5, 2005 placing 12.5 percent of its capital. Baidu.com shares had a placement price of 27.8 per share. At the close of the NASDAQ session that day, Baidu.com shares were trading at 122.54 (a 353% appreciation). It was the best performance on the first trading day of a foreign company in NASDAQ history to date. Baidu.com is often referred to as "China's Google" because of its resemblance to it. In fact, Google owned 2.6% of the company for a while, but ended up selling it. Market value: 40B (July 2019).

Facebook vs. Tencent

Facebook, Inc. is a US company offering online social networking and social media services based in Menlo Park, California. Their website was launched on February 4, 2004 by Mark Zuckerberg. Initially the founders limited the membership of the website to Harvard students, but later expanded it to institutions of higher education in the Boston area, Ivy League schools and Stanford University. In February 2012, it went public in a 104 billion public offering, the highest for a start-up company. Most of its revenue comes from on-screen ads. Facebook can be accessed from a wide range of Internet-connected devices such as PCs, laptops, tablets and smartphones. Once registered, users can create a personalized profile indicating their name, occupation, schools attended, etc. Users can add other users such as "friends," exchange messages, post status updates, share photos, videos and links, use multiple software applications (apps), and receive notifications of other users' activity. Facebook has more than 2.2 billion active users per month. On April 9, 2012, Facebook acquired Instagram for one billion and in February 2014 purchased WhatsApp mobile messaging for 16 billion. Market value: 560B (July 2019).

Tencent is a multinational Chinese company whose subsidiaries provide Internet products and services. Tencent is a social network and much, much more. It is the largest Internet portal in China and currently the company with the highest market value surpassing the giant Alibaba. To get a rough idea of the services provided by Tencent, its technological capacity and its penetration of the Chinese market, we could imagine a company that integrates services from Facebook, Google, Whatsapp, Netflix, Spotify and the largest in video games. The products and services of Tencent's company are grouped into seven main business lines: Instant Messaging, Online Multimedia, Mobile and Telecom Value Added Services, Interactive Entertainment Service, E-Commerce and Online Advertising Service. Among the most popular are QQ, which is China's largest social networking and instant messaging service, and SOSO, an equivalent to the Google search engine. Tencent Games, a subsidiary of Tencent Holdings, leads the global ranking for video game revenue worldwide. Tencent was founded by Ma Huateng and Zhang Zhidong in November 1998 as Tencent Inc. and Tencent Holdings Ltd. It was listed on the Hong Kong Stock Exchange on June 16, 2004. On July 10, 2008 Tencent Holding was added to the Hang Seng index. It currently holds over 400 patents. Market value: 460B (July 2019).

The Huawei case

The US conflict with Huawei is key to understanding the country's technological war with China, the commercial implications, and the battle for technological supremacy. In order to have the big picture, we will begin with a description of the Huawei Company, its characteristics and its importance in China's economy and worldwide.

Huawei Technologies Co., Ltd. is a Chinese high-tech multinational private company specializing in research and development (R&D), electronics production and marketing of communications equipment. It also provides customized network solutions for operators in the telecommunications industry. It was founded in 1987 by Ren Zhengfei. Huawei Technologies Co., Ltd. supplies 35 of the world's largest telecommunications operators and invests 10% of its annual revenues in research and development. In addition to its R&D centers in Shenzhen, Shanghai, Beijing, Nanking, Xi'an, Chengdu and Wuhan in China, Huawei Technologies Co., Ltd. also has R&D centers in Sweden, United States, Ecuador, Ireland, Colombia, Mexico, India and Russia.

Huawei Technologies has been included in the list of most respected companies by "The Reputation Institute" and published by Forbes magazine in the United States in May 2007. The list of the most respected companies covers various industries such as consumer products, electrical and electronic, automotive, retail, pharmaceutical, computer, financial, aerospace, etc. In the telecommunications sector six companies have been listed and Huawei Technologies is one of the six most respected telecommunications companies in the world.

Huawei started operations as a distributor of imported PBX products (Private Branch Exchange). In 1989 it began the development and subsequent sale of its own PBX. After accumulating knowledge and resources in the telephone exchange business, Huawei managed to position itself as an important link in the telecommunications market in 1993 by launching its digital telephone switch with a capacity of more than ten thousand circuits. Until then, Chinese domestic telecommunication companies were not able to build switches with such capacity. Huawei switches were the first to be installed only in small towns and rural areas. In 1994 Huawei established itself in the long distance transmission equipment business, launching its own HONET integrated access network and SDH product line.

> **Synchronous digital hierarchy** (SDH) and Synchronous optical networking (SONET) are standardized protocols that transfer multiple digital bit streams synchronously over optical fiber using lasers or highly coherent light from light-emitting diodes (LEDs). At low transmission rates data can also be transferred via an electrical interface. The method was developed to replace the plesiochronous digital hierarchy (PDH) system for transporting large amounts of telephone calls and data traffic over the same fiber without the problems of synchronization.

In 1996 Huawei won its first overseas contract supplying basic telephony products to Hong Kong-based Hutchison-Whampoa. The United States alleged in 2000 that Huawei had installed a telecommunications system in Iraq that may have violated United Nations sanctions. Since 2001 Huawei has increased its speed of expansion in the foreign market. In 2004, Huawei's overseas sales surpassed domestic sales. Huawei has strategic partnerships with Siemens for TD-SCDMA product development. In 2003 Huawei started a strategic partnership called Huawei-3Com with 3Com for the manufacture of Internet protocol-based routers and switches.

> **TD-SCDMA** (Time division synchronous code division multiple access) is a mobile telephone standard for wireless network operators who want to move from a second generation (2G) wireless network to a third-generation (3G).

Huawei and the US security firm Symantec announced in May 2007 the signing of the joint venture to develop security equipment and data storage for operators in the telecommunications market. Huawei controlled 51% of the new company that would be named Huawei-Symantec Inc. Symantec held the remaining 49% of the shares of the new company. The company was established in the city of Chengdu. In May 2008, Huawei joined Optus in developing a mobile innovation center in Sydney, Australia, to accelerate the adoption of high-speed mobile and wireless broadband.

In the following years Huawei continued its expansion both within China and internationally. Its business lines have grown and its technology reaches levels that can be considered as a spearhead worldwide. At its 2019 HDC conference Huawei announced that its Mobile Services reached 100 Million active users outside of China and announced development projects that will support the further growth of Huawei's partnership-ecosystem.

In May 2018, the Trump administration issued an executive order invoking national security grounds to prohibit the government from hiring foreign technology providers. It also put Huawei on the "black list," which prohibits US technology companies from supplying it with semiconductors, key components of its business, as well as technology transfers. The development and manufacture of high technology is impossible without semiconductors, and that is the last sector in which the United States remains the undisputed leader. **China manufactures only 16% of the semiconductors it uses,** of which only half are produced by its own companies. In 2018, Chinese imports of microchips surpassed 300 billion dollars, more than petroleum. Each smartphone has up to 20 microchips. For example, the Huawei P30 Pro includes integrated circuits produced in the United States, Japan and Taiwan and only one processor made in mainland China.

The ultimate purpose of Donald Trump's government is to create a fence around Huawei to limit its growth. However, the Chinese government's support for Huawei and president Trump's need to continue trade negotiations forced the US government to cease its punishment of Huawei. On June 29, 2019 Donald Trump announced the suspension of the veto on the company so US companies will be able to continue doing business with Huawei.

The Trump administration's measures brought negative consequences for Huawei, including a fall in the stock market, a severe blow to the trademark and a significant devaluation in the exchange and resale market. The company said it would continue to provide security upgrades, focus on improving its usual value offering and soon have an operating system of its own. It is important to note that the blockade unleashed such a nationalist sentiment that some Chinese customers using Apple phones bought a Huawei phone. According to the China Daily portal, Huawei continues to grow and improve its economic indicators despite the restrictive measures imposed against it by the Trump Administration in order to curb its global expansion. The company's revenues in the first half of 2019 reached 58.3 billion, an increase of 23.2% compared to the first half of 2018.

Huawei is not just a tech company, but one of China's technological champions. It is better known for the production and sale of smartphones than for its research and production of networks especially in the area of 5G. And this is precisely the issue that worries the United States and reveals that the real battle is in the field of 5G, where Huawei is key to having patents and a score of contracts to facilitate technology and be the largest manufacturer of telecommunications equipment in the world with 28% of the market. **Given this fact, 5G technology is key in the fight for technological supremacy.**

The fifth-generation cellular technology, 5G, boasts download speeds 10 times as fast as 4G. It will vastly increase the connections between devices at a speed that make self-driving vehicles and interconnected home appliances possible. Huawei, which began developing the technology in 2009, has been leading in this area.

Huawei, which had revenue of US105 billion in 2018 and employs nearly 200,000 people, is considered one of the first Chinese firms to make its name globally.

Getting tough on perhaps the nation's most beloved company in many Chinese minds, marked the beginning of a hostile tech cold war and fundamentally changed the nature of the battle with the US.

Without a clear map the antagonistic move to ban Huawei could have catastrophic consequences for US consumers, the American semiconductor industry and, more importantly, the global advancement of 5G, which will change the way humans live and communicate.

The technological cold war

The "cold war" was a political, economic, social, military, informational and scientific confrontation that began at the end of World War II between the Western (capitalist) bloc led by the United States and the Eastern (communist) bloc led by the Soviet Union.

It originated between 1945 and 1947 during the post-war tensions and lasted until the dissolution of the Soviet Union (beginning of Perestroika in 1985, Chernobyl nuclear accident in 1986, fall of the Berlin Wall in 1989 and failed coup d'état in the USSR in 1991). Neither of the two blocks took military action against the other, which is why it was called the "cold war".

The reasons for this confrontation were essentially ideological and political. The Soviet Union financed and supported revolutions, guerrillas and socialist governments, while the United States gave open support and propagated destabilizations and coups d'état, especially in Latin America and Africa. In both cases human rights were seriously violated.

Although these confrontations did not unleash a world war, the gravity of the economic, political and ideological conflicts marked much of the history of the second half of the twentieth century. The two superpowers certainly wished to implement their model of government all over the planet.

The English writer George Orwell used "cold war" as a general term in his essay "You and the Atomic Bomb" published on October 19, 1945 in the British newspaper Tribune. In a world threatened by nuclear war, Orwell referred to James Burnham's predictions of a polarized world.

The first use of the term to describe specifically the geopolitical confrontation between the Soviet Union and the post-war United States was in a speech by Bernard Baruch, a financial and influential US presidential adviser, on April 16, 1947. In the speech Baruch said: "Let us not deceive ourselves: we are immersed in a cold war". The term was popularized by columnist Walter Lippmann with his book The Cold War.

The new Cold War is technological. What began as a trade war between the United States and China in 2018 with the imposition of tariffs on a growing number of products and in August 2019 escalated into a currency war, has evolved to show the complexity of the confrontation between the two powers, where the United States has put the large Chinese companies in the technology sector, such as Huawei, ZTE and Tencent, in the spotlight of their actions.

The success of Chinese technology companies such as Alibaba, Huawei or Tencent in the global economy threatens the dominance of US companies in the sector so far. Huawei has already overtaken Apple as the world's second largest smartphone manufacturer, behind only Korean Samsung. Moreover, the Palo Alto powerful firm has had to lower its revenue forecasts for the first time since 2015 because of the impact of the Chinese slowdown on its sales.

The dimensions of this confrontation go beyond commercial rivalry and into geopolitics. The Silicon Valley model where innovation and technological development have relied on private financing capable of taking risks may succumb to the model of Shenzhen, the city of China that is home to some of those technological giants that grew under state protection, the forced transfer of technology from companies that want to do business in the country and a large, cheap and skilled workforce.

US and China are two opposing models, one based on private initiative and the other driven by the public sector. To give a definitive impulse to its model, in 2015 Chinese Prime Minister Li Keqiang launched the Made in China 2025 plan to give a definitive impulse to the country's industry. Three years later, president Xi Jinping reformulated the plan to turn China into a technological superpower - in aerospace, robotics, biotechnology and computing - on that horizon, with an estimated budget of 300 billion. It is a program that, as the US Council on International Relations recognizes in a recent report, represents an existential threat to US technological leadership. And Washington, under president Donald Trump, has come under attack. The United States is not going to give up global technological supremacy without a fight, and the Huawei case shows that this battle has already begun.

In the war that the United States and China have for technological supremacy, the first blows were thrown by the United States. These blows failed to defeat China and rather have produced the strengthening of the warrior spirit in China. The Huawei ban and tariffs on Chinese goods will not slow China. We have seen that they really serve to stimulate its new innovation system and boost scientific research aimed at becoming more independent.

Another consequence will be an acceleration of China's attempt to rebalance its economy away from external demand and investment towards domestic consumption. This started in 2008 with the global financial crisis and has become increasingly necessary as China's middle class develops. Since then large-scale government-led infrastructure investments, measures to increase household income, reduction of income tax, and improvements to social welfare systems have helped grow domestic consumption.

When Trump first announced tariffs in 2018, China's domestic consumption was responsible for 76.2% of its GDP growth, and the Chinese stock market absorbed the impact and bounced back after an initial sharp decline. Since then, the Chinese government has introduced new policies to boost domestic consumption further, including more tax cuts, improved childcare, and elderly care initiatives and incentives. **So the trade war has helped China's efforts to redistribute wealth and restructure its economy.**

The trade war has also rallied the Chinese public around its government. US treatment of Chinese companies has been perceived as bullying and people have compared it to the way that the British Empire forced unfair trade practices on China in the 19th century. This topic is incredibly emotive in Chinese society and has boosted domestic support for the government.

The war for technological supremacy has just begun. 5G technology is an important hill that both countries want to conquer **but the most important battle is the conquest and mastery of Artificial Intelligence.** The country that dominates this technology will be the first world power.

Nouriel Roubini, Professor of Economics, Stern School of Business, New York University, analyzes the consequences of the Sino-American conflict and writes them in an interesting article published in collaboration with Project Syndicate. This is his conclusion:

"The global consequences of a Sino-American cold war would be even more severe than those of the Cold War between the US and the Soviet Union. Whereas the Soviet Union was a declining power with a failing economic model, China will soon become the world's largest economy, and will continue to grow from there. Moreover, the US and the Soviet Union traded very little with each other, whereas China is fully integrated in the global trading and investment system, and deeply intertwined with the US, in particular.

A full-scale cold war thus could trigger a new stage of de-globalization, or at least a division of the global economy into two incompatible economic blocs. In either scenario, trade in goods, services, capital, labor, technology, and data would be severely restricted, and the digital realm would become a "splinternet," wherein Western and Chinese nodes would not connect to one another. Now that the US has imposed sanctions on ZTE and Huawei, China will be scrambling to ensure that its tech giants can source essential inputs domestically, or at least from friendly trade partners that are not dependent on the US.

In this balkanized world, China and the US will both expect all other countries to pick a side, while most governments will try to thread the needle of maintaining good economic ties with both. After all, many US allies now do more business (in terms of trade and investment) with China than they do with America. Yet in a future economy where China and the US separately control access to crucial technologies such as AI and 5G, the middle ground will most likely become uninhabitable. Everyone will have to choose, and the world may well enter a long process of de-globalization.

Whatever happens, the Sino-American relationship will be the key geopolitical issue of this century. Some degree of rivalry is inevitable. But, ideally, both sides would manage it constructively, allowing for cooperation on some issues and healthy competition on others. In effect, China and the US would create a new international order, based on the recognition that the (inevitably) rising new power should be granted a role in shaping global rules and institutions.

If the relationship is mismanaged – with the US trying to derail China's development and contain its rise, and China aggressively projecting its power in Asia and around the world – a full-scale cold war will ensue, and a hot one (or a series of proxy wars) cannot be ruled out. In the twenty-first century, the Thucydides Trap would swallow not just the US and China, but the entire world." (https://bit.ly/2kjdfA9)

Jack Ma - Elon Musk debate on AI

Ma Yun or Jack Ma was born on 10 September 1964 in Hangzhou, Zhejiang, China. He began studying English at a young age by conversing with English-speakers at Hangzhou international hotel. He would ride 70 miles on his bicycle to give tourists tours of the area to practice his English for nine years. Ma is the co-founder and was the executive chair of Alibaba Group, a multinational technology conglomerate. Ma is a strong proponent of an open and market-driven economy. Ma is seen as a global ambassador for Chinese business and as such is frequently listed as one of the world's most powerful people by Forbes. He also serves as a role model for startup businesses. In 2017, he was ranked second in the annual "World's 50 Greatest Leaders" list by Fortune. On 10 September 2018, he announced that he will retire from Alibaba and pursue educational work, effective in one year, with Daniel Zhang succeeding him as executive chairman. Jack Ma formally retired on 10 Sep from Alibaba, the Chinese e-commerce giant he founded that helped transform the way hundreds of millions of people shop and made him one of the world's richest men.

Elon Reeve Musk was born and raised in Pretoria, South Africa, Musk moved to Canada when he was 17 to attend Queen's University. He transferred to the University of Pennsylvania two years later where he received an economics degree from the Wharton School and a degree in physics from the College of Arts and Sciences. He began a Ph.D. in applied physics and material sciences at Stanford University in 1995 but dropped out after two days to pursue an entrepreneurial career. He subsequently co-founded Zip2, a web software company, which was acquired by Compaq. He holds South African, Canadian, and US citizenship and is the founder, CEO, and lead designer of SpaceX, co-founder, CEO, and product architect of Tesla, co-founder of Neuralink; founder of The Boring Company; co-founder and co-chairman of OpenAI; and co-founder of PayPal. In December 2016, he was ranked 21st on the Forbes list of The World's Most Powerful People. He is listed by Forbes as the 40th-richest person in the world.

Many waited with bated breath as Jack Ma and Elon Musk, two of the greatest tech minds of the generation, came together at the World Artificial Intelligence Conference in Shanghai on Wednesday, August-28-2019. As expected, the energy was high and the discussion, at times, tense. In an hour long conversation, **the men behind Alibaba and Tesla had a war of words over Artificial Intelligence, Mars, and the future.**

"I think AI is going to open a new chapter of this society of the world that people try to understand ourselves better rather than the outside world," Ma said. He added: "I'm quite optimistic. And I don't think Artificial Intelligence is a threat. I don't think AI is something terrible. But human beings are smart enough to learn that."

But Musk disagreed, using the rapid advancement of video games as an example of just how daunting AI really is. "If you go back 40 years ago, 50 years ago maybe, you had Pong: That was just two rectangles and a square. Now you've got photorealistic, real-time simulations with millions of people playing simultaneously," he said. "If you assume any rate of improvement at all, these games will be indistinguishable from reality. You will not be able to tell the difference. Either that or civilization will end." Musk added that he wasn't all defeatist, saying: "I'm a naturally optimistic person, to be clear. I'm not saying, 'Hey, doom and gloom.' I'm just saying this is the apparent pattern. The rate of change of technology is incredibly fast. It is outpacing our ability to understand it."

The hot topic in the hour-long talk was AI, which has provoked increasing concern among scientists such as late British cosmologist Stephen Hawking who warned that it will eventually turn on and "annihilate" humanity.

"Computers may be clever, but human beings are much smarter," Jack Ma said. "We invented the computer, I've never seen a computer invent a human being." While insisting that he is "not a tech guy," the Alibaba founder added, "I think AI can help us understand humans better. I don't think it's a threat."

Musk countered, "I don't know, man, that's like, famous last words."

Tesla CEO said "the rate of advancement of computers in general is insane", sketching out a vision in which super-fast, artificially intelligent devices eventually tire of dealing with dumb, slow humans. "The computer will just get impatient if nothing else. It will be like talking to a tree," Musk said. Mankind's hope lies in "going along for the ride" by harnessing some of that computing power, he said, as he offered an unabashed plug for his Neuralink Corporation. Neuralink aims to develop implantable brain-machine interface devices, which conjures images of The Matrix, whose characters download software to their brains that instantly turns them into martial arts masters. "Right now we are already a cyborg because we are so well-integrated with our phones and our computers," said Musk. "The phone is like an extension of yourself. If you forget your phone, it is like a missing limb."

Jack Ma focused much of his comments on how machine learning could act as a force for good. He said it was something "to embrace" and would deliver fresh insights into how people think. "When human beings understand ourselves better, then we can improve the world better," he explained. Furthermore, he predicted AI would help create new kinds of jobs, which would require less of our time and be centered on creative tasks. "I think people should work three days a week, four hours a day," he said. "In the artificial intelligence period, people can live 120 years. At that time we are going to have a lot of jobs which nobody will want to do. So, we need artificial intelligence for the robots to take care of the old guys. So that's my view about jobs, don't worry about it, we will have jobs."

By contrast, Elon Musk suggested that mass unemployment was a real concern. "AI will make jobs kind of pointless," he claimed. "Probably the last job that will remain will be writing AI, **and then eventually, the AI will just write its own software.**" He added that **there was a risk that human civilization could come to an end** and ultimately be seen as a staging post for a superior type of life. "You could sort of think of humanity as a biological boot loader for digital super-intelligence," Musk explained. "A boot loader is... sort of like the minimal bit of code necessary for a computer to start. "You couldn't evolve silicon circuits. There needed to be biology to get there." To avoid such a fate we needed to find a way to connect our brains to computers so that we could "go along for the ride with AI" he said.

As a final summary of the debate between Jack Ma and Elon Musk on Artificial Intelligence, we can note the following:

Musk and Ma disagreed most about the potential risks of AI. Ma argued that compared to humans, computers are just a toy, adding that the best resource in the world is the human brain. "It's impossible that humans could be controlled by machines. They're machines that are invented by humans," Ma said.

Musk noted that he very much disagrees with Ma's stance. Arguing his point, Elon Musk said that humans are capable of creating things that are superior to people. Humans are not the last step in evolution and people must be wary of thinking that they are smarter than they really are. "The most important mistake smart people make is that they think they're smart. Computers are already smarter than people. We just keep moving the goalposts," he stated.

-9-

THE FOUR WAVES

In the evolution of humankind there have been important events that have meant disruptive changes such as the control of fire. However, **the four big waves before the arrival of Strong Artificial Intelligence (SAI) are:**

1. **Homo habilis** (Applying intelligence to use a stick as a tool)
2. **Agriculture** (Food production under human control)
3. **Industrial Revolution** (Application of the machine to replace physical force)
4. **AI Revolution** (Application of AI to replace intellectual force)

In this chapter we will study the four most important waves in the evolution of the human being. We will dedicate a little more space to the Industrial Revolution that took place in England because this change was transformative. Its effect was felt in the economy, the production of goods, social relations and the whole life of the human being. The benefits of the Industrial Revolution did not reach all the people within a country or all countries equally. This gave birth to social classes, bourgeoisie and proletariat, within a country, as well as developed and emerging countries in the concert of nations. This Industrial Revolution had several stages that are known as first, second and third revolution. In reality, **it was a long process that lasted a total of approximately 240 years,** that is, from 1760 to 2000.

From the 21st century onwards, the Fourth Wave in the development of humanity took hold. It is characterized by the intensive use of the personal computer, Internet, cellular telephony, the Intelligent Factory and the application of Artificial Intelligence in almost all the activities of society. **This wave is the AI Revolution**. Some authors identify it as Industry 4.0 or the Fourth Industrial Revolution. We consider it a step further than a new stage of the Industrial Revolution that began in England in 1760 because the intensive use of computers, the Internet **and the application of Artificial Intelligence mark a great change**. The Industrial Revolution was the substitution of the physical force of the human being by a machine. **The AI Revolution is the substitution of the intellectual force by AI technology.** We are currently living in this stage. This wave is the prelude to the Fifth Wave that will arrive with Strong Artificial Intelligence by 2040.

Homo habilis

The First Wave was caused by an ancestor of the human being who used his brain with an incipient intelligence and his prehensile hand to pick up a stone, a bone or a stick as a weapon or tool. He was Homo habilis (from the Latin homo, 'man', and habilis, 'skillful'). A hominid who lived in Africa during a period between 1.5 and 2.5 million years ago and whose species became extinct in the process of evolution of the human genus. The period in which Homo habilis lived corresponds to the Pleistocene, a time in which extensive ice sheets of ice covered the highest latitudes of the planet, especially in the northern hemisphere, alternating with periods in which these areas were partially uncovered. During the Pleistocene there were interglacial periods lasting thousands of years in which the earth's climate was more benign and conducive to life.

We can consider that Homo habilis is, as its name well indicates, the first living being on Planet Earth with sufficient skill to use his hand to hold a tool, conserve it and improve it. **This fact marks the first great application of the intelligence of the human being** in his economic and social development.

When it comes to Artificial Intelligence, the focus is on the brain. However, **the hand deserves to be highlighted** as the most important part of the anatomy where intelligence is manifested. We can say that it is the part of the body that allows man to express his intelligence and reach the quality of human being. It would not be bold to say that the hand is an extension of the brain and reciprocally, thanks to the hand, the human brain has been able to develop.

A team led by scientists Louis and Mary Leakey uncovered the fossilized remains of a unique early human between 1960 and 1963 at Olduvai Gorge in Tanzania. The type specimen, OH 7, was found by Jonathan Leakey. Because this early human had a combination of features different from those seen in Australopithecus, Louis Leakey, South African scientist Philip Tobias and British scientist John Napier declared these fossils a new species, and called them Homo habilis (meaning 'handy man') because they suspected that it was this slightly larger-brained early human that made the thousands of stone tools also found at Olduvai Gorge.

Early Homo had smaller teeth than Australopithecus, although their tooth enamel was still thick and their jaws were still strong, indicating that their teeth were still adapted for chewing some hard foods (possibly only seasonally when their preferred foods became less available). Dental studies suggest that the diet of Homo habilis was flexible and versatile. They were capable of eating a broad range of foods, including some tougher foods like leaves, woody plants and some animal tissues. However, they did not routinely consume or specialize in eating hard foods like brittle nuts or seeds, dried meat or very hard tubers.

Like the majority of the Australopithecus, Homo habilis possessed elongated arms, possibly suggesting continued reliance on an arboreal environment. While the digits were still curved, they had increased gripping capabilities for tool manufacture and use, as evidenced by the pronounced attachment site for the flexor pollicis longus muscle, which acts to flex the thumb.

Homo habilis. Physical characteristics:

- Height: average 3 ft. 4 in - 4 ft. 5 in (100 - 135 cm)
- Weight: average 70 lbs. (32 kg)
- Rounded skull.
- Spadiform incisors.
- Large molars with thick enamel.
- Absence of diastema (space or gap between two teeth).
- Foramen magnum (occipital hollow) further towards the center.
- Incisors larger than Australopithecus.
- Short face.
- Curved fingers and toes (indicating that they climbed trees).
- Greater neurocranial capacity 650 cm^3.

What is the border that divides a primate from a Homo habilis? Where did the spark of intelligence ignite? Barbara Helm Welker writes on this interesting subject in her book "The history of our tribe, Hominini" and provides answers to the questions: Where did we come from? What were our ancestors like? Why do we differ from other animals? How do scientists trace and construct our evolutionary history? This is one of the central ideas of her book:

"The real skill comes with having the manual dexterity to do so, making a tool that can accomplish a variety of uses, and the ability to teach others...We go on and on about encephalization in the hominin lineage and technological advancements in the archaeological record over time, but what may have been the true dividing line between ourselves and the apes, whether bipeds or not, was the ability to teach our young, kin, and other group members and thus increase their chance of survival. The vehicle for developing a theory of mind is language. Human children develop a theory of mind at three or four years of age. Prior to that time, they do not realize that they or others may have incomplete information." (https://bit.ly/2m1ZBBG)

Agriculture

From his origin until the beginning of the Neolithic, approximately 10,000 years ago, man procured his food as a hunter-gatherer. Hunting prey was the basis of his diet. He also collected wild fruits and roots for consumption. His diet also included vegetables, leaves, stems, shoots and wild grains. For the purpose of this topic, agriculture encompasses the domestication of plants and animals.

Primitive man lived in harmony and equilibrium with nature. When he moved due to the migrations of the species or the cycle of the seasons, he adapted to the changing conditions of the climate and the environment. **When he became sedentary, he faced new conditions and restrictions that had to be resolved.**

In its initial phase, agriculture developed differently in the regions of the world where human beings lived, depending on the climate, the species of the vegetable and the animal kingdom that nature offered. Rice was domesticated in China between 11,500 and 6,200 B.C., followed by beans and soybeans. In Europe, wheat, barley, peas, lentils, chickpeas and flax were grown. Pigs were domesticated in Mesopotamia in 11,000 B.C., followed by sheep. Cattle were domesticated in Turkey and Pakistan around 8,500 B.C. Sugar cane and some root vegetables were grown in New Guinea around 7,000 B.C. In the Andes, potatoes, beans and coca were brought into cultivation between 8,000 and 5,000 B.C. In the same period, bananas were cultivated in New Guinea. Other examples were corn in Mesoamerica around 4,000 B.C and cotton in Peru by 3,600 B.C. Camels were possibly domesticated around 3,000 B.C. in Somalia and Arabia.

In the middle Ages in both Europe and Asia, agriculture was transformed with the use of improved techniques and the spread of crops such as sugar cane, rice, cotton and fruit trees. After 1492, a global exchange of previously local crops and livestock breeds occurred. Maize, potatoes, sweet potatoes and manioc were the key crops that spread from the New World to the Old, while varieties of wheat, barley, rice and turnips traveled from the Old World to the New. There had been few livestock species in the New World, with horses, cattle, sheep and goats being completely unknown before their arrival with Old World settlers.

Crops moving in both directions across the Atlantic Ocean caused population growth around the world and a lasting effect on many cultures in the Early Modern period. Maize and cassava were introduced from Brazil into Africa by Portuguese traders in the 16th century, becoming staple foods, replacing native African crops. After its introduction from South America to Spain in the late 1500s, the potato became a staple crop throughout Europe by the late 1700s. Potatoes allowed farmers to produce more food and initially added variety to the European diet. The increased supply of food reduced disease, increased births and reduced mortality, causing a population boom throughout the British Empire, the US and Europe.

Agriculture allows a much greater density of population than can be supported by hunting and gathering and allows for the accumulation of excess production to be kept for winter use or to be sold for profit. The ability of farmers to feed large numbers of people whose activities have nothing to do with material production was the crucial factor in the rise of surplus production, specialization, advanced technology, hierarchical social structures, inequality and standing armies. Agrarian societies thus support the emergence of a more complex social structure.

In agrarian societies, some of the simple correlations between social complexity and the environment begin to disappear. One view is that humans with this technology have moved a large step toward controlling their environments, are less dependent on them, and hence show fewer correlations between environment and technology-related traits. A rather different view is that as societies become larger and the movement of goods and people cheaper, they incorporate an increasing range of environmental variation within their borders and trade systems. But environmental factors may still play an important role as variables that affect the internal structure and history of a society. For example, the average size of agrarian states will depend on the ease of transportation, major cities will tend to be located at trade nodes and the demographic history of a society may depend on disease episodes.

Until recent decades, the transition to farming was seen as an inherently progressive one: people learned that planting seeds caused crops to grow and this new improved food source led to larger populations, sedentary farm and town life, more leisure time and so to specialization, writing, technological advances and civilization.

Dan Albone constructed in England the first commercially successful gasoline-powered general purpose tractor in 1901. The 1923 International Harvester Farmall tractor marked a major point in the replacement of draft animals (particularly horses) with machines. Farmall was a model name and later a brand name for tractors manufactured by the American company International Harvester (IH).

Since that time, self-propelled mechanical harvesters (combines), planters and other equipment have been developed, further revolutionizing agriculture. These inventions allowed farming tasks to be done with a speed and on a scale previously impossible, leading modern farms to output much greater volumes of high-quality produce per land unit.

The Green Revolution was a series of research, development, and technology transfer initiatives, between the 1940s and the late 1970s. It increased agricultural production around the world, especially from the late 1960s. The initiatives, led by Norman Borlaug and credited with saving over a billion people from starvation, involved the development of high-yielding varieties of cereal grains, expansion of irrigation infrastructure, modernization of management techniques, distribution of hybridized seeds, synthetic fertilizers, and pesticides to farmers. It also resulted in a huge population increase in countries like Africa, India and China. Something that Borlaug had foreseen as the unfortunate legacy of his work.

The Industrial Revolution

The Industrial Revolution was the process of economic, social and technological transformation that began in the eighteenth century in England and that gradually extended to Western Europe, then to the United States and ended up covering almost the entire world. **This period of industrial transformation begins in 1760 and ends in the year 2000** to begin the Fourth Wave driven by Artificial Intelligence.

This process of change has gone through several stages. We will study the characteristics of the process of the Industrial Revolution, dedicating more space to the First Revolution that took place in England, which caused a disruptive change with a powerful impact on the life of society. This stage was founded on the introduction of James Watt's steam engine (patented in 1769).

During this period, the greatest set of economic, technological and social transformations in the history of humanity from the Neolithic period saw the passage from a rural economy based fundamentally on agriculture and commerce to an urban, industrialized and mechanized economy.

There is still discussion among historians and economists about the dates of the great changes set in train by the Industrial Revolution. The most accepted beginning of what we could call the **First Industrial Revolution could be placed in the second part of the 18th century (1760)**, while its conclusion could be placed in the middle of the 19th century. The Second Industrial Revolution would start from the middle of the 19th century to the beginning of the 20th century, with 1914 standing out as the most accepted date of completion, the year of the beginning of the First World War. A new impetus in 1960 with digital technology (computers) caused a third stage that lasted until the year 2000. In the year 2000 the AI Revolution started.

The beginnings of European industrialization are to be found in the Modern Age. From the 16th century onwards, there was an advance in trade, financial methods and banking, as well as technical progress in navigation, printing and watchmaking. However, these advances were always hampered by constant epidemics and long wars, as well as famines that did not permit the dispersion of new knowledge nor great demographic growth.

The Renaissance marked another turning point, with the appearance of the first capitalist societies in Holland and northern Italy. It was from the middle of the 18th century that Europe began to distance itself from the rest of the world and to establish the base of the future industrial society due to the then still primitive development of heavy industry and mining. The alliance of traders and farmers increased productivity, which in turn led to an accentuated population explosion from the nineteenth century onwards. The Industrial Revolution was characterized by the transition from an agricultural and manual economy to a commercial and industrial one whose ideology was based on reason and scientific innovation. Here it is important to emphasize these two concepts: reason and innovation, concepts that appear again in the 21st century as the engines of technological change and the basis of Artificial Intelligence.

Another main driver of the Revolution was born of necessity. Although in some places in Europe, such as Great Britain, an industrial base already existed, the Napoleonic Wars consolidated European industry. Due to the war, which spread throughout most of Europe, imports of many products and raw materials were suspended. This forced governments to put pressure on their industries and the nation in general to produce more and better than before, developing previously non-existent industries.

The first industrial areas appeared in Great Britain at the end of the 18th century, extending to Belgium and France at the beginning of the 19th century and to Germany and the United States at the middle of the century, to Japan from 1868 and to Russia, Italy and Spain at the end of the century. Among the causes were some as disparate as the notable absence of major wars between 1815 and 1914, the acceptance of the market economy and the consequent birth of capitalism, the break with the past, a certain monetary balance and the absence of inflation.

The Industrial Revolution originated in England because of several factors whose determination is one of the most important issues. The United Kingdom was one of the countries with the greatest availability of essential raw materials, especially coal, an essential material for feeding the steam engine that was the great motor of the early Industrial

Revolution, as well as the blast furnaces of the iron and steel industry.

As ideological, political and social factors, English society had gone through the so-called crisis of the 17th century in a particular way: while southern and eastern Europe established absolute monarchies, the English civil war (1642-1651) and the subsequent Glorious Revolution (1688) determined the establishment of a parliamentary monarchy (ideologically defined by John Locke's liberalism) based on the division of powers, individual freedom and a level of legal security that provided sufficient guarantees for the private entrepreneur.

As a strategic factor during the 18th century, England built a naval fleet which, after the Battle of Trafalgar, became the master of the seas and a very extensive colonial empire. Despite the loss of the Thirteen Colonies, set free in the War of Independence of the United States (1776-1781), it controlled, among others, the territories of the Indian subcontinent, an important source of raw materials for its industry, notably the cotton that fed the textile industry, as well as a captive market for the products of the metropolis. The patriotic song Rule Britannia (1740) explicitly stated: rule the waves.

In spite of all the above factors, the Industrial Revolution would not have been able to prosper without the development of transport, which would carry the goods produced in the factory to the markets where they were consumed.

These new forms of transport became necessary not only for internal trade, but also for international trade, since in this epoch the great national and international markets were created. International trade was liberalized, especially after the Treaty of Utrecht (1713), which liberalized trade relations between England and other European countries and Latin America. Privileged companies and economic protectionism were put to an end, and an imperialist policy and the elimination of trade union privileges were advocated. In addition, ecclesiastical, stately and communal lands were disentailed in order to put new lands on the market and create a new concept of ownership. **The Industrial Revolution increased foreign markets and a new international division of labor.**

As a consequence of industrial development new groups or social classes were born: the proletariat (the industrial workers and poor peasants) and the bourgeoisie, owners of the means of production and holders of most of the income and capital. This new social division led to the development of social and labor problems, popular protests and new ideologies that demanded an improvement in living conditions.

The Industrial Revolution marked a turning point in history, modifying and influencing all aspects of daily life in one way or another. Both agricultural production and nascent industry multiplied, while production time decreased. From 1800 onwards, wealth and per capita income multiplied as never before in history. Until then per capita GDP had remained practically stagnant for centuries.

From this point began a transition that would put an end to centuries of labor based on manual work and the use of animal traction, these being replaced by machinery for industrial manufacturing and for the transport of goods and passengers.

The Industrial Revolution took on a renewed momentum at the end of the 19th century (1870), known as **Second Industrial Revolution.** At this time, new technological systems were introduced, most significantly electrical power and telephones. It was a period of rapid industrial development, primarily in Britain, Germany and the United States, but also in France, Netherlands, Italy and Japan. It was characterized by the build out of railroads, large-scale iron and steel production, widespread use of machinery in manufacturing, greatly increased use of steam power, widespread use of the telegraph, use of petroleum and the beginning of electrification. It also was the period during which modern organizational methods for operating large scale businesses over vast areas came into use.

The Third Industrial Revolution is the shift from mechanical and analogue electronic technology to digital electronics which began anywhere from the late 1950s to the late 1970s with the adoption and proliferation of digital computers and digital record keeping that continues to the present day. Implicitly, the term also refers to the sweeping changes brought about by digital computing and communication technology during and after the latter half of the 20th century.

Industrial Revolution. Impact on industry and society:

- Transfer of the population from the countryside to the city
- International migration
- Sustained population growth

- Serial production
- Expansion of capitalism
- Emergence of large companies
- Deterioration of the environment
- The steam locomotive as an icon of change.
- Serial car production
- The automobile as a means of transport and symbol of social status
- Application of science and technology to the invention of achines.
- Use of new energy sources, mainly coal.
- The revolution in transport: railways, steamboats and automobiles.
- The emergence of an urban proletariat.
- Extensive use of the personal computer
- Expansion of the Internet to within reach of almost everyone
- Development of high-tech companies
- Information available through search engines, maps and GPS
- Development of cellular telephony
- Increased use of renewable energies.
- New energy storage technologies.
- Intelligent grid development.
- Transport based on the electric vehicle.

AI Revolution

We are in the midst of the AI Revolution. Without determining an exact date, it is accepted that it began at the dawn of this century. Its full development would take place in the following two decades. **Artificial Intelligence is the central element of this transformation**, intimately related to the growing accumulation of large amounts of data, the use of algorithms to process them and the massive interconnection of digital systems and devices.

Researchers and writers have not reached agreement on the name to be given to this period of profound transformation. For **Andrew D. Maynard**, director of the Risk Innovation Lab at Arizona State University, the name is Fourth Industrial Revolution. For **Professor Klaus Schwab** it is Industry 4.0. **For the author of this book it must be AI Revolution because Artificial Intelligence is at the center of all transformation**. Also, it is a disruptive change that affects not only industry and companies. It is a revolution that reaches the whole of society: governments, companies, civil organizations and people's lives. The AI Revolution is changing everyone and its effect will be even deeper and more radical when it matures into Strong Artificial Intelligence.

Professor Klaus Schwab has the merit of being the first to describe in a book the period he calls **Industry 4.0.** In honor of Professor Schwab, we will describe the time in which we now live, taking into account his book. We must add that we agree with the description in the book of the present time. However, we consider that it falls short of mentioning the impact of Artificial Intelligence not only on industry but on society as a whole

In his book **"The Fourth Industrial Revolution,"** Klaus Schwab, (Ravensburg, Germany March 30, 1938, German economist and businessman) founder and CEO of the World Economic Forum describes how this revolution is fundamentally different from the previous ones that were characterized primarily by advances in the manufacturing industry. Industry 4.0 technologies have great potential to connect billions of people to the web, dramatically improve the efficiency of businesses and organizations, and help regenerate the natural environment through better information management. (https://amzn.to/2moYbS4)

Professor Klaus Schawb's book is structured in three main chapters:

The Fourth Industrial Revolution: a very brief chapter that tries to explain what the Fourth Industrial Revolution is and to argue that it is a phenomenon that is already among us and that provokes deep and systemic changes.

Drivers: where key technologies are identified and briefly described, technologies that are grouped into three sections, those of a physical nature (autonomous vehicles, 3D printing, advanced robotics and new materials), digital (Internet of Things, blockchain) and biological (genetic editing).

Impact: where, as the title clearly expresses, the impact of these technologies is analyzed from various points of view.

The book ends with an annex that talks about 23 concrete changes, assessing the probability of occurrence towards 2025 that the experts assign to them, and the negative and positive consequences that can be expected from them.

The term Industry 4.0 was created in Germany to refer to the digital transformation of industry, also known as "Intelligent

Factory" or "Industrial Internet". This concept of a new industrial structuring or Industry 4.0 was first dealt with at the Hannover Fair (industrial technology exhibition) in 2011. In 2013 a report detailing this concept and its implications was supported by a select research group.

The Intelligent Factory is the result of the fusion of the virtual and physical worlds. The building blocks are intelligent products, characterized by electronics, embedded software and connectivity. They are called cyber-physical systems and have the capacity to interact with other systems and with humans. The software allows them to self-manage and make decentralized decisions. Equipped with sensors, they capture information about their environment, use and status that they can then provide to those who manufacture or manage their service. Cyber-physical systems can offer intelligent services and establish new business models taking advantage of innovative combinations of intelligent services to increase the creation of value, either up or down the value chain. These same principles apply to the machines that manufacture them, the cyber-physical production systems that make up the "Intelligent Factory". They are machines with the capacity for communication, personalization, adaptation to the environment and flexibility.

The concept of Industry 4.0 expresses the idea that the world is in the preliminary step of what will be the Fifth Wave in the evolution of humankind. After the development of steam engines and mechanization (second half of the 18th century), after the development of electricity for domestic and industrial purposes (end of the 19th century), and after automation (20th century), the current stage of industrial transformation is sustained by the so-called Intelligent Factory. This is characterized by the interconnection of machines and systems at the production site itself. It is characterized also by a fluid exchange of information with the outside world, whether with the level of supply and demand from markets, customers, competitors, and/or with other intelligent factories.

It corresponds to a new way of organizing the means of production. The objective to be achieved is the implementation of a large number of "Intelligent Factories" capable of greater adaptability to production needs and processes, as well as a more efficient allocation of resources, thus opening the way to a new wave with the advent of Strong Artificial Intelligence.

Industry 4.0 is not an already consolidated and experienced reality. It is a new milestone in industrial development that could mark important social changes in the coming years, making extensive use of the Internet and cutting-edge technologies. Its primary aim is that of developing industrial plants and energy generators that are smarter and more respectful of the environment, as well as with production chains that are much better connected to each other and to supply and demand markets. Industry 4.0 is developing in a small number of countries, although others are gradually joining them.

Effects on economy and society:

- The Intelligent Factory will be fully functional.
- Smart cities will be common.
- Houses and buildings will be intelligent
- 10% of consumer products will be made in 3D printers
- 90% of the world's population will have constant access to the Internet
- Autonomous vehicles.
- 50% of home Internet traffic will be directed to things.
- The first AI will be used in a company's board of directors.
- 10% of people will wear clothing connected to the Internet
- The first car made in a 3D printer will appear
- Doctors will partially be replaced by intelligent software.
- Bankers and brokers mostly replaced by AI systems.

Inequality in economic development

The effect of the Industrial Revolution has not been the same among the nations of the world. Countries that have promoted industrialization and technology have succeeded in increasing their per capita income and their level of economic development. Non-industrialized countries with poor technological development have low incomes and their population often suffers from famine.

England was the first country to have an Industrial Revolution and its economic power strengthened significantly over the following centuries. This power even allowed it to dominate other countries in Asia, Africa and America.

The United States, Europe, Japan, South Korea, Canada, China and other countries have managed to industrialize their economy and strengthen their technological development.

The result is an increase in the income and standard of living of the population.

The world's economic development registers a deep inequality that becomes greater as the gap in technological development widens. This inequality can also occur within the same country. In China we find the modern city of Shenzhen which is immersed in the Fourth Industrial Revolution with an impressive technological development. On the other hand, there are regions of agricultural economy which have not been industrialized. Shenzhen is the capital of Artificial Intelligence in China and is also the city with the fastest economic growth.

Artificial Intelligence will be the determining factor in the economic development of countries, companies and people.

The economic gap will widen even more between those who take advantage of the benefits of Artificial Intelligence and those who are left out.

The development of countries, companies and individuals will be in accordance with the application of Artificial Intelligence.

However, most countries in the world do not have a plan for the development of Artificial Intelligence. Irakli Beridze, director of the Center for Artificial Intelligence and robotics of the United Nations, estimates that of the 193 member states of the UN, only about thirty have a national strategy for the development of this technology.

The Organization for Economic Cooperation and Development has 26 countries that have a plan for the development of Artificial Intelligence. On its list are the United States, Sweden, Turkey, Singapore, India, Hungary and Italy. There is no Spain nor Mexico, both of which are important members of that organization.

Actions to promote Artificial Intelligence

Emerging countries are relatively lagging behind in the development of information technology and in particular Artificial Intelligence. If they do not accelerate the pace, they will lose the opportunity to use this powerful engine to boost their economic, technological, political and social development. Most importantly, they will once again be under the economic power of the countries and companies that dominate technology as happened in the Industrial

Revolution, with the aggravating factor that this time the domination will be broader and deeper. In the Industrial Revolution, steam and electricity replaced muscular force. Now Artificial Intelligence will replace the mind of the human being.

To promote the development of technology and in particular Artificial Intelligence, the emerging countries will be required to implement a strategy that executes the following actions:

1. Assign to Artificial Intelligence a high level of priority in government plans and policies as China and France have done.

2. Establish a national plan for the development of AI with clear and precise objectives; assign units of measurement to avoid vague and diffuse concepts; set a short, medium and long term time, that is, two, five and ten years at least; assign roles, responsibilities and the involvement of officials to the highest level of government.

3. Include in the plan the government, companies, universities, research centers, non-governmental organizations, investors and, of course, students, entrepreneurs and people interested in the development of AI to achieve synergy at the national level.

4. As France has done, allocate a significant part of the budget to encourage research, innovation and development of Artificial Intelligence. We consider that 1% of GDP should be allocated to this plan.

5. Establish a comprehensive program to support students, researchers and entrepreneurs in the field of Artificial Intelligence. Create a scholarship program, repatriation of professionals and an investment fund to help entrepreneurs. Support AI research centers.

6. Reward the outstanding and open up opportunities for AI products to be widely disseminated and placed on the national and international markets.

7. Encourage the study of AI in universities by creating specific careers for the study of AI at undergraduate and graduate levels.

8. If we consider that the countries of Latin America do not have the strength that is manifested in the countries of Western Europe, agreements could be established among countries to share experiences and balance deficiencies in order to advance with a firmer step.

9. Open the doors to immigrants who have knowledge of AI so that they can be integrated as teachers in education centers and also so that they can set up businesses.

Tos ovide opportunities for the creation and development of companies, both in tax matters and in the processing of permits and licenses.

11. Encourage the registration of patents

12. Establish a legal framework for the handling of personal information, data banks, social networks and big data in order to create, from the beginning, a solid and transparent basis for the storage, transfer and use of information.

13. Take the necessary measures to ensure that people displaced by robots and machines equipped with AI are not affected. One solution to this problem is to retrain workers in factories and offices.

14. Assign a public body to audit data and information to prevent misuse and protect users against cyber-attacks.

15. Legislate on Artificial Intelligence to prevent AI-based systems from causing harm to humans.

Milena Kabza, Narodowy Bank Polski, writes in an article published on the Internet: "A country that strategically implements AI technologies can obtain an advantage over others, because it will be able to develop faster — in particular due to changes taking place in the labor market. In the future, the cities in such a country could function more efficiently, because autonomous cars and intelligent infrastructure will optimize traffic. The largest companies will have the best data concerning consumer behavior, and the residents will live longer, because AI will revolutionize the diagnosis and treatment of diseases. Meanwhile, the sphere of national defense and security will be different than today, because autonomous weapons will replace soldiers and pilots, and war will be waged in cyberspace." (https://bit.ly/2lTlp2x)

-10-

FROM AI REVOLUTION TO STRONG AI

AI Revolution is the path to reach Strong Artificial Intelligence. The path to the most disruptive change in human history. This path began some years ago and will end with the advent of Strong Artificial Intelligence.

It is important to understand the AI Revolution in order to appreciate the magnitude of the Fifth Wave in the History of humanity. When the change occurs it will be too late to take precautionary or safeguard measures. Now is the time to think, legislate and put into action measures to control and maintain dominance over Artificial Intelligence..

In this chapter we will review the new technologies that drive AI in order to establish effective control over each of them, including legislation on their application. We will study the benefits and dangers of AI to take the good it offers us and avoid falling into the dangers it presents; we will review the work being done by organizations for the control of Artificial Intelligence such as OpenAI and finally we will make a call for reflection: Is humanity prepared to cede the supremacy of intelligence to an inanimate entity? Does it really want to do so? Is it aware of the dangers of this adventure?

New technologies to boost AI

Artificial Intelligence is spreading strongly in all activities of society. Every day there is news of the application of AI in medicine, education, robotics, architecture, banking, industry, agriculture, finance, communications, economy, transport and everything. Governments and companies allocate enormous financial resources to research and development of Artificial Intelligence. New technologies are geared towards the development of AI. The companies that stand out the most are those that use AI in their production, communication and administration processes. Society is enraptured by technology. Artificial Intelligence is nourished by technology. As a result, society frenziedly promotes Artificial Intelligence.

The Institute of Electrical and Electronics Engineers (IEEE), the world's largest technical professional organization for the advancement of technology presents a list of the most important advances in **technology for the year 2019.**

The top 10 technology trends predicted by IEEE to reach adoption in 2019 are:

Deep learning accelerators such as GPUs (Graphics Processing Unit), FPGAs, (Field-Programmable Gate Array) and more recently TPUs (Tensor Processing Unit). More companies have been announcing plans to design their own accelerators, which are widely used in data centers. There is also an opportunity to deploy them at the edge, initially for inference and for limited training over time. This also includes accelerators for very low power devices. The development of these technologies will allow machine learning (or smart devices) to be used in many IoT devices and appliances.

Assisted transportation. While the vision of fully autonomous, self-driving vehicles might still be a few years away, increasingly automated assistance is taking place in both personal and municipal (dedicated) vehicles. Assisted transportation is already very useful in terms of wide recognition and is paving the way for fully autonomous vehicles. This technology is highly dependent on deep learning accelerators for video recognition.

The Internet of Bodies (IoB). IoT and self-monitoring technologies are moving closer to and even inside the human body. Consumers are comfortable with self-tracking using external devices (such as fitness trackers and smart glasses) and with playing games using augmented reality devices. Digital pills are entering mainstream medicine, and body-attached, implantable, and embedded IoB devices are also beginning to interact with sensors in the environment. These devices yield richer data that enable more interesting and useful applications, but also raise concerns about security, privacy, physical harm, and abuse.

Social credit algorithms. These algorithms use facial recognition and other advanced biometrics to identify a person and retrieve data about that person from social media and other digital profiles for the purpose of approval or denial of access to consumer products or social services. In our increasingly networked world, the combination of biometrics and blended social data streams can turn a brief observation into a judgment of whether a person is a good or bad risk or worthy of public social sanction. Some countries are reportedly already using social credit algorithms to assess loyalty to the state.

Advanced (smart) materials and devices. We believe novel and advanced materials and devices for sensors, actuators, and wireless communications, such as tunable glass, smart paper, and ingestible transmitters, will create an explosion of exciting applications in healthcare, packaging, appliances, and more. These technologies will also advance pervasive, ubiquitous, and immersive computing, such as the recent announcement of a cellular phone with a foldable screen. The use of such technologies will have a large impact in the way we perceive IoT devices and will lead to new usage models.

Active security protection. The traditional method of protecting computer systems involves the deployment of prevention mechanisms, such as anti-virus software. As attackers become more sophisticated, the effectiveness of protection mechanisms decreases as the cost increases. However, a new generation of security mechanisms is emerging that uses an active approach, such as hooks that can be activated when new types of attacks are exposed and machine-learning mechanisms to identify sophisticated attacks. Attacking the attacker is a technological possibility as well, but is almost always illegal.

Virtual reality (VR) and augmented reality (AR). These related technologies have been hitting the mainstream in some respects for a number of years. For a well-known example, Pokemon Go is a game that uses the camera of a smartphone to interpose fictional objects in real-world surroundings. Gaming is clearly a driver of these technologies, with other consumer devices becoming affordable and commonplace. VR and AR technologies are also useful for education, engineering, and other fields. However, there has been a Catch-22 in that there is a lack of applications resulting from the high cost of entry, yet the cost has stayed high due to a lack of applications. With advertisements for VR headsets appearing during prime-time television programs, we may have finally reached a tipping point.

Chatbots. These Artificial Intelligence (AI) programs simulate interactive human conversation using key pre-calculated user phrases and auditory or text-based signals. Chatbots have recently started to use self-created sentences in lieu of pre-calculated user phrases, providing better results. Chatbots are frequently used for basic customer service on social networking hubs and are often included in operating systems as intelligent virtual assistants. We have recently witnessed the use of chatbots as personal assistants capable of machine-to-machine communications as well. In fact, chatbots mimic humans so well that some countries are considering requiring chatbots to disclose that they are not human. Industry is looking to expand chatbot applications to interaction with cognitive-impaired children as a way to provide therapeutic support.

Automated voice spam (robocall) prevention. A robocall is a phone call that uses a computerized auto dialer to deliver a pre-recorded message, as if from a robot. Spam phone calls are an ongoing problem of increasing sophistication, such as spoofing the caller ID number of the victim's family and business associates. This is leading people to regularly ignore phone calls, creating risks such as true emergency calls going unanswered. However, emerging technology can now block spoofed caller ID and intercept questionable calls so the computer can ask questions of the caller to assess whether he or she is legitimate.

Technology for humanity (specifically machine learning). We are approaching the point where technology can help resolve societal issues. We predict that large-scale use of machine learning, robots, and drones will help improve agriculture, ease drought, ensure the supply of food, and improve health in remote areas. Some of these activities have already started, but we predict an increase in adoption rate and the reporting of success stories in the next year. "Sensors everywhere" and advances in IoT and edge computing are major factors contributing to the adoption of this technology (Edge computing is a distributed computing paradigm which brings computation and data storage closer to the location where it is needed to improve response). Recent events, such as major fires and bridge collapses, are further accelerating the urgency to adopt monitoring technologies in fields like forests and smart roads.

Below is a list that the IEEE considers very promising for the year 2020:

Digital twins. These are software representations of assets and processes to understand, predict, and optimize performance for improved business outcomes. A digital twin can be a digital representation of any characteristic of a real entity, including humans. The choice of which characteristics are digitized is determined by the intended use of the twin. Digital twins are already being used by many companies: according to analysts, 48% of companies in the IoT space have already started adopting them. This includes digital twins for very complex entities, such as an entire smart city (for example, Digital Singapore). Digital twins are also expected to play a transformational role in healthcare over the next three years.

Real-time ray tracing. RT2 has long been considered the Holy Grail for rendering computer graphics realistically. Although the technique itself is quite mature, it was too computer-intensive to perform in real time until recently—so all ray-traced scenes had to be scripted and rendered in advance. In 2018, we witnessed the debut of a consumer product family with RT2 capabilities. In the next couple of years we expect to see incremental iterations until true RT2 is widespread. Initially, we expect the growth to be driven by consumer applications, such as gaming, followed by professional applications, such as training and simulation. Combined with VR, this technology could open up new frontiers in high-fidelity visual simulations.

Serverless computing. This is used to refer to the family of lambda-like offerings in the cloud, such as AWS Lambda, Google Cloud Functions, Azure Functions, or Nuclio. "Serverless" is the next step in the continuum along the line of virtualization, containers, and micro services. Unlike IaaS (Infrastructure as a service), in serverless computing the service provider manages the resources at a very fine granularity (all the way down to an individual function). End users can focus on the functions and don't have to pre-allocate instances or containers or manage them explicitly. While it's still at an early stage of adoption, there's appeal on both sides (better resource utilization for the providers, and pay-for-what-you-use for the users), so we expect that it will pick up rapidly and we will start seeing significant adoption in the next couple of years.

> **AWS Lambda** is an event-driven, serverless computing platform provided by Amazon as a part of Amazon Web Services. It is a computing service that runs code in response to events and automatically manages the computing resources required by that code.

Between 2020 and 2038. That is, **in the second part of the Fourth Wave or AI Revolution** there will be surprising advances in technology that will change the life of society. However, as surprising as they may seem, nothing will be comparable to the profound change in the evolution of humanity that will come with Strong Artificial Intelligence. That is, when the intelligence of an inanimate being is superior to that of the human being.

These are some of the surprising **technologies that we will see from 2020 onwards** and that will pave the way for the most profound and disruptive change in the history of humanity:

-**Unmanned vehicles**. It is expected that by 2020 there will be about 10 million unmanned vehicles. Many car manufacturers have already started to implement some of the functions of automatic driving in their vehicles.

-**Parts of the human body will be printed with 3D** technology for transplanting. 3D printing technology already has undergone great changes. It uses cartridges filled with a suspension of living cells, and smart gel that adds structure and creates a biological tissue.

-**Ultra-fast 5G** Internet from drones with solar panels. Google is working on drones with solar panels, handing out ultra-fast Internet project called Project Sky bender. Theoretically, the drones will provide Internet services 40 times faster than 4G networks, allowing the transfer of gigabytes of data per second.

-**Construction workers are going to print 3D residential areas**. The first ever 3D-printed house is located in Texas. It was built in just 24 hours. After this successful experiment, the company got official permission to use 3D building technology and wants to start the mass production of houses. The company wants to focus on poor countries in South America.

-**Education**. Textbooks are digitized with the help of AI, early-stage virtual tutors assist human instructors and facial analysis gauges the emotions of students to help determine who's struggling or bored and better tailor the experience to their individual needs.

-**Cooking** is perfectly suited to AI since it basically just requires knowledge of how a list of ingredients are combined in different ways, in different amounts. Products like the Hello Egg can not only help find and execute recipes more easily, but watch your eating and cooking habits to design meal plans that improve health.

-**Media.** Journalism is harnessing AI, too, and will continue to benefit from it. Bloomberg uses Cyborg technology to help make quick sense of complex financial reports. The Associated Press employs the natural language abilities of Automated Insights to produce 3,700 earnings reports stories per year — nearly four times more than in the recent past.

-**Pay with your face**. Advanced AI face recognition algorithms will soon be quick enough and cheap enough to support millions of transactions per day, but machine learning can teach a computer to recognize more than faces.

-**Manufacturing**. AI powered robots work alongside humans to perform a limited range of tasks like assembly and stacking, and predictive analysis sensors keep equipment running smoothly.

-**Mass production of flying cars**. This project is experimental but Japanese developers hope that there will be flying drone taxis in Tokyo by 2020. Inventors want to create cars that will land and take off vertically and their speed will be approximately 125 mph.

-**Healthcare**. In the comparatively AI-nascent field of healthcare, diseases are more quickly and accurately diagnosed, drug discovery is sped up and streamlined, virtual nursing assistants monitor patients and big data analysis helps to create a more personalized patient experience.

-**Bionic insects**. Scientists are developing bionic remedies for insects through which they can be controlled. These could then be sent to remote places to find people who are victims of earthquakes and other natural disasters.

William Henry Gates III, Bill Gates, is well known for making sweeping futuristic predictions in his own annual letter. For 2019 Bill's predictions fell into three categories--climate change mitigation, healthcare, and **Artificial Intelligence**-- and ranged from technologies that are hitting the commercial market to ones still in research. Here is his list:

1. **Robot dexterity**: Robot hands that are better equipped to manipulate unfamiliar objects.

2. **New-wave nuclear power**: Advanced fusion and fission reactors that could help mitigate carbon emissions.
3. **Predicting preemies**: A blood test that can predict if a pregnant woman is at risk of a premature birth.
4. **Gut probe in a pill**: A small, swallow able device that can capture images of the gut without anesthesia (even in children and infants).
5. **Custom cancer vaccines**: A treatment that uses the body's own immune system to identify a tumor by its unique mutation, which could effectively shut down many types of cancers.
6. **The cow-free burger**: Plant-based and lab-grown meat alternatives that could drastically cut carbon emissions.
7. **Carbon dioxide catcher**: Technologies that can capture carbon dioxide from the air and utilize it in new ways.
8. **An ECG on your wrist**: Technology advances that allow people to continuously monitor their hearts with wearable devices.
9. **Sanitation without sewers**: Energy-efficient toilets that can operate without a sewer system and treat waste on the spot in developing worlds. (More than 2 billion people lack access to a clean toilet, according to Gates's 2019 annual letter)
10. **Smooth-talking AI assistants**: New advances in capturing semantic relationships between words are making machines better at understanding natural language.

Technologies for Strong Artificial Intelligence

The surprising developments we saw in the previous section are only the beginning of what we will see in the coming years promoting Artificial Intelligence. There's much more to come, more than anyone, even the most prescient prognosticators, can fathom but even with all these technologies nothing will be comparable with Strong Artificial Intelligence.

The Fifth Wave is underway. Satya Nadella, Director of Microsoft, says bluntly: "Artificial Intelligence moves at a steady pace and does not stop. It depends on the human being whether it has a positive effect or whether it ends up destroying humanity."

All this strength and enthusiasm accelerates the development of AI and directs it towards the Strong Artificial Intelligence that will give rise to the Fifth Wave. In spite of the risks involved, human beings insist on achieving it.

We have studied the technologies that are already in operation and that drive Artificial Intelligence. However, there are other technologies that are in the laboratories or in the process of experimentation **that will be the sustenance of Strong Artificial Intelligence**. We will review the five technologies with the greatest impact on the development of Artificial Intelligence: AI Chips, 5G technology, quantum computing in the cloud, encoding data in DNA and AI software to reach the Fifth Wave in the evolution of humanity.

AI chips

Artificial Intelligence is based on software that can theoretically run on any hardware. That is, on any chip or microprocessor with the right power; so it might seem wrong to say that to run AI programs you need a special chip. However, the design, capacity and speed of microprocessors oriented to Artificial Intelligence have shown that they respond better to the needs posed by AI algorithms with sophisticated technologies such as deep learning or neural networks. Taking this into account, some companies such as Intel and Nvidia, as well as startups and some universities such as the Massachusetts Institute of Technology (MIT) are focusing research on the production of special chips for Artificial Intelligence.

Jeff Bezos, CEO of Amazon, brings together technology elites each year at the MARS private conference. The last meeting took place in California where futuristic projects were presented. Among all the presentations was Eyeriss, the new AI chip resulting from the collaboration between Nvidia and MIT researchers. Eyeriss is a microprocessor specifically designed to increase the power of AI algorithms. The new chip stood out for its efficiency and flexibility, as well as for its handling of deep learning techniques.

The Mars Society is an American worldwide volunteer-driven space-advocacy non-profit organization dedicated to promoting human exploration and the settlement of the planet Mars. MARS is a yearly event hosted by Amazon Founder and CEO Jeff Bezos. MARS brings together innovative minds in machine learning, automation, robotics, and space to share new ideas across these rapidly advancing domains.

Eyeriss is an energy-efficient deep convolutional neural network (CNN) accelerator that supports state-of-the-art CNNs, which have many layers, millions of filter weights, and varying shapes (filter sizes, number of filters and channels). The test chip featured a spatial array of 168 processing elements (PE) fed by a reconfigurable multicast on-chip network that handled many shapes and minimized data movement by exploiting data reuse.

At the Consumer Electronics Show (CES-2019) held in Las Vegas, Intel has revealed that it is working in collaboration with Facebook to produce a new AI chip during the second half of this year. Intel's microprocessor promises compatibility with major AI software systems and greater efficiency for automated learning tasks than generic chips. However, experts warn that Intel will have to compete with the processor launched by Nvidia last year, as well as with other leading companies and small startups that will begin to flood the market with specialized AI chips this year.

One of those small startups has surprised the industry with the production of a high capacity chip specially designed to execute Artificial Intelligence algorithms. In August 2019 the company **Cerebras announced the big news:** "Cerebras Systems Unveils the Wafer-Scale Engine (WSE. The largest chip ever built with 1.2 Trillion Transistor Wafer-Scale Processor for AI. The World's Largest Chip at More Than 56 Times the Size of an NVIDIA V100."

The Cerebras WSE has an area of 46,225 mm² and houses 1.2 trillion transistors. All the cores are optimized for AI workloads and the chip consumes a whopping 15 KW of power. According to Cerebras, the chip is around 1000 faster than traditional systems simply because communication can happen across the scribe lines instead of jumping through hoops (interconnect, DIMM, etc.).

The WSE contains 400,000 Sparse Linear Algebra (SLA) cores. Each core is flexible, programmable, and optimized for the computations that underpin most neural networks. Programmability ensures the cores can run all AI algorithms in the constantly changing machine learning field. The 400,000 cores on the WSE are connected via the Swarm communication fabric in a 2D mesh with 100 PB/s of bandwidth. Swarm is a massive on-chip communication fabric that delivers breakthrough bandwidth and low latency at a fraction of the power draw of traditional techniques used to cluster graphics processing units. It is fully configurable;

software configures all the cores on the WSE to support the precise communication required for training the user-specified model. For each neural network, Swarm provides a unique and optimized communication path.

The WSE has 18 GB of on-chip memory, all accessible within a single clock cycle, and provides 9 PB/s memory bandwidth. This is 3000x more capacity and 10,000x greater bandwidth than the leading competitor. More cores, more local memory enables fast, flexible computation, at lower latency and with less energy. This would allow a massive speedup in AI applications and would reduce training times from months to just a couple of hours. This is truly revolutionary, there is no doubt about it, assuming they can deliver on their promise and start delivering this to customers soon. The Cerebras WSE is being manufactured on a TSMC 300mm wafer using their 16nm process which means this is cutting edge technology and just one node behind giants like NVIDIA. Of course, with 84-interconnected blocks that house over 400,000 cores, the process it's manufactured on simply does not matter. The engineers behind the chip believe it can be used in giant data centers and help accelerate the progress of Artificial Intelligence in everything from self-driving cars to talking digital assistants like Amazon's Alexa.

Technological competition between the United States and China continues. A week after the announcement of Cerebras, **Huawei launched the chip Ascend 910, "The world's most powerful AI processor"** The Ascend 910 is a new AI processor that belongs to Huawei's series of Ascend-Max chipsets. Huawei announced the processor's planned specs at its 2018 flagship event, Huawei Connect. After a year of ongoing development, test results now show that the Ascend 910 processor delivers on its performance goals with much lower power consumption than originally planned. For half-precision floating point (FP16) operations, Ascend 910 delivers 256 Tera FLOPS. Despite its unrivaled performance, Ascend 910's max power consumption is only 310W. "Ascend 910 performs much better than we expected," said Eric Xu, Huawei's Rotating Chairman, "Without a doubt, it has more computing power than any other AI processor in the world."

Huawei defines AI as a new general purpose technology, like railroads and electricity in the 19th century, and cars, computers, and the Internet in the 20th century. The company believes that AI will be used in almost every sector of the economy. According to Xu, AI is still in its early stages of development, and there are a number of gaps to close before AI can become a true general purpose technology. Huawei's AI strategy is designed to bridge these gaps and speed up adoption on a global scale.

> **FLOPS.** Floating point operations per second. Is a measure of computer performance useful in scientific computations that require floating-point calculations.

Alibaba, the e-commerce giant in China, enters the competition to produce an AI chip. On September 25 Alibaba Group Holdings Ltd said it has developed a new chip that specializes in machine-learning tasks and which will be used to enhance services for its cloud computing division.

Called Hanguang 800, the company's first self-developed AI chip is currently being used within Alibaba to power product search, automatic translation, and personalized recommendations on the e-commerce giant's web sites.

"The launch of Hanguang 800 is an important step in our pursuit of next-generation technologies, boosting computing capabilities that will drive both our current and emerging businesses while improving energy-efficiency," Alibaba CTO Jeff Zhang said in a statement. The chip was developed by DAMO Academy, a research institute Alibaba launched in late 2017, and T-Head, the company's specialized semiconductor division.

Alibaba's foray into the chip sector comes amid efforts by Beijing to promote China's semiconductor industry and reduce the country's reliance on foreign imports of core technologies.

5G technology

5G is known more for everything that has been written as promise and risk than for its reality. For several years announcements have been made about its arrival on the market but the promise has not yet been fulfilled. However it's coming and will be very important in communications. **The 5G is the fifth generation of wireless communication technologies and standards.** It is the Internet that some cell phones use to connect to the network anywhere. Actually, it is a development or evolution of the current 4G/LTE.

The 5G network provides three fundamental things: more transmission capacity, less latency and greater reliability, so it can be the basis for supporting Strong Artificial Intelligence.

The idea behind this development is to make phone calls, send messages and, above all, surf the Internet at a much higher speed than currently possible, all while allowing more devices to be connected at the same time. This fifth generation of wireless communications is the one that will allow to see a web page with a speed so fast that we should be able to upload videos in Ultra HD almost without blinking. The official standard has already been approved, and promises to be 10 to 20 times faster than current mobile connections.

In addition to increasing speed, 5G networks will offer lower latency, greater reliability and better connectivity from more places; also it will offer greater capacity, allowing more users and more devices to be connected at the same time. The resulting infrastructure will make the Internet of Things scalable, with more than 20 billion "things" including buildings, cars, machines and appliances that can be connected to the network by the time 5G debuts globally in 2020, up from 4.9 billion in 2015.

> **Latency** is a time interval between the stimulation and response or from a more general point of view, a time delay between the cause and the effect of some physical change in the system being observed. Latency is physically a consequence of the limited velocity with which any physical interaction can propagate. The magnitude of this velocity is always less than or equal to the speed of light.

This means that interactions with the Internet or the cloud will be almost instantaneous. Added to the download speeds, this will mean that clicking on a photo in the cloud would take the same amount of time to open on the mobile as if it were in the memory. But speed is not the only advantage that will change the rules of the game. The most important thing is that 5G is being built from the ground up to ensure a reliable signal with predictable low latency. This reliability is what makes 5G a particularly useful network for communication between devices, so it is expected to mark the beginning of a new wave of automation. The possibility of better communication not only between people, but between things, is what will create the conditions for Strong Artificial Intelligence.

Jeff Weisbein, founder and CEO of digital media company Best Techie said: "The application of 5G technology will result in massive changes for both consumers and enterprises. 5G networks will offer consumers incredible broadband speeds at home (up to 20 GB/s). It will also enable companies to make advancements such as even smarter, better connected cars, advancements in medical technologies and improved retail experiences through personalization. Technologies such as AI and machine learning offer great potential, but require high bandwidth and low latency to achieve optimal performance. The same is true for technologies like virtual reality and augmented reality, which can offer a customer experience like nothing before with 5G technology"

Huawei is a leader in 5G technology and has recently signed a contract to install the 5G network in Russia as it has with other European countries. This is one of the reasons why the United States is aiming to stop Huawei as part of the trade negotiation with China.

On September 26 Huawei Technologies Co Ltd said it has started making 5G base stations without US components and that total production of 5G base stations should more than double next year as more countries introduce the technology.

The company will start mass production of US component-free 5G base stations next month, founder and CEO Ren Zhengfei told a forum.

"We carried out the testing in August and September, and from October on we will start scale production," Ren said, adding that initially it would begin making 5,000 US component-free 5G base stations a month.

Annual production next year is expected to hit 1.5 million units, compared with 600,000 estimated for this year (2019) which includes those made with US components and those without.

Quantum computing in the cloud

In chapter 5 we refer to quantum computing (QC). Here we will add an interesting difference that will make it more accessible to users and will allow greater and faster advances towards Strong Artificial Intelligence: **quantum computing in the cloud.**

Let's remember the basics of QC. The idea of quantum computation arose in 1981 when Paul Benioff proposed to take advantage of the laws of quantum theory in the field of computation. This means that, instead of working with a single bit, as in digital computing where values are 0 and 1, in quantum computing the value can be 0 or 1 or both at the same time. This is called superposition. This superposition does mean that it has a greater range of information processing than traditional computers.

Quantum computing is a different computing paradigm than classical computing, it makes use of qubits instead of bits; therefore it creates different combinations with totally different results. This means that some problems that have not been solved with a digital computer can be solved by quantum computing.

During the Consumer Electronic Show (CES-2019), IBM introduced what is presumed to be the first quantum computer for commercial use. Its name is Q System One. It is the first commercial quantum computer originally designed with a 20 qubit quantum chip. The IBM system includes a self-calibrated quantum processor with a processing capacity of up to 50 qubits; a cryogenic environment that keeps the equipment at -273 degrees centigrade; information reading and writing instruments that use microwaves; software or firmware that contains the most basic instructions of the computer and a digital interface to interact with the machine and connect it to the cloud.

High-speed quantum computers could accelerate the discovery of new drugs, decipher the most complex cryptographic security systems, design new materials, model climate change and accelerate the process to reach Strong Artificial Intelligence.

There is currently no consensus on the best way to make them real or affordable to a mass market. Therefore, IBM's project to facilitate quantum computing in the cloud is of great importance. Currently **there are already 100,000 users** of Q System One.

Physicists, engineers and computer scientists in large companies, startups and universities are working on projects to develop quantum computing in the cloud. In addition to IBM, there are other QC projects. These are some of the most important:

Google unveiled its new quantum computing chip called Bristlecone. This chip comes with 72 qubits, the second highest so far. The next closest competitor is IBM with a 50-qubit quantum computer. The difference is only about 22 qubits, but the real difference in computing power is enormous. Google maintains the state of qubits using superconducting circuits that are maintained at temperatures lower than what is typically seen in outer space. Google believes this is the best way to insulate these bits from environmental changes.

Rigetti computing is a startup company that has come up with a quantum processor operating with a whopping 128 qubits. Recently, Rigetti also introduced a Quantum Cloud Service or QCS that builds on its existing quantum computing in the cloud programming toolkit. This service brings together both traditional and quantum computers on a single cloud platform to help users create applications using the power of qubits.

QuTech is a Dutch research organization that has been making rapid strides in the world of quantum computing. Led by Prof. Leo Kouwenhoven and located in the Delft University of Technology, this research unit has created qubits that they believe can be protected from external disturbances. In fact, Kouwenhoven claims that their qubits will be stable in all conditions just like knots in a rope, so researchers can come up with ways to harness them.

Microsoft is taking a much different approach to quantum computing. Instead of trying to stabilize the flaky qubits, it is developing a new kind of qubit called topological qubit that will be more suited to mass production of quantum computers. Named Station Q, this research team led by Michael Freedman, is based on the discovery of subatomic particles in the Netherlands in 2012.

Technology is advancing at dizzying speed. I just finished writing information about the Google´s quantum computer when this news was published on September 22 that breaks speed records: "Google's Quantum Supremacy to Render All Cryptocurrency & Military Secrets Breakable". The news written by Joseph Watson and published in Science & Tech says: "Google's announcement that it has achieved "quantum supremacy" with a 53-qubit quantum computer greases the skids for all cryptocurrency and military secrets protected by cryptography to be breakable in a stunning new development that will change the world.

The Big Tech corporation's new quantum processor took a mere 200 seconds to complete a computing task that would normally require 10,000 years on a supercomputer. The 53-qubit quantum computer can break any 53-bit cryptography in seconds, meaning Bitcoin's 256-bit encryption is vulnerable once Google scales its quantum computing to 256 qubits, something their own scientists say will be possible by 2022." (https://bit.ly/2m1bbNN)

If this were the only technology news all year round it would be spectacular and enough to cause a stir. However, there is so much important tech news that it could go unnoticed.

Quantum computing is in its initial stage but it will surely be one of the main technologies that Strong Artificial Intelligence will rely on in the Fifth Wave.

Encoding data in DNA

The volume of data produced by society grows exponentially. This enormous amount of data is the raw material for big data technology to convert into useful information for Artificial Intelligence algorithms but it is also a flow that represents a big problem for its storage, retrieval, processing and delivery of results.

> **DNA** Deoxyribonucleic acid is a molecule composed of two chains that coil around each other to form a double helix carrying genetic instructions for the development, functioning, growth and reproduction of all known organisms and many viruses. DNA and ribonucleic acid (RNA) are nucleic acids.

A study by Seagate, a manufacturer of hard drives and storage media, predicts a 10-fold increase in global data volume by 2025. The study, entitled Data Age 2025, conducted by IDC and sponsored by Seagate, forecasts that by 2025 data generation will total 163 zettabytes (ZB equals $10*21$ bytes).

This situation is a challenge to take advantage of new opportunities using this data and the ideas it generates, while at the same time requiring strategic options on the collection, use and location of the information. In addition, the number of consumers and businesses creating, sharing and accessing data across devices and the cloud will continue to far exceed expectations.

In addition, while consumers were the primary creators of the world's largest volume of data, the Data Age 2025 study predicts that the trend will change, with companies creating 60% of the world's information by 2025. In this new landscape, business leaders will be able to access new and unique business opportunities, powered by this abundance of data and the unparalleled insights it provides; however, they will also have to make strategic decisions about data collection, utilization and location.

To solve this problem, Microsoft, the leading software company, is working on a project with the University of Washington to produce a hard disk of DNA. Even if this might seem fantastic, it is necessary to say that Microsoft is not the first company to work with the idea of a DNA hard disk, but the first to produce it in a functional way and demonstrate its functioning.

The researchers recorded something as simple as the word "Hello" which in binary is represented as 01001000 01000101 01001100 01001100 0100111111. This sequence of bits was encoded in DNA bases: A for adenine, G for guanine, C for cytosine and T for thymine. The hard disk then synthesizes this code and stores it in a liquid for later retrieval. The technology is at the research stage but will be ready and functional to support the development of Strong Artificial Intelligence.

Eleonore Pauwels, a renowned researcher at the Wilson Center (Global Fellow / Science and Technology Innovation Program, Citizen Health Innovators project), published an interesting article on the Internet asking "What Happens When Artificial Intelligence Meets Cutting-Edge Genetics?" This is her answer:

"The United States has been precision medicine's worldwide champion, conducting most of the research that first deciphered our genome about fifteen years ago. This could change with China's heavy investment and capacity-building in the increasing convergence of Artificial Intelligence and new genetic technologies. This golden combination of AI and genomics data has the potential to drive precision medicine to new heights by helping unravel the mysteries of why our bodies react to different chemicals, viruses, and environments, thus recommending the best medicines and treatments.

As China establishes itself as a real competitive force in precision medicine, the US needs to anticipate and understand what this competition means in terms of ownership of medical innovation and personal data protection. Which nation will be the first to own and patent cancer diagnostics and therapeutics vital to our future? Can our science policy and diplomacy encourage US-China collaborative research efforts? The stakes are also high in terms of biosecurity, as genetic and computing research is inherently dual-use and therefore a strategic piece in a nation's security arsenal. While it will be crucial to leverage genomic data for future health, economic and biodefense capital, these data will also have to be well managed and protected. How do we foster, at a science policy level, a US-China dialogue, involving norms and values, about personal data-sharing and protection? In life sciences and genomics, the answer will require creativity and anticipation with the goal of building collaborative practices instead of walls. Which political and economic incentives can help us make this commitment to collaboration a win-win game for both nations?

In 2016, the Chinese government launched a 9 billion and 15-year effort that aims at turning China into a global leader in harnessing computing and AI technologies for interpreting genetic and health data. This investment eclipses a similar precision medicine initiative by the Obama administration which started with a 215 million investment in the president's 2016 Budget and might not be pursued by president Trump's new administration. But this is more than a race in numbers. Working with companies in China and abroad, most of them in the US, Chinese investors and tech leaders are getting access to ever growing amounts of patients' genetic data and developing the machine-learning tools needed to turn these data into sophisticated diagnostics and therapeutics. Liquid biopsies for diagnosing cancer, for instance, are predicted to become the next commercial gold rush in healthcare. By one estimate, the market is expected to be worth 40 billion in 2017. Increasingly, the US-China relationship will not be defined by the ownership of 20th century manufacturing industries but by a race in genetic and computing innovation that will drive the economy of the future." (https://bit.ly/2mDLNsR)

AI software

It is true that the microprocessor, the Internet transmission speed and the computer are essential parts to develop Artificial Intelligence systems. However, **the most important AI component is software**. To write innovative systems and AI applications that succeed in the market the key is software.

The G2 portal contains specialized information for software developers with Artificial Intelligence. Consult it for valuable information. (https://www.g2.com/)

This is part of what it says: "Artificial intelligence (AI) has gradually been making its way into business software and will continue to for the foreseeable future. These intelligent applications have incorporated machine and deep learning algorithms into their everyday functionality to better automate tasks for the user. Automating these processes saves the user time and energy, makes their job simpler, and allows employees to work more efficiently and productively. While there are some that believe AI is out to replace their jobs, they will be pleasantly surprised that, in most cases, this is a false assumption. Instead, the application of AI will simply make their jobs easier.

Artificial intelligence (AI) is becoming a staple of all business software, whether users are aware of it or not. Often, AI and machine learning capabilities are embedded inside applications and provide users with functionality such as automation or predictive capabilities. These intelligent applications make the processes and tasks conducted by businesses and employees simpler and easier with the help of AI, but it is important to differentiate between tools that are AI-enabled, and those that help develop intelligent applications.

AI software is the latter. It provides developers with tools to build intelligent applications, whether that be adding machine learning or speech recognition to a solution, or creating an entirely new application from scratch with the help of an AI platform. These developer tools are often algorithms, libraries, or frameworks of code, or developer kits that can help users create machine and deep learning functionality for software. The use of AI in software will eventually become nothing more than a norm: a feature that is not considered revolutionary, but one that is considered necessary. The software world is striving to reach that norm with the use of AI developer tools.

Those who believe that the widespread use of AI in business will be the downfall for human employees are mistaken. Instead, AI software will help improve the employee experience and offer streamlined, automated ways for workers to complete manual, mundane tasks. It will help companies work smarter and make more intelligent decisions. AI software provides software engineers with the tools to building these solutions that will help benefit employees in all areas of business."

Software for coding AI applications has developed rapidly in recent years and now there is a wide range of possibilities that we can classify into four groups:

1. **Artificial Intelligence platforms**: These will provide the platforms for developing an application from scratch. Many built-in algorithms are provided with the system. Drag and drop facility makes them easy to use.
5. **Chatbots**: This software creates the effect that a human being is the one who maintains the conversation.
6. **Deep learning software**: It includes speech recognition, image recognition etc.
7. **Machine learning software**: Machine learning is the technique which will make the computer learn through data.

This is a list of some of the best software for AI development:

✓ IBM Watson
✓ Cloud Machine Learning Engine
✓ Azure Machine Learning
✓ Apache Prediction IO
✓ Salesforce Einstein

But what if instead of searching through menus within programs like Microsoft Excel, our AI computers could understand the problem we're trying to solve and write the software to solve it? It's a hyper-futuristic idea, but one that has recently seen progress from Microsoft Research and the University of Cambridge. Microsoft and Cambridge built an algorithm capable of writing code that would solve simple math problems. The algorithm, named Deep Coder, would be able to augment its own ability by also looking at potential combinations of code for how a problem could be solved. In the future, the Microsoft and Cambridge team says they want this system to understand the nuances of complete coding languages and be able to write software.

What if the computer learns to write **its own Artificial Intelligence software** to do everything it wants?

The Bayou project points in that direction. Computer scientists at Rice University have created a deep-learning, software-coding application that can help human programmers navigate the growing multitude of often-undocumented application programming interfaces, or APIs.

Known as Bayou, the Rice application was created through an initiative funded by the Defense Advanced Research Projects Agency aimed at extracting knowledge from online source code repositories like GitHub.

> **GitHub** is a company that provides hosting for software development version control using Git. It is a subsidiary of Microsoft. **Git** is a distributed version-control system for tracking changes in source code during software development.

Designing applications that can program computers is a long-sought grail. "People have tried for 60 years to build systems that can write code, but the problem is that these methods aren't that good with ambiguity," said Bayou co-creator Swarat Chaudhuri, associate professor of computer science at Rice. "You usually need to give a lot of details about what the target program does, and writing down these details can be as much work as just writing the code. Bayou is a considerable improvement," he said.

Bayou is based on a method called neural sketch learning, which trains an artificial neural network to recognize high-level patterns in hundreds of thousands of Java programs. It does this by creating a "sketch" for each program it reads and then associating this sketch with the "intent" that lies behind the program. When a user asks Bayou questions, the system makes a judgment call about what program it's being asked to write. It then creates sketches for several of the most likely candidate programs the user might want.

Man-machine symbiosis

The aim of Elon Musk is to enhance human cognitive abilities through Artificial Intelligence to turn the human being into a kind of cyberborg or cybernetic organism.

Recently Elon Musk surprised the world with a new project and a new company: **Neuralink.** A Nano biotechnology company that aims to integrate the human brain with Artificial Intelligence. The company was founded in 2016 and first became known to the general public in March 2017. The company focuses on creating devices that can be implanted in the human brain with the ultimate purpose of helping humans fuse with software and keep pace with advances in Artificial Intelligence. **This symbiosis could improve memory or allow more direct interaction with Artificial Intelligence computers.**

Sometimes his ideas may seem unrealistic delusions of grandeur. However, he have shown that his ideas are well-centered, achievable, and can even become productive enterprises. Examples include PayPal, Tesla, and more.

The man-machine symbiosis that seemed to be the product of science fiction is beginning to become part of our daily lives, and Musk's dreams seem a little closer to becoming reality. For now, they already have the support of a company, financial resources and highly trained staff working every day to achieve their goal.

The big new project is to develop technology that allows the brain to be connected to a computer. Neuralink is the startup entrusted, since 2017, with the development of an implant system using threads with the potential to contribute to the treatment of various brain disorders and ambitious challenges for the future of humanity.

Although its main motivation is to favor advances in the field of medicine, Neuralink could mean the definitive symbiosis between the human brain and Artificial Intelligence. The possibility of making an implant in a person's brain tissue would allow it to be able to complete reading and writing operations and to handle a large volume of data.

Among the multiple medical applications it includes restoring mobility to people with an amputated limb through the use of intelligent prostheses, as well as helping those with some type of hearing or visual impairment.

The implantation of Neuralink will be possible by means of a surgical robot that simulates the operation of a sewing machine. The highly flexible and thin threads would give the brain the ability to communicate wirelessly with external connected devices.

Neuralink will provide real-time monitoring with unprecedented freedom of action. Musk's company expects the first human trials to begin in 2020 through collaboration with leading universities and academic institutions.

Perhaps the future of Artificial Intelligence is not a rivalry between man and computer, but a symbiosis in which both parties add the best of each to produce a superior entity.

Elon Musk said he is concerned that the development of Artificial Intelligence will end up leaving human beings behind. That's why he wants to add a "layer" of Artificial Intelligence to our own intelligence. Will the future of humanity be a society of cyborgs? **Does Musk's brilliant brain already have a layer of Artificial Intelligence?**

Neuralink is not the only project to generate man-machine symbiosis. Facebook also wants to connect the human being with the computer.

Facebook said on September 23, 2019 it bought New York-based CTRL-labs, a start-up that is exploring ways for people to communicate with computers using brain signals, in a deal that was valued at one billion. Facebook said it intends to use the neural interface technology of CTRL-labs in developing a wristband that connects to other devices intuitively. "The vision for this work is a wristband that lets people control their devices as a natural extension of movement," Facebook said.

Media reports said CTRL-labs is working with brain science and machine learning to create interfaces for people to **control and manipulate computers by thinking**. Its development-stage wrist-worn device uses sensors to track gestures and would act as an input device.

OpenAI

OpenAI is a not-for-profit Artificial Intelligence research company that aims to promote and develop friendly Artificial Intelligence in a way that benefits humanity as a whole: "**Our mission is to ensure that artificial general intelligence (AGI) benefits all of humanity, primarily by attempting to build safe AGI and share the benefits with the world.**"

The organization aims to "collaborate freely" with other institutions and researchers by making its patents and research open to the public. Founders Elon Musk, Sam Altman, Reid Hoffman and Peter Thiel **are motivated in part by concerns about the existential risk of Artificial Intelligence.**

In October 2015, Musk, Altman and other investors announced the organization providing more than one billion to the company to fund its operations. On April 27, 2016, OpenAI released a public beta version of "OpenAI Gym," its research platform for enhanced learning. On December 5, 2016, OpenAI launched Universe, a software platform for measuring and training an AI's general intelligence across the world's supply of games, websites and other applications.

During the Dota 2 International 2017 tournament OpenAI allowed a bot trained in machine learning techniques to play a 1-on-1 demonstration game against a professional Dota 2 player, Danil "Dendi" Ishutin, who played against the computer and lost. After the demonstration, Greg Brockman explained that the robot had learned by playing against itself for two weeks in real time, and that the learning software was a step in the direction of creating software that can handle complex tasks "like being a surgeon."

Some scientists, such as Stephen Hawking, Raymond Kurzweil and Stuart Russell believe that if Artificial Intelligence one day gains the ability to redesign at an ever-increasing rate, an unstoppable "burst of intelligence" could lead to human extinction. **Musk characterizes AI as humanity's greatest existential threat**. With this in mind, the founders of OpenAI structured their objectives as a non-profit organization so that they could focus their research on creating a plan for humans and the world **to receive the benefits of AI and avoid its dangers**.

> **OpenAI states that** "it is difficult to understand how much AI could benefit society at the human level," and that it is equally difficult to understand "how much it could harm society if it were built or misused".

Safety research cannot be safely postponed: "because of AI's amazing history, it is difficult to predict when AI at the human level might be within reach". OpenAI asserts that AI "must be an extension of individual human will and, in the spirit of freedom, be distributed as widely and equitably as possible" Co-Chair Sam Altman hopes the project will surpass human intelligence.

Microsoft recently announced that it is joining the Ethical Artificial Intelligence project proposed by OpenAI with a billion dollars. OpenAI and Microsoft expressed the vision of an Artificial Intelligence that works so that people can solve the great problems that afflict humanity, such as climate change. Sam Altman, CEO of OpenAI, indicated that the goal of this effort is to allow Artificial Intelligence to be "implemented without risks and in a safe way and that this provides economic benefits that are widely distributed."

Benefits and dangers

In the evolution of Artificial Intelligence there are several stages whose effects can be distinguished to take advantage of them, take precautions or limit them so that they benefit and do not cause harm to humanity.

Towards the middle of the last century, when Turing unveiled his famous test to determine if a computer could emulate the human being or when the young students of Dartmouth

College astonished the world with the software that could make the computer play Chess or demonstrate mathematical theorems, everything was surprise, wonder and astonishment for what it was thought that a machine endowed with a certain degree of intelligence could achieve.

In the second decade of the next century Artificial Intelligence accelerates its pace. Robots multiply in factories to increase productivity, large companies develop systems to provide customer support, banks invest large sums of money to produce intelligent systems and simplify their operations. Governments realize the potential of Artificial Intelligence and set up programs to promote it. It is at this time when Artificial Intelligence is synonymous with productivity, efficiency, cost savings, and wealth generation. **The countries that join the AI at this stage will be placed at the top of the table of innovation, development and welfare**. They will be those that dominate the world and, as always, those who remain at the end of the table will suffer shortages, hunger and misery. China stands out as the government that provides the most support for the development of AI by elevating it to the highest category among its government policies.

In this stage of the evolution of Artificial Intelligence there are applications to replace the human being in routine tasks. Large computer companies produce digital assistants such as Siri, Cortana, Alexa, Assistant or Bixby that cause astonishment because they can act as a result of a conversation in natural language. Artificial Intelligence begins to grow like moisture and society receives frequent and surprising news about its sensational achievements: it can detect cancer at an early stage, it makes decisions on the stock market better than an experienced broker, it can drive a car without a driver, it can make an airplane fly and land, it can act as a lawyer in a civil trial, it can do things that astonish humanity and the human being is enraptured with Artificial Intelligence. Humanity does not realize what awaits it in the future when AI becomes Strong Artificial Intelligence.

But beware: **Artificial Intelligence can be like the fierce wolf in sheep's clothing**, so it's best if humanity now takes the necessary precautions to limit its power and keep it under its control.

Researchers, scientists and philosophers who are close to the development of Artificial Intelligence have understood this situation and have raised their voices to warn humanity of the danger represented by Artificial Intelligence if it is allowed to advance in full freedom to take control of the most delicate activities of the human being: in politics that means the power to influence society, military strategy, the privacy of people, the stock market, the economy, medicine, jurisprudence and even philosophy, logic, ethics, morals and art; in short, all sensitive or high-risk activities where decisions must be taken by human beings before AI dominates and controls Planet Earth.

On July 18, 2018, the leaders of the technological world signed a document in which they pledge "not to participate in or support the development, manufacture, sale or use of autonomous lethal weapons." The announcement was made in Stockholm, Sweden, as part of the Annual International Conference on Artificial Intelligence. Tesla Director Elon Musk, Skype co-founder Jaan Tallinn and other global technology leaders signed the document, which was signed by more than 2,400 people and 160 companies from 36 countries involved in the development of Artificial Intelligence. They include representatives from the Massachusetts Institute of Technology (MIT), Boston University, UC Berkeley and Cambridge University. The initiative was organized by the Future of Life Institute (FLI), a non-profit organization of which the main Artificial Intelligence researchers from all over the world are part and which seeks to alert about the development of this type of system. Although they highlight the benefits and advances of new technologies, they stress that it is necessary to regulate their development and, above all, ensure that machine learning is not used without any kind of control because it could lead to a dangerous scenario for the world.

Some companies have also become aware of the risks posed by AI and have committed themselves in a particular way to a Decalogue of measures to limit it and not allow it to pose a danger to humanity. Google is perhaps the most important and the one that has set out its position most clearly. On June 7, 2018 Google issued a document to publicize the principles or "commandments" that will underpin the research, innovation and production of systems based on Artificial Intelligence. In its introductory part, it stresses that its commitment to the future lies in this technology and that it is necessary to set rules for its proper use through seven principles. "We announce that these seven principles will guide our work forward. These are not theoretical concepts; they are concrete standards that will actively govern our product research and development and impact our business decisions."

It is important to note that Google assures that it will not use AI for the development of applications that may cause harm such as the development of weapons or technologies capable of gathering information for espionage that contravene international rules or violate human rights. **In the document Google states that AI is its bet for the long term:**

1. Be socially beneficial.

    The expanded reach of new technologies increasingly touches society as a whole. Advances in AI will have transformative impacts in a wide range of fields, including healthcare, security, energy, transportation, manufacturing, and entertainment. As we consider potential development and uses of AI technologies, we will take into account a broad range of social and economic factors, and will proceed where we believe that the overall likely benefits substantially exceed the foreseeable risks and downsides.

    AI also enhances our ability to understand the meaning of content at scale. We will strive to make high-quality and accurate information readily available using AI, while continuing to respect cultural, social, and legal norms in the countries where we operate. And we will continue to thoughtfully evaluate when to make our technologies available on a non-commercial basis.

2. Avoid creating or reinforcing unfair bias.

    AI algorithms and datasets can reflect, reinforce, or reduce unfair biases. We recognize that distinguishing fair from unfair biases is not always simple, and differs across cultures and societies. We will seek to avoid unjust impacts on people, particularly those related to sensitive characteristics such as race, ethnicity, gender, nationality, income, sexual orientation, ability, and political or religious beliefs.

3. Be built and tested for safety.

    We will continue to develop and apply strong safety and security practices to avoid unintended results that create risks of harm. We will design our AI systems to be appropriately cautious, and seek to develop them in accordance with best practices in AI safety research. In appropriate cases, we will test AI technologies in constrained environments and monitor their operation after deployment.

4. Be accountable to people.

We will design AI systems that provide appropriate opportunities for feedback, relevant explanations, and appeal. Our AI technologies will be subject to appropriate human direction and control.

5. Incorporate privacy design principles.

We will incorporate our privacy principles in the development and use of our AI technologies. We will give opportunity for notice and consent, encourage architectures with privacy safeguards, and provide appropriate transparency and control over the use of data.

6. Uphold high standards of scientific excellence.

Technological innovation is rooted in the scientific method and a commitment to open inquiry, intellectual rigor, integrity, and collaboration. AI tools have the potential to unlock new realms of scientific research and knowledge in critical domains like biology, chemistry, medicine, and environmental sciences. We aspire to high standards of scientific excellence as we work to progress AI development.

We will work with a range of stakeholders to promote thoughtful leadership in this area, drawing on scientifically rigorous and multidisciplinary approaches. And we will responsibly share AI knowledge by publishing educational materials, best practices, and research that enable more people to develop useful AI applications.

8. Be made available for uses that accord with these principles.

Many technologies have multiple uses. We will work to limit potentially harmful or abusive applications. As we develop and deploy AI technologies, we will evaluate likely uses in light of the following factors:

- ✓ Primary purpose and use: the primary purpose and likely use of a technology and application, including how closely the solution is related to or adaptable to a harmful use
- ✓ Nature and uniqueness: whether we are making available technology that is unique or more generally available
- ✓ Scale: whether the use of this technology will have significant impact

✓ Nature of Google's involvement: whether we are providing general-purpose tools, integrating tools for customers, or developing custom solutions

AI applications Google will not pursue

In addition to the above objectives, Google will not design or deploy AI in the following application areas:

1. Technologies that cause or are likely to cause overall harm. Where there is a material risk of harm, we will proceed only where we believe that the benefits substantially outweigh the risks, and will incorporate appropriate safety constraints.
2. Weapons or other technologies whose principal purpose or implementation is to cause or directly facilitate injury to people.
3. Technologies that gather or use information for surveillance violating internationally accepted norms.
4. Technologies whose purpose contravenes widely accepted principles of international law and human rights.

UNESCO. The United Nations Educational, Scientific and Cultural Organization is also concerned about the effects of Artificial Intelligence. Its Director, Audrey Azoulay, announced her intention to focus the agency's attention on the ethical challenges presented by Artificial Intelligence. "Unesco can be on the front line to help define a framework to ensure the conformity of Artificial Intelligence systems with fundamental rights," she said during a session of the agency's Executive Board and expressed her intention that the organization "guide researchers in the development of programs and help governments to establish public policies." During a visit to China Audrey Azoulay called for a global meeting on Artificial Intelligence because "there is a need for a global debate on the consequences of the large-scale use of Artificial Intelligence and its application in fields such as military, security or individual freedoms. We must have this discussion on the ethics of Artificial Intelligence, and we cannot have it without China because China is a strategic partner of UNESCO." said Audrey Azoulay.

Developed country governments, global institutions and the world's leading companies are already taking steps to interact with Artificial Intelligence. It's time to get informed and make decisions.

Attraction to risk

In the next two decades humanity will be on the path to Strong Artificial Intelligence. The human being will be in love with technology and will dedicate its intelligence, enthusiasm and financial resources to strengthen it. Even knowing that there are great risks and dangers in Strong Artificial Intelligence, human beings will strive to reach it. They well know that it will cause problems and that at some point it will take control of the critical activities of humanity, but as if all this did not concern them, they will give themselves over in a mad frenzy to reach it.

Cristina Llagostera published in the prestigious Spanish newspaper El País an interesting article to explain why risk attracts human beings. Here we take its essence to try to find the explanation to the human being's effort to produce an inanimate entity with an intelligence equal or superior to his own.

"What can drive a person to set almost impossible goals, to drive recklessly at high speed or to engage in gambling? To expose oneself to an uncertain or dangerous situation is a behavior that is difficult to explain, however, some people feel a special attraction towards risk, like an irresistible magnet that pushes them to live to the limit and to repeatedly compromise their safety.

Sociology talks about the culture of risk. This expression indicates that the technological development of recent decades has not been accompanied by a greater sense of security, but rather the opposite: change and uncertainty have become a constant. As a result, risk is perceived and more present than ever, generating in some cases an exacerbated need for control or, at the other extreme, lifestyles coupled with a taste for novelty and strong sensations.

This yearning for intensity is characteristic of a society that tends to excess and needs increasingly powerful stimuli. The attraction for risk can go from hobbies, sports or activities that carry certain danger, to the necessity to test relationships, to undertaking risky conduct, to provoking continuous economic or professional troubles. Exposure to risk is perceived by the organism as a threat to survival. As a consequence, adrenaline is triggered, muscles are stretched, breathing is shaken, heart rate increases and the person remains alert, vigilant, focusing his attention on the danger...This yearning for intensity is characteristic of a society that tends to excess. Accustomed as we are to a very high level of activation, more and more impacting stimuli are needed to produce sensations... The fearlessness to take risks is a prerequisite for progress, but it is necessary to distinguish when it becomes a necessity that can reach alarming limits." (https://bit.ly/2miEM5e)

The Pew Research Center Survey

The Pew Research Center is a nonpartisan American think tank (referring to itself as a "fact tank") based in Washington, D.C. It provides information on social issues, public opinion, and demographic trends shaping the United States and the world. It also conducts public opinion polling, demographic research, media content analysis, and other empirical social science research. The Pew Research Center does not take policy positions, and is a subsidiary of The Pew Charitable Trusts.

The Pew Research Center carried out an extensive survey to obtain the opinion of experts related to Artificial Intelligence. PRC submitted the question: As emerging algorithm-driven artificial intelligence continues to spread, will people be better off than they are today?

Some 979 technology pioneers, innovators, developers, business and policy leaders, researchers and activists answered this question in a canvassing of experts conducted in the summer of 2018.

It is interesting to know the answers. There are optimists and pessimists. Positive and negative. All colors and flavors. If you want to know the thinking of experts on the interesting subject of Artificial Intelligence visit the PRC website that presents the results: (https://pewrsr.ch/2I6Sgd4).

We've extracted some as a sample:

> **Baratunde Thurston**, futurist, former director of digital at The Onion and co-founder of comedy/technology start-up Cultivated Wit, said, "For the record, this is not the future I want, but it is what I expect given existing default settings in our economic and sociopolitical system preferences. ... The problems to which we are applying machine learning and AI are generally not ones that will lead to a 'better' life for most people. That's why I say in 2030, most people won't be better due to AI. We won't be more autonomous; we will be more automated as we

follow the metaphorical GPS line through daily interactions. We don't choose our breakfast or our morning workouts or our route to work. An algorithm will make these choices for us in a way that maximizes efficiency (narrowly defined) and probably also maximizes the profitability of the service provider. By 2030, we may cram more activities and interactions into our days, but I don't think that will make our lives 'better.' A better life, by my definition, is one in which we feel more valued and happy. Given that the biggest investments in AI are on behalf of marketing efforts designed to deplete our attention and bank balances, I can only imagine this leading to days that are more filled but lives that are less fulfilled. To create a different future, I believe we must unleash these technologies toward goals beyond profit maximization. Imagine a mapping app that plotted your work commute through the most beautiful route, not simply the fastest. Imagine a communications app that facilitated deeper connections with people you deemed most important. These technologies must be more people-centric. We need to ask that they ask us, 'What is important to you? How would you like to spend your time?' But that's not the system we're building. All those decisions have been hoarded by the unimaginative pursuit of profit."

Thad Hall, a researcher and coauthor of "Politics for a Connected American Public", added: "AI is likely to have benefits – from improving medical diagnoses to improving people's consumer experiences. However, there are four aspects of AI that are very problematic. 1) It is likely to result in more economic uncertainty and dislocation for people, including employment issues and more need to change jobs to stay relevant. 2) AI will continue to erode people's privacy as search becomes more thorough. China's monitoring of populations illustrates what this could look like in authoritarian and Western countries, with greater facial recognition used to identify people and affect their privacy. 3) AI will likely continue to have biases that are negative toward minority populations, including groups we have not considered. Given that algorithms often have identifiable biases (e.g., favoring people who are white or male), they likely also have biases that are less well-recognized, such as biases that are negative toward people with disabilities, older people or other groups. These biases may ripple through society in unknown ways. Some groups are more likely to be monitored effectively. 4) AI is creating a world where reality can be manipulated in ways we do not appreciate. Fake videos, audio and similar media are likely to explode and create a world where 'reality' is hard to discern. The relativistic political world will become more so, with people having evidence to support their own reality or multiple realities that mean no one knows what the truth is."

Robert Epstein, senior research psychologist at the American Institute for Behavioral Research and Technology and the founding director of the Loebner Prize, a competition in artificial intelligence, said, "By 2030, it is likely that AIs will have achieved a type of sentience, even if it is not human-like. They will also be able to exercise varying degrees of control over most human communications, financial transactions, transportation systems, power grids and weapon systems. As I noted in my 2008 book, 'Parsing the Turing Test,' they will reside in the 'InterNest' we have been building for them, and we will have no way of dislodging them. How they decide to deal with humanity – to help us, ignore us or destroy us – will be entirely up to them, and there is no way currently to predict which avenue they will choose. Because a few paranoid humans will almost certainly try to destroy the new sentient AIs, there is at least a reasonable possibility that that they will swat us like the flies we are – the possibility that Stephen Hawking, Elon Musk and others have warned about. There is no way, to my knowledge, of stopping this future from emerging. Driven by the convenience of connectivity, the greed that underlies business expansion and the pipedreams of muddle-headed people who confuse machine-like intelligence with biological intelligence, we will continue to build AIs we can barely understand and to expand the InterNest in which they will live – until the inevitable – whatever that proves to be – occurs."

Time to decide the way forward

From Homo habilis the intelligence of man has been the force that has allowed him to win on Planet Earth. Intelligence has inspired him to deposit a seed in the earth, take care of it, water it, raise the harvest and nourish himself with its already ripe fruits. It has allowed him to think about using the energy of steam to increase his physical strength and to use it to move machines and looms. It has led him to invent the production chain to make industry more efficient, to use oil in an internal combustion engine that moves vehicles at high speeds to be transported over long distances. It has led him to produce a machine to process information at dizzying speeds in order to increase thinking ability. It has given him the ingenuity to light up the night and turn it into day, to communicate at great distances, to process information and obtain results in seconds, to continue discovering and inventing all kinds of devices to improve his standard of living. And now, after all he has achieved, the human being is one step away from giving the precious gift of intelligence to an inanimate being. The first question that arises is: Can the human being create an inanimate being with an intelligence equal to or greater than his own?

The scientists and builders of Artificial Intelligence do not agree. There are those who think that a machine may have Specific Artificial Intelligence but that it will never have Strong Artificial Intelligence. There are those who consider that the probability exists but that it will take several centuries to reach and, finally, there are those who think that the advances in this field and the technologies that are being developed leads to the conclusion that Strong Artificial Intelligence will be a reality before the end of the present century.

Ramón López de Mántaras belongs to the group that says no. His experience in the study of Artificial Intelligence is impressive: Research Professor at the Consejo Superior de Investigaciones Científicas (CSIC), Director of the Instituto de Investigación en Inteligencia Artificial (IIIA) at the CSIC, Master of Sciences in Computer Engineering at the University of California-Berkeley, PhD in Physics at the Universidad Paul Sabatier in Toulouse and PhD in Computer Science at the Universidad Politécnica de Catalunya. He is one of the pioneers of Artificial Intelligence in Spain, author of numerous scientific articles in the field of Artificial Intelligence and member of the Editorial Board of the main scientific journals in AI.

At a conference organized by BBVA on the subject of Artificial Intelligence, Ramón López de Mántaras was asked: can Artificial Intelligence think like a human? His answer was a resounding NO and he added "We can train it to do something very well, but if that same system is trained for anything else, it forgets the first one". He considers this failure to be the so-called "catastrophic oblivion", and López de Mántaras considers it the limit of this technology, which many fear. Books published by López de Mántaras: https://amzn.to/2lYWXwJ

Raymond Kurzweil (Massachusetts, February 12, 1948) is an inventor, businessman, writer and scientist specializing in Computer Science and Artificial Intelligence. Since 2012 he has been Director of Engineering at Google. He is an expert systems technologist and an eminent futurist. He is currently president of the computer company Kurzweil Technologies which is dedicated to developing electronic conversation devices and applications for people with disabilities and promoter of the University of Silicon Valley Singularity.

Kurzweil predicts that a computer will pass the Turing test by 2029, demonstrating intelligence, self-awareness and emotional richness indistinguishable from a human being. This moment has been called technological singularity (a term popularized by mathematician, computer sci-fi author Vernor Vinge). Kurzweil foresees that the first Strong Artificial Intelligence will be built around a computer simulation of a human brain, which will be possible thanks to a scanner guided by nanobots. A machine equipped with Artificial Intelligence could perform all human intellectual tasks and would be emotional and self-conscious. **Kurzweil argues that such AI will inevitably become more intelligent and powerful than that of a human being.** He suggests that AI will show moral thought and respect for humans as their ancestors. According to his predictions, the line between humans and machines will blur as part of technological evolution. Cybernetic implants will greatly improve man, equip him with new physical and cognitive skills, and allow him to interact directly with machines. Kurzweil has written interesting books on Artificial Intelligence. Check them out on Amazon: https://amzn.to/2kMGFHe

Ben Goertzel is the founder and CEO of SingularityNET, a blockchain-based AI marketplace project. Goertzel is also the chief scientist of the financial prediction firm Aidyia Holdings; chairman of AI software company Novamente LLC, a privately held software company; chairman of the Artificial General Intelligence Society and the Open Cog Foundation; research professor in the Fujian Key Lab for Brain-Like Intelligent Systems at Xiamen University of Technology, China; chair of the Artificial General Intelligence (AGI) conference series, and an American author and researcher in the field of Artificial

Intelligence. Goertzel published a book about the Artificial General Intelligence: https://amzn.to/2morpjX

Goertzel wrote on his website Singularity Hub an article with the title "From Here to Human-Level Artificial General Intelligence in Four (Not All That) Simple Steps". These are his conclusions:

"In the 15 years **since I first introduced the term artificial general intelligence** (AGI), the AI field has advanced tremendously. We now have self-driving cars, automated face recognition and image captioning, machine translation and expert AI game-players, and so much more.

However, these achievements remain essentially in the domain of "narrow AI"—AI that carries out tasks based on specifically-supplied data or rules, or carefully-created training situations. AIs that can generalize to unanticipated domains and confront the world as autonomous agents are still part of the road ahead.

The question remains: **what do we need to do** to get from today's narrow AI tools, which have become mainstream in business and society, to the AGI envisioned by futurists and science fiction authors?

While **there is a tremendous diversity of perspectives** and no shortage of technical and conceptual ideas on the path to AGI, there is nothing resembling an agreement among experts on the matter.

For example, Google DeepMind's chief founder Demis Hassabis has long been a fan of relatively closely brain-inspired approaches to AGI, and continues to publish papers in this direction. On the other hand, the OpenCog AGI-oriented project that I co-founded in 2008 is grounded in a less brain-oriented approach—it involves neural networks, but also heavily leverages symbolic-logic representations and probabilistic inference, and evolutionary program learning.

The bottom line is, just as we have many different workable approaches to manned flight—airplanes, helicopters, blimps, rockets, etc.—there may be many viable paths to AGI, some of which are more biologically inspired than others. And, somewhat like the Wright brothers, today's AGI pioneers are proceeding largely via experiment and intuition, in part because we don't yet know enough useful theoretical laws of general intelligence to proceed with AGI engineering in a mainly theory-guided way; the theory of AGI is evolving organically alongside the practice.

In a talk I gave recently at Josef Urban's AI4REASON lab in Prague I outlined "Four Simple Steps to Human-Level AGI." The title was intended as dry humor, as actually none of the steps are simple at all. **But I do believe they are achievable within our lifetime, maybe even in the next 5-10 years.** Better yet, each of the four steps is currently being worked on by multiple teams of brilliant people around the world, including but by no means limited to my own teams at SingularityNET, Hanson Robotics, and OpenCog.

The good news is, I don't believe we need radically better hardware, nor radically different algorithms, nor new kinds of sensors or actuators. **We just need to use our computers and algorithms in a slightly more judicious way by doing the following.**

1. Make cognitive synergy practical

    We have a lot of powerful AI algorithms today, but we don't use them together in sufficiently sophisticated ways, so we lose much of the synergetic intelligence that could come from using them together. By contrast, the different components in the human brain are tuned to work together with exquisite feedback and interplay. **We need to make systems that enable richer and more thorough coordination of different AI agents at various levels into one complex, adaptive AI network.**

2. Bridge symbolic and sub symbolic AI

    I believe **AGI will most effectively be achieved via bridging of the algorithms used for low-level intelligence,** such as perception and movement (e.g., deep neural networks), with the algorithms used for high-level abstract reasoning (such as logic engines).

3. Whole-organism architecture

    Humans are bodies as much as minds, and so achieving human-**like AGI will require embedding AI systems in physical systems** capable of interacting with the everyday human world in nuanced ways.

4. Scalable meta-learning

    AGI needs not just learning but also learning how to learn. An AGI will need to apply its reasoning and learning algorithms recursively to itself so as to automatically improve its functionality. Ultimately, the ability to apply learning to improve learning should allow AGIs to progress far beyond human capability. At the moment, meta-learning remains a difficult but critical research pursuit. At SingularityNET, for instance, we are just now beginning to apply OpenCog's AI to recognize patterns in its own effectiveness over time, so as to improve its own performance.

If my perspective on AGI is correct, then once each of these four aspects is advanced beyond the current state, **we're going to be there—AGI at the human level and beyond...** I find this prospect **tremendously exciting, and just a little scary... We are venturing into unknown territory here**, not only intellectually and technologically, but socially and philosophically as well. Let us do our best to carry out this next stage of our collective voyage in a manner that is wise and cooperative as well as clever and fascinating." (https://bit.ly/2mnqlwU)

The author of this book thinks that the human being will be able to create an inanimate being with an intelligence superior to his own and the best thing we can do now is to prepare to live with Strong Artificial Intelligence in the Fifth Wave of the evolution of humanity.

The danger represented by Artificial Intelligence must not be an impediment to its use and exploitation for the benefit of humanity. Fire itself represents a danger and has been one of the most important elements for human progress and well-being.

Just as fire must be controlled in its use and application, AI must be controlled and regulated to submit to the domain of humanity. **The first step is to become aware of the benefits and dangers of Artificial Intelligence and this is the primary objective of this book.**

In the history of humanity two sources of energy have been produced whose effects have been fundamental in its development: fire and nuclear energy. We can say that AI will be more important and of greater transcendence than fire and nuclear energy in the future of humanity.

Humanity faces the greatest dilemma in its evolution. Now is the time for countries, companies and individuals to make the decision to consider Artificial Intelligence as a fundamental part of their development plans or life projects.

Epilogue

For hundreds of thousands of years, human beings have mastered the Planet Earth and have managed to dominate other living beings thanks to their greater intellectual capacity. The spark of intelligence allowed Homo habilis to use a stone, a stick or a bone as a primeval tool or as a defense weapon.

The slow but constant development of their intelligence has led them to mold mud, melt metal, carve wood, till the earth, domesticate animals, build dens, produce fire at will and control it, cover their bodies to protect themselves from bad weather, prepare and conserve their food, learn to increase their knowledge, educate their children, invent writing to communicate and preserve their memories, store water, and use plants and other remedies to take care of their health.

Their intelligence has been an inexhaustible factor in taking them across the seas, flying like birds and conquering space. Their brilliant intellect has allowed them to produce and control electricity, to unleash the force of atoms, to reach the stars and to land on the Moon. It has inspired them to achieve refined expressions of intelligence such as religion, music, literature, philosophy, logic, ethics, poetry and to develop common sense.

But now, incredible as it may seem, they are working with great care to give an inanimate being the great power of intelligence. In a few years, an instant in comparison with the existence of the Universe, human beings will produce a machine with intelligence and the capacity to learn, to improve itself and to become the most intelligent entity on Planet Earth.

How will this singularity affect human beings? Will they be able to control Strong Artificial Intelligence? Will they share the dominion of Planet Earth in a symbiosis? Or will they submit to an Intelligence superior to their own? Now is the time to act to influence the destiny of humanity.

www.ingramcontent.com/pod-product-compliance
Lightning Source LLC
Chambersburg PA
CBHW071238050326
40690CB00011B/2170